GENDER REGIMES IN TRANSITION IN CENTRAL AND EASTERN EUROPE

Gillian Pascall and Anna Kwak

First published in Great Britain in November 2005 by

The Policy Press
University of Bristol
Fourth Floor
Beacon House
Queen's Road
Bristol BS8 1QU
UK

Tel +44 (0)117 331 4054
Fax +44 (0)117 331 4093
e-mail tpp-info@bristol.ac.uk
www.policypress.org.uk

British Library Cataloguing in Publication Data
A catalogue record for this book is available from the British Library.

Library of Congress Cataloging-in-Publication Data
A catalog record for this book has been requested.

ISBN 1 86134 625 5 hardcover

Gillian Pascall is Professor of Social Policy at the University of
Nottingham, UK. **Anna Kwak** is a professor at the Institute of Applied
Social Sciences, University of Warsaw, Poland.

Cover design by Qube Design Associates, Bristol.
Printed and bound in Great Britain by MPG Books, Bodmin.

Contents

List of tables and figures

Tables

Figures

Acknowledgements

We would like to thank the British Council and the Polish State Committee for Scientific Research who, through the Polish–British Partnership Programme, gave us a grant for travel in order to undertake the qualitative research for the study 'Gender relations of care: parents and social policy in Poland' on which we draw for this book. We also appreciate the support given to the project by the School of Sociology and Social Policy, University of Nottingham, UK. Now that our book is being published we would like to express how much we appreciate such help, which allowed us to translate our ideas into reality.

We also would like to thank Dorota Całka, Magdalena Leśniewicz-Bieńczyk, Iwona Skubis, Renata Bartosik, Anna Dyrała and Anna Górna for their part in the research.

We are particularly grateful to colleagues who have supported the study in a variety of ways, through their interest, through time given to commenting on proposals and drafts, and help with translation. Among these we would particularly like to thank: Robert Dingwall, Frances Camilleri, Jane Lewis, Andrzej Mościskier and Robert Pascall.

Acknowledgements

ONE

Introduction: gender and the family under communism and after

This book explores the nature of the gender regimes emerging in the new Central and Eastern European (CEE) member states of the European Union, and in particular in Poland, in the aftermath of communism. It asks about gender equalities and inequalities in the welfare regimes of the new CEE welfare states and specifically about the extent to which the support for mothers and their care responsibilities, which characterised CEE countries under communism, has survived the transition from communism. The transition has primarily been seen as a transition of economics and politics, with liberalisation of markets and of civil society. But it is also a transition of social welfare structures and of households and of the gender relations and assumptions within both. What assumptions are now made about the state's role in social welfare, about the gender relations of earning and caring and about the social policies that should support earning and caring? How well do emerging structures in practice support paid and unpaid work and gender equality in both? And how may they best be developed in the context of continuing social and economic change as well as in the context of a European Union now expanding to include Central, Eastern and Western Europe?

The welfare regimes of Central and Eastern Europe in the communist era had a distinctive gender character. State socialist societies sought women's labour for economic development. They enabled it through education systems oriented to producing highly qualified women and men (UNICEF, 1998), through workplace social provision and through state-guaranteed entitlements such as parental leave and benefits, kindergartens and nurseries and strong family allowance systems (Fajth, 1996; Haney, 2002). Under communism these societies retained an unreconstructed domestic division of labour that left women with a famed 'double burden'. The established pattern of gender relations across Central and Eastern Europe was of dual earner households, supported by state and enterprise welfare structures. Social policies and households in Western Europe have been, broadly speaking, moving from the male breadwinner model of the family and towards assumptions relating to dual earners, although the practice in most countries is of one-and-a-half earners, with men fully in paid labour, and women bending paid labour to unpaid (Lewis, 2001a, 2001b, 2002). But countries of Central and Eastern Europe have had dual earner household systems since the post–Second World War period, along with soviet domination. These are now being transformed in the transition from communism. Could they be moving in the opposite direction, as the underpinning structures of the communist era are unpicked? Is there a 're-traditionalisation' in governments and their social policies and in household practices and family values? What are the current patterns in CEE countries and what are their implications for parents attempting to earn and to care for children?

Across Europe, issues of how work and welfare structures can accommodate care have come to the fore. The Organization for Economic Co-operation and Development (OECD) has published *A caring world: The new Social Policy Agenda* (1999) and the International Labour Office (ILO) has produced *Care work: The quest for security* (Daly, 2001). For the European Union, Esping-Andersen – much criticised for leaving unpaid care work and gender issues out of earlier work – has proposed a new European welfare architecture (Esping-Andersen, 2001). In *Why we need a new welfare state*, he now finds a need for a "child-centred social investment strategy" and a "new gender contract", a woman-friendly policy and the need to change "both gendered choices and societal constraints" (Esping-Andersen et al, 2002, pp 26-67, 68-95, 95). The Council of the European Union and Ministers for Employment and Social Policy have carried a resolution for the new millennium on the balanced participation of women and men in family and working life, agreeing to support a "new social contract on gender in which the de facto equality of men and women in the public and private domains ... will be reflected in all European Union policies" (Council of the European Union, 2000, introduction, para 11). This appears to show official policy in Europe not only engaging in a politics of private life but also embracing men's participation in care on the same basis as women's. Meanwhile, anxieties about the demographic situation, with an ageing population and declining fertility, bring women's labour market participation to the fore as a solution to Europe's labour market needs. The Social Policy Agenda and the Lisbon strategy have brought issues of work and care into focus, with their aim of increasing quality employment through social policies, and the strategy of the Open Method of Coordination now developing comparative measures of childcare across Europe (see

Chapter Seven). These seem to show unprecedented international concern, even consensus, about the need for social policies to support women's labour market participation, about the gap in care created by the demise of the male breadwinner family (Lewis, 2002), the need for care in the context of family change, the need for welfare states to support care (Williams, 2004) and the threat of declining birth rates.

In former communist countries, care issues are particularly dramatic although their history is somewhat different (Hantrais, 2002a). A World Bank publication *Gender in transition* examines changes in taxation and benefit systems "designed to compensate women for their reproductive and nurturing activities ... to promote fertility and foster equilibrium between women's employment and childbearing" (Paci, 2002, p 32). It argues that "the reduction of state support for nurturing and childcare has shifted back to women the entire responsibility for these functions. Coupled with continuing high participation rates, this has increased the dual burden on women and increased demands on their time" (Paci, 2002, p xii; see also World Bank, 2001). A paper for the United Nations Economic Commission for Europe (UNECE) on *Gender aspects of changes in the labor markets in transition economies* makes connections between care issues in transition countries and fertility rates:

> By the end of the 1990s all transition countries have the lowest fertility rates in Europe, and in the world. ... Though factors behind demographic trends are complex, re-designing of a market-based family support system in which responsibilities and costs of having children would be shared among the state (central and local levels), private sector and households is an important policy priority. (Ruminska-Zimny, 2002, p 9)

It appears widely accepted among the international agencies that reducing support for parents and children has made earning and caring particularly difficult in the former communist countries and that whether to have children at all has become a question for would-be parents.

If care is one reason for the contemporary importance of these issues, another is the historic enlargement of the European Union, with the new accessions of 2004. The widening of the European Union is primarily an expansion to the east. Of the then 13 accession and candidate countries[1], 10 are former communist regimes, and new welfare architecture for Europe will need to accommodate the countries of Central and Eastern Europe as well as Western Europe. The strength of European Union social policy is open to debate (Streek, 1995; Walby, 1999), but European gender policy has been its most admired aspect (Neilson, 1998; Rossilli, 1997, 1999, 2000). The Treaty of Rome committed member states to the principle that men and women should receive equal pay for equal work (Article 119), and – after a rather slow start – the string of directives on equal pay, equal treatment at work and, more recently, on working time, parental leave, and part-time work is just some of the innovative legislation emanating from the European Union and concerned with key issues for gender equality (Duncan, 2002; Pascall and Manning, 2002). From 2004, with 10 candidate countries joining, the European Union has been transformed into a union of East and West, including the greater part of the former communist bloc of Europe (Ingham and Ingham, 2002; Mair and Zielonka, 2002). From the point of view of gender in households and of the gender regimes embedded in welfare systems, East and West have very different histories and contemporary conditions. And most CEE countries now face a new transition into a wider European Union, which has its own agenda of economic, political and social policies relating to gender.

What is the nature of the regimes?

One task of this book is to examine what kind of welfare states are emerging in post-communist countries. If care is at the centre of European debates about ageing populations and women's labour market participation, it is also at the centre of debates about welfare regimes and gender. It has been argued – mainly in relation to Western Europe – that welfare states have been underpinned by assumptions about gender. Most western welfare systems were rooted in a Beveridgean system in the post-Second World War era, which assumed men as breadwinners and women as carers. Social policies in strong male breadwinner countries, such as the UK and Ireland, assumed and tended to support traditional gender roles, while Scandinavian regimes began to encourage women's labour market participation and a dual earner model from the 1960s (Lewis, 1992, 1997, 2001b; Sainsbury, 1996; Crompton, 1999; O'Connor et al, 1999). Daly and Rake (2003) have offered a comparative analysis of gender and the welfare state whose systematic account of relations between welfare states and gender greatly enriches our understanding of these relationships in Western Europe and the US. Gornick and Meyers in *Families that work: Policies for reconciling parenthood and employment* (2003) map and measure Western

European policies for an American audience. Most such analyses have been rooted in Western Europe, although with some writing about Canada, Australia and the US. This literature provides useful tools with which to understand the emerging regimes of CEE countries, although there is little writing that connects the debates about gender to former communist countries (Pascall and Manning, 2000; Haney, 2002). It is particularly interesting and important to do this because of the distinctive set of social policy assumptions around gender under communism. The book explores what assumptions the new CEE states make about gender, and what kind of gender regimes are now emerging.

The gender regimes of the communist era appeared, on the surface, to be like Scandinavian ones, with women's high labour market participation and gender pay gaps of around 80%: in these respects they were comparable with Sweden (UNICEF, 2001, p 14). But there were differences, with an unreconstructed household division of labour within households, no civil society and no women's movement. There were pressures to bring women into the labour market but no pressures to bring men into household and care work. The experience of gender equality as an imposition from authoritarian governments rather than as an objective of social movements made communist dual earner regimes feel very different from the inside (Ferge, 1998). Not even Scandinavian countries have achieved gender equality within households but, under communism, CEE countries had a clearly distinctive pattern: extreme domestic inequality (probably associated with the repression of civil society and the women's movement), combined with social and legal provisions to support women's participation in the labour market, and legal equalities in marriage and divorce (clearly stemming from soviet domination and authoritarian governments) (UNICEF, 1999; Gershuny, 2000).

While the rest of Europe is moving – at different rates and to different degrees – towards a dual earner model in social policy assumptions and practices, the trajectory of CEE countries is clearly different and perhaps contradictory. Does the withdrawal of the state bring back the male breadwinner model in the former communist countries, and, if so, what are the implications for gender equality? After communism, government spending and support for families declined and the development of civil society was slow. Are they still dual earner households, or have they been 're-traditionalised', with women's paid employment becoming more fragile, motherhood likely to take women out of the labour market, and domestic ideals re-established? A strong undercurrent in the literature about transition from communism sees women as losers in the trend towards markets and away from socially supported motherhood: "In the short run at least, women in East Central Europe stand to lose economic, social welfare and reproductive rights" (Einhorn, 1993, p 1). This undercurrent comes to the surface in a theory of 're-traditionalisation', which proposes that traditional gender ideologies are likely to translate into gender inequities in the labour market and in domestic divisions (Glass and Kawachi, 2001). But some statistical comparisons of the early transition period failed to find such consistent trends against women (van der Lippe and Fodor, 1998). How does the evidence now, 15 years after transition, show women's position in CEE countries?

How much diversity is there in gender assumptions and policies after communism? Should we understand these countries as emerging into difference as they separate themselves from the communist past, or as sharing a common path away from communism and into the European Union? Clearly, social policy making has moved from socialist authority to a diversity of states. The communist period brought relative uniformity, although differences may have been repressed beneath the surface and ready to emerge with the end of soviet authority. The 15 years since the end of communism may have brought distinctive policy regimes across CEE countries. Alternatively, the long experience of communism may leave lingering similarities, with some aspects of the communist past still written into constitution and policy, expectations and the need for women's employment, gender relations in households and expectations and demands of the state. Transition itself – while it brings the possibility of difference – is in some ways a common process: for all these countries it involves a move from state- and employer-provided welfare systems to a mixed economy with a reduction in state support for children and parental employment. We will use the theoretical literature on gender in welfare regimes to help understand these issues while drawing on quantitative data from the European Union, the TransMONEE project and the European Foundation for the Improvement of Living and Working Conditions (Dublin) to compare the emerging regimes across policy issues and nations. Chapter Two in particular, looks at the place of Poland among the new CEE member states of the European Union, and how Poland compares, in key dimensions, with countries of Western Europe.

Is there a re-traditionalisation in state policies, re-invoking traditional families?

Poland forms an important and interesting example of gender regimes in transition. It is the largest among the countries to join the European Union, with a population of nearly 40 million, contributing around half of the new population of 74.3 million in the expanded Europe (European Commission, 2004a). Polish economic policies have given a strong push to developing markets, and there has been a consequent reduction in support for families, for parents, and in particular for mothers in the labour market. Poland was the first country to re-establish its GDP to pre-1989 levels, but its current economic position is in the middle ranking of the new CEE member states, and well below the EU15. There have been ideological forces in favour of traditional families, with the influence of the Roman Catholic Church and the Solidarity Party seeing the traditional family as a way to assert Polish national identity after Russian and soviet domination. Assumptions in Polish governments' underlying policies for work, care, income and time incline towards the traditional; and women's role in paid work has probably never been as strong in Poland as in other CEE countries. TransMONEE data on pre-primary enrolments show that Polish 3- to 6-year-olds are rather more likely to be in kindergarten now than they were 10 years ago, but a lot less likely than children from Hungary or the Czech Republic. Enrolments in 2001 were around 50% in Poland and about 87% in Hungary (TransMONEE data, see Chapter Two). Women's employment now is especially reduced by the generally high levels of unemployment and by the assumption that women/mothers are unreliable workers. Nothing in the policy environment ensures respect for women's employment rights. Ideals of motherhood are elevated while policies for fatherhood are few (see Chapter Three). Many women appear to be dependent on men within households. Working hours for men and women make parenting very difficult. Women's place in public life is marginal and the expectations of a developing civil society have been fulfilled for men more than for women. If anywhere among CEE countries we could find evidence of re-traditionalisation – a return to pre-communist policies in governments and values in households – we might expect to find it in Poland.

Approach

We shall use empirical data: quantitative data, including official comparative data on European Union member states, such as the structural indicators and European Commission published sources (European Commission, 2004a), the TransMONEE data from UNICEF's Innocenti Research Centre in Florence and data about work from the European Foundation for the Improvement of Living and Working Conditions, and qualitative data recently gathered in Poland.

Accession to the European Union brings comparative statistical data across the 25 countries, with the structural indicators and new publications highlighting the CEE new member states (European Commission, 2004a). The TransMONEE data and publications such as *Women in transition* (UNICEF, 1999) give us a wide-ranging view of transition from communism across the 27 countries of the former communist region, and essential information about the situation of women and the changing policies of governments. The European Foundation for the Improvement of Living and Working Conditions' report on the *Working conditions in the acceding and candidate countries* (Paoli and Parent-Thirion, 2003) and their *Quality of life in Europe* studies (including Alber and Fahey, 2004; Alber and Köhler, 2004; Fahey and Spéder, 2004) now offer comparative data across Europe on work, including unpaid parenting work, and on attitudes to social policies, allowing comparisons between individual CEE countries as well as across East and West. This data will be used to discuss the nature of the gender regimes emerging in CEE countries and to compare them with the countries of Western Europe.

We see these quantitative and qualitative data sources as complementary rather than competitive. They engender different kinds of data and have different strengths and weaknesses rather than being "separate paradigms" (Bryman, 1988, p 172). In this case, the quantitative data will enable us to draw a very broad picture of the gender implications of the transition from communism across the countries of Central and Eastern Europe and to address the increasingly significant questions about these countries in the European Union. The qualitative data enable us to see transition from within, to gain insight into the experience of transition from communism through the accounts of some of those most powerfully affected by it. The changes of social policy in the transition period are likely to be most strongly felt by women who are mothers of young children and at the same time are paid workers. This is a critical group for understanding the impact of transition on gender relations. The impact of transition on their time, income, security and ability to care for their children raises key policy issues.

We therefore discuss these issues from the perspective of people inside the transition from communism. Our qualitative study was of 72 respondents, who were mothers with at least one child under seven and either employed or on maternity leave. We wanted to understand some of the variety of situations in Poland where the changing economic and political situation has affected people in different ways, and we therefore interviewed equal numbers of respondents in contrasting locations: Warsaw, which is the fastest developing city in Poland, economically and politically, and Skierniewice, which is a provincial town in central Poland, 75 kilometres from Warsaw and with a population of approximately 49,000. In Skierniewice, around twice as many people worked in agriculture as in Poland as a whole in 2001. But on key dimensions Skierniewice is typical of Poland in the transition period. Since 1990, it has been experiencing a reduction of workplaces as businesses have closed and employment in general has been reduced. The level of unemployment is typical of Poland, and, as elsewhere, is highest among those aged 18-34, and higher among women than among men. Administrative reform in January 1999 made Skierniewice a county capital. The interviews were semi-structured. The Skierniewice interviewers had difficulty with the respondents' suspicion of tape-recorders and they therefore recorded the interviews through notes. The Warsaw interviews were tape-recorded and transcribed. All were translated into English. All respondents were given pseudonyms to protect the confidentiality of the interviews. This qualitative research was concerned with the respondents' understanding of the social, political and economic context and its impact on them as mothers; with the impact of the transition from communism on gender relations of care in households; with their strategies for negotiating the consequences of the state's reduction of social support; and their perceptions of policies that would enable parenting. We make no claims about the statistical representativeness of our sample of mothers and inferences about the statistical significance of our conclusions cannot be drawn.

The reader should always ask about the similarities and differences between the experience of these mothers in Poland and of mothers elsewhere. Chapter Two locates Poland within the new CEE member states by reference to some well-established quantitative measures of gender equality, and Chapter Three locates our study in comparison with quantitative studies in Poland. In the qualitative data we are concerned with the social processes from the point of view of mothers, and are attempting to develop an understanding of these processes inductively from the data. We do try to represent the diversity of views offered by the mothers in interviews: "the content or map of the range of views, experiences, outcomes of the phenomena under study and the factors that shape or influence them" and it is this which may be inferred to the wider population (Ritchie and Lewis, 2003, p 269). The mothers offered accounts of their experience as mothers, and of their memories of their own mothers' mothering under communism. Of course, these are very different data: accounts of the past may be romanticised and we need to bear this in mind. There is not very much good evidence about the quality of welfare systems under communism, when damaging information may well have been suppressed. But the respondents' accounts of the past may also be read as a perspective on the present, whether this is of improving living standards or a childcare system more like a sieve than a safety net. Through these dual strategies we address questions about the gender implications of broad social change across the transition countries and women's experience of parenting in the post-communist situation, as well as their judgements of the ways that social policies have affected them and might better support them. What are the key debates?

Is a welfare state possible after communism?

We ask to what extent the withdrawal of the state is seen as representing an enlargement of civil society and freedom or, alternatively, is perceived as a reduction of essential support to families? The collapse of authoritarian governments across Central and Eastern Europe and the former Soviet Union chimed with the spread of liberal economics and politics and liberal values in the West. The values of a welfare state – the very idea of a welfare state – have been challenged by the spread of free markets and individualism, and have widely undermined government commitment to social objectives, people's faith in their governments to meet social needs, and governments' faith in their people to vote for any agenda besides low taxation and individual choice. But in CEE countries in particular, after the years of authoritarian government, domination from above and from beyond national borders, the idea of a welfare state is problematic: "The values underpinning social policy have been more de-legitimated or more corrupted than in the stable liberal democracies" (Ferge, 1998, p 177).

The collapse of authoritarian governments brought damage to economies and GDPs, to public finance and to services. In the years following the transition from communism, GDP in Central Europe (CE) dropped by nearly a fifth and in the Baltic states and South-Eastern Europe (SEE) by a quarter. Central Europe is the only part of the region to have recovered economically to its pre-transition level. The Baltic states and SEE are now at about 80% of their GDP level of 1989. Governments have spent a diminishing proportion of these reduced GDPs. The gender regimes of the soviet era were built on very high levels of public expenditure of around 55% of GDP in the countries of Central and South-Eastern Europe. The comparable figures now are 45% in CE and 40% in SEE (UNICEF, 2001, pp 13-16). The policy consequences have been described for Hungary as reduced spending on education, health, pensions and child benefits, and pluralisation of welfare instruments (Ferge and Tausz, 2002; Szeman, 2003). These changes threaten the previously high levels of support for women's employment and motherhood, family benefits and spending on health and education.

But how are these changes perceived on the ground? The freedom to develop in civil society has been widely expected to bring women into organisations with a feminist agenda. But there has not been a major movement involving women or a development of women's organisations identifying themselves as feminist (Ferge, 1998; Fuszara 2000a, 2000b, 2000c; Watson, 2000a, 2000b). The relative lack of these, and of women in positions in formal politics, may suggest that women are not identifying with gender equality or with the agenda of support for combining work and family that has developed in the West. How do women perceive the state and its withdrawal from services? Do they see the reduction in welfare provision as an increase in choice and control, an increase in the autonomy of households and families, or as a failure of the state's function (Fodor, 2002, pp 372-3)? What do they see as appropriate to the state now, after the authoritarian regime?

Is there re-traditionalisation at the level of the household?

There is little question about the distribution of work in CEE households during the communist period, or about people's sense of maternal and paternal roles. Governments wanted women to be workers but they also wanted them to be mothers. All the structures developed to enable this were to enable women to sustain their roles in the household, not to enable any change in the domestic division of labour. The lack of outside influence and public debate made an unfriendly environment for the development of feminist identity in women or any change in men's identity as breadwinners that would bring them to see themselves as being responsible for childcare. These perceptions are supported by time-budget data that emphasise the dual load of women, leading to long working hours (UNICEF, 1999; Gershuny, 2000).

But there is room for debate about the post-communist period. Most commentators emphasise a lack of change inside households, while dramatic change outside has brought diminishing support for mothers of young children and has led to heavy workloads, with mothers unsupported by the state or their partners:

> The communist state espoused an egalitarian ideology and enshrined equality rights in legislation, but its promise was unfulfilled in the daily lives of women. With civil society weak and the family shut against the state, there was little space for women's equality to develop and grow from the grassroots. (UNICEF, 1999, p 1)

In Poland in particular, these trends have been identified as 're-traditionalisation' (Glass and Kawachi, 2001). These authors note the high level of women's unemployment in Poland, and the greater likelihood of being unemployed for mothers, despite their higher levels of qualification, which does not apply to fathers. They also comment on the (less-pronounced) tendency for women to describe their main activity as 'keeping house'. All of these could add up to a return to a male breadwinner model of the household, with men's employment prioritised over women's; men seeing themselves as breadwinners; and women content to return to domesticity after the rigours of soviet working-motherhood. The high and increasing levels of women's unemployment are indeed a significant trend in Poland and may lead to women's dependence within families. But there is little evidence about the extent to which these trends come about through women's own choices, and little evidence about the sense people have of themselves, their mentalities or identities as carers and earners.

Our qualitative data do not include women who described themselves as unemployed, although some respondents were on parental leave and their labour market attachment seemed fragile. Our discussion of these questions is mainly in terms of households where both partners have jobs and we may therefore have excluded people with the most traditional orientations. But Poland is a good test case of re-traditionalisation among CEE countries, in the sense that Poland has been identified as having more cultural and political pressures, rejecting the communist past, embracing the Roman Catholic Church, restricting abortion, and with high levels of women's unemployment (see Chapter Three). And we are able through our qualitative data to explore people's sense of themselves as workers and carers, to ask about traditional mentalities as well as traditional opportunities.

If the accounts given, of Poland in particular, tend to emphasise the continuation of traditional patterns of household work and care, there are some contradictory indications. Bjornberg and Sass (1997; Erler and Sass, 1997, pp 39-40), in a quantitative study of families with small children, early in the transition period, in countries across Europe including Poland and Hungary, found fathers second only in importance to mothers in the families' childcare arrangements. The fathers' importance was also well ahead of formal childcare in Poland and ahead of grandmothers everywhere. Clearly, grandmother care is important and can be one way in which traditional gender arrangements are continued. But these data raise questions about the notion that traditional patterns are maintained in households. The European Foundation for the Improvement of Living and Working Conditions has produced new evidence about the distribution of care work in households, suggesting that men in the candidate countries are more likely than men in the West to spend some time on childcare (Paoli and Parent-Thirion, 2003). So there is an alternative possibility to explore in relation to emerging households: far from being havens of tradition in a fast-moving world, the households of CEE countries may be re-inventing themselves more rapidly than those in Western Europe.

A new social policy regime? Or an old one?

We also discussed social policy issues with our respondents in Poland: what particular policies and what kind of social policy environment would they like to see? Do they agree with the policies of their governments? Do they want policies to enable women to leave the labour market and care for children? Do they want state support for a dual earner model of the family? And if so, is this for a model in which there is equal care between men and women as well as equal paid employment? What kind of welfare regime do women expect in the aftermath of authoritarian government? And, now civil society is more developed, what are women's expectations of the household division of labour, and how this should be supported through social policies?

There is some evidence that the pressures of the current social, economic and political context in Poland are bringing men into care roles in households, and some evidence from our respondents of strong expectations: respondents were vocal about their husbands' responsibilities for their children. This might bring with it an assumption that social policies should support men's role in unpaid work. They were also vocal about the time pressures on men and women trying to raise children in contemporary Poland. Do these add together into policy proposals involving men as carers? Or do women look for state support in moulding their own lives to fit their children's needs? The history of gender relations in households under communism might lead us to expect that a traditional model would emerge in debates about forms of support for working parenthood; while the contemporary picture of more involved fathers could bring with it more sense of the need for state policies to support more equal care in the household, along with more equal work outside it.

There are many dilemmas in the debates we had with these mothers of young children. Support for parents in the communist era was much more comprehensive, in terms of time, cost, culture, education and benefits, than anything they could muster now. Many respondents looked back with nostalgia to the security it represented. But it was also communist, authoritarian and the product of an occupying power. To the extent that the communist policies continue in the present, their effects are very different and often damaging. Discussions around periods of parental leave illustrate these issues very powerfully: in the very free market of contemporary Poland, women may want and need parental leave to accommodate the care of young children but they also see leave entitlements as exposing women to discrimination. Our respondents often saw themselves as having more choice than their own mothers but they were very aware of having less security. In employment themselves, they acknowledged the diverse situations of women in contemporary Poland: they pointed to the risks of unemployment to young women in general and to mothers in particular. Many described great difficulty meeting the demands of employers and the needs of their children. These difficulties were evident in most of our respondents' discussions of having children post-communism. Many commented on their own difficulties, but also on the difficulties of those in harsher circumstances in a more divided Poland, and on the national evidence of declining birth rates. Many respondents were outraged by the present situation and wanted change. These qualitative data are supported by quantitative evidence from the European Foundation for the Improvement of Living and Working Conditions, which suggests that dual earner families are under pressure (Alber and Fahey, 2004).

What sources of change in social policy are there? How much evidence is there of women involved in political action to express their dissent or demanding more positive policies from national government or local authorities? National governments and international agencies have shown concerns about declining birth rates. Could these concerns bring some defence for the systems that have supported women as mothers and their children? Does the development of civil society bring changes in the way gender relations are perceived and acted on by governments and households? Chapter Seven also explores the impact of European Union membership. Gender equality has been among the most prominent issues of the European Union's social agenda and it has been extending from a concern with the labour market to a concern with the issues of childcare and working time that often underlie women's position in the labour market. Will a European social agenda bring support to gender equality across the CEE countries?

New directions: gender regimes in the countries of Central and Eastern Europe

This book connects with a literature about comparative welfare states and a literature about gender. The countries of Central and Eastern Europe have often been excluded from these comparative literatures, although expansion of the European Union to the east makes these issues of great moment. Esping-Andersen, in *Why we need a new welfare state* (Esping-Andersen et al, 2002), now acknowledges the importance of a 'child-centred investment strategy' and a 'new gender contract'; but in what was designed as a 'new architecture for Europe' it is difficult to find any accommodation for those countries of Central and Eastern Europe that joined in May 2004. A cluster of books have been written in response to the collapse of the former Soviet Union, some of which focused on women and changing gender relations: Corrin (1992) *Superwomen and the double burden*; Mueller and Funk (eds) (1993) *Gender politics and post-communism*; Einhorn (1993) *Cinderella goes to market*; Moghadam (ed) (1993) *Democratic reform and the position of women in transitional economies*; Łobodzińska (1995) *Family, women and employment in Central-Eastern Europe*; Buckley (ed) (1997) *Post-soviet women: From the Baltic to Central Asia*; Gal and Kligman (eds) (2000) *Reproducing gender: politics, publics, and everyday life after socialism*.

Lynne Haney's (2002) *Inventing the needy: Gender and the politics of welfare in Hungary* investigates the changing welfare regimes in Hungary from 1948-96 and offers a fascinating account of changing gender regimes from the inside, drawing on interviews, documentary data and correspondence to elucidate the changing perceptions of need under communism and after in Hungary. There has been little to analyse and document on the relations between welfare states and gender across Central and Eastern Europe, although this is a crucial aspect of the changes that are occurring in CEE countries.

This book is embedded in a contemporary literature about issues of welfare regimes, transition from communism and an expanding Europe, but its focus on gender regimes in Central and Eastern Europe is new, distinctive, and, in the context of the widening of Europe, of great contemporary importance. The book thus connects with major theoretical issues about comparative welfare states as well as with key contemporary issues arising from the expansion of the European Union to include the countries of Central and Eastern Europe that are in transition from communism. But first, this chapter closes with discussion of some aspects of the social and economic and family context of gender under communism and in transition.

Gender under communism

Countries of the former soviet region have common legislative roots that produce an amount of common history of social policy and family law. Measures to secure the 'emancipation' of women in the former Soviet Union were embodied in resolutions of the 1920 Congress of the Comintern, and later extended to other soviet states. These measures covered issues of paid employment, motherhood and the liberalisation of laws on marriage and the family (Molyneux, 1990, p 25).

Soviet states' emphasis on labour participation as a route to emancipation led to social policy regimes that could be seen as support systems for women as paid employees and as mothers. Services were targeted first at the need for women's labour. Legislation in Poland, for example, was intended to "minimise existing conflicts between occupational and family obligations by granting more privileges, extended maternal and childcare paid leave of absence, family allowances, family support funds, restriction of pregnant and nursing women's working hours, and free health care" (Łobodzińska, 1995, p 7).

State subsidies for nurseries and kindergartens were important to women's labour market participation but the wage structure also pushed women into the labour market: in Hungary, 20% women worked outside the home in 1941 and 60% in 1965, while the figure was 75% for Budapest women (rural women were classified as housewives, but worked on farms):

> Full employment policies positioned work as a basic need
> for men and women alike; the wage structure made work
> a practical need for families; and the system of price subsidies
> defined what families needed to survive materially. These
> interpretations were linked to the larger demands of
> industrialisation and production. Thus, national-level
> policies also fulfilled the economic needs of the regime. In
> doing so, they often satisfied the needs of different social
> groups in contrasting ways – class position and family
> structure clearly affected the allocation of centralised
> services. A similar dynamic characterised the distribution of
> enterprise-based benefits in the period. (Haney, 2002, p 39)

Pro-natalist policies followed this emphasis on women's employment. From the 1970s, demographic issues loomed larger and policies to encourage motherhood ensued, especially in Hungary (Molyneux, 1990, p 27). Indeed, Haney argues for Hungary that the characterisation of regimes in terms of pre- and post-transition, state socialism/welfare capitalism is too simple, with a transformation from a welfare society in the post-Second World War period to a maternalist one in the 1960s (Haney, 2002, pp 4-5).

The official constitutional position of women under communism was of equality with men: marriage and family law were liberalised, sexually exploitative images and writing prohibited, and equal opportunity for women was promoted. However, despite these wide-ranging laws that framed women as equals, by the 1980s the official conception of gender relations was entrenching difference rather than equality:

> The particular issue of gendered divisions in employment
> and in the home was never seriously tackled by government
> policies. Instead, in most countries, while the material effects
> of inequality (women's double burden) were deplored, the
> divisions themselves – far from being seen as socially
> constructed – were increasingly talked of as natural, even
> desirable, by planners and populace alike, as a reaction to
> the extremism of earlier years. (Molyneux, 1990, p 43)

Social policies' challenge to traditional roles had more impact on public life – especially women's participation in paid employment – and traditional motherhood and maternal responsibility were simultaneously idealised and sustained. Women's responsibilities were to bear and to raise children. The regimes could be characterised as sustaining women's roles as mothers and as workers:

> Because of the impossibility of free public discourse, gender
> relations never became a public issue. In public life, work,
> studies, culture and politics, women had become (almost)
> equal, and they may have felt (almost) equal. But in the
> private sphere, in partner relations, within the family and
> the interpersonal arena, traditional ways of constructing
> men and women's roles remained, by and large, untouched.
> (Ferge, 1998, p 221)

Gender in transition economies

State support for this notion of gender equality makes these provisions
problematic now, in the context of the rejection of soviet models. The
transition from communism has had dramatic effects everywhere on a
number of aspects of gender relations and the system of social policies
that supported soviet-style gender equality. Economic damage to state
revenues and political challenges to public services have undermined
the social policies that supported women as workers and mothers:
"The values underpinning social policy have become more de-
legitimated or more corrupted than in the stable liberal democracies"
(Ferge, 1997b, p 177). Employment and the welfare systems that went
with it are much less secure. While these changes have removed the
foundations on which women's roles in paid work, motherhood and
care were constructed, what is coming in their place is more diverse.

Economic transformation brought falling GDPs everywhere, around
20% in Central Europe, but more severely elsewhere, with Latvia's
falling to 51% of its 1989 figure by 1995. Equally, economic growth
has been re-established everywhere; but Poland recovered to its 1989
level in 1996 and was 30% above it by 2002, while Latvia and Lithuania
were still 24% and 27% below their 1989 figure (TransMONEE data,
2003) (Figure 1.1).

The threat to social spending on education, health and childcare,
and thus to the key structures which supported the gender regimes, is
obvious. Public expenditure cuts and welfare state restructuring in
the early transition period took place in the context of falling GDPs
and increasing inequalities (Ferge and Juhasz, 2004). In Central Europe,
government expenditure has diminished in most countries, but has
remained high as a percentage of GDP: at transition Czechoslovakia
had government spending at around 60.1% of GDP, which by 2002
had fallen to 46.6% in the Czech Republic and 48.4% in Slovakia.

Figure 1.1: Real GDP growth

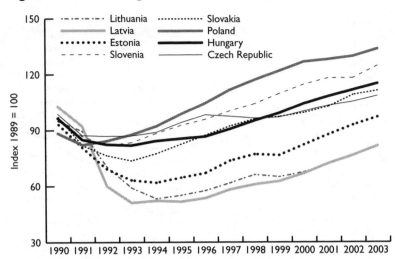

Source: TransMONEE database, www.unicef-icdc.org/resources

Hungary's reduction was less dramatic, from 57.5% of GDP to 53.5% during this period, while Poland's expenditure rose slightly, from nearly 40% in 1990 to 44.1% in 2002 (Figure 1.2).

Changes in GDP and in public expenditure have provided a turbulent context for social policies, even in countries which have maintained relatively high government spending, such as Hungary. TransMONEE data suggest that expenditure on health services (Figure 1.3) and education (Figure 1.4) have been broadly sustained across these areas as a proportion of GDP, bearing in mind that GDPs themselves are much lower.

To the extent that state welfare spending has been sustained, it has had to compensate for increasing inequalities in the capacity of individuals to sustain their own welfare through earnings, in terms of income and security. The employment ratio – the proportion of those aged 15-59 in employment – shows a steady decline across the 1990s in all countries (Figure 1.5). Although these particular data do not tell us about the gender distribution of this decline (which is discussed in Chapter Two), they do indicate increasing difficulty for individuals in supporting themselves.

There are also increasing inequalities in people's ability to support themselves. The transition has brought opportunities for individuals and – in most countries now – a growth in GDP. But inequalities of earnings and income show a tendency to rise across these countries, with increasing Gini coefficients (Figure 1.6).

Figure 1.2: General government expenditure

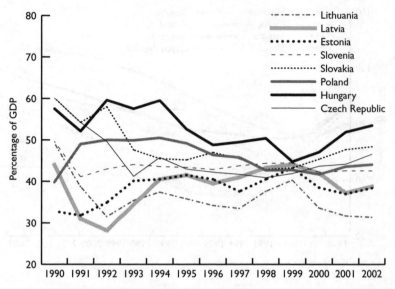

Source: TransMONEE database, www.unicef-icdc.org/resources

Figure 1.3: Public expenditures on health

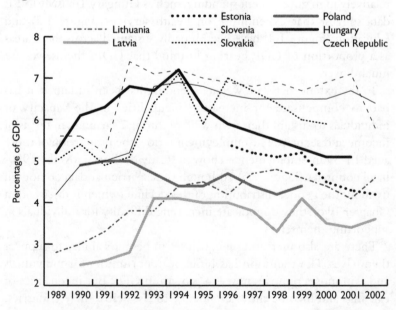

Source: TransMONEE database, www.unicef-icdc.org/resources

Figure 1.4: Public expenditures on education

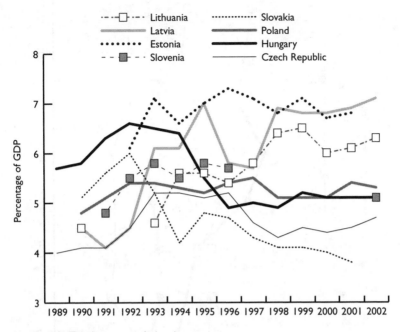

Source: TransMONEE database, www.unicef-icdc.org/resources

Figure 1.5: Employment ratio

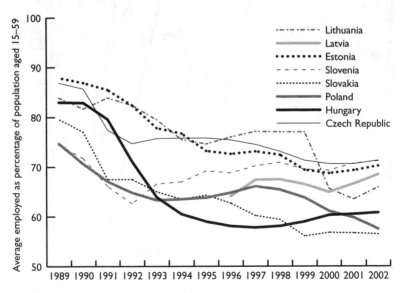

Source: TransMONEE database, www.unicef-icdc.org/resources

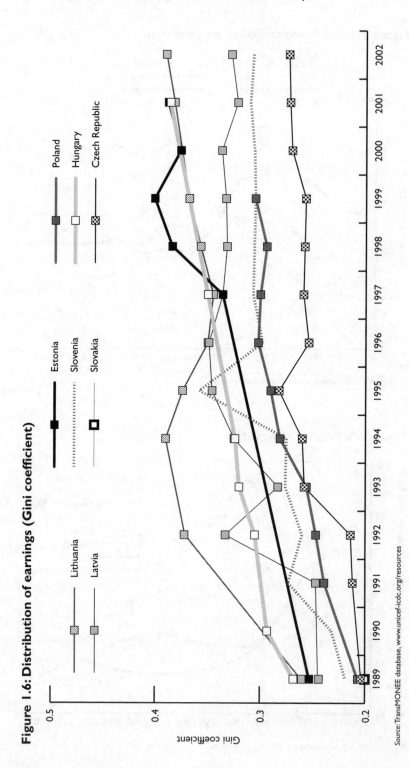

Figure 1.6: Distribution of earnings (Gini coefficient)

Source: TransMONEE database, www.unicef-icdc.org/resources

The broad social and economic picture that can be drawn of the CEE countries joining Europe is one of economic turmoil and recovery, with a growth in per capita incomes in most countries, and states – especially those in Central Europe – retaining high public spending and protecting public services, especially health and education. But there has also been a reduction in labour market participation and a growth in inequality and unemployment through policies influenced by international agencies such as the World Bank and the International Monetary Fund (Ferge and Juhasz, 2004; Potucek, 2004). The recent socioeconomic conditions are in contrast with those of the EU15 countries that have experienced steady improvements in real income and a decrease in inequalities. The result is wide differences in living standards between the new CEE member states and the EU15. In 2002, according to purchasing power standards, the highest living standards are in Slovenia and the Czech Republic at around 60% of the EU15 average, while the lowest are in Latvia at less than 40%. In this respect, Poland ranks in the lower middle range of new CEE member states, with living standards just over 40% of the EU15 average (European Commission, 2004a, p 16). Figure 1.7 shows the GDP per capita in the period since transition.

Figure 1.7: GDP per capita

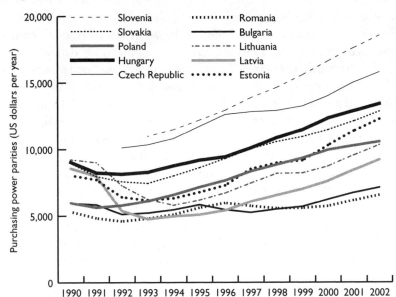

Source: TransMONEE database, www.unicef-icdc.org/resources

Marriage and cohabitation in transition societies

Male breadwinner families have been challenged by state policy dating back to the 1920s. The 'emancipation' of women in the former Soviet Union was seen first in Communist Party resolutions and by officials in terms of encouraging women to work outside the home (as well as in it), and identifying women's exclusion from paid employment as a key to their oppression (Molyneux, 1990, p 25). In CEE countries, these developments came with the spread of soviet domination and the post-1948 reforms:

> Like those enacted in other Eastern European countries, Hungary's reforms ended decades of patriarchal family law that codified female dependence on men. They constituted a new family form that served as the basis for the era's policy regime. Rhetorically, the 1949 Hungarian Constitution guaranteed women equal rights, equal working conditions, increased legal protection, and new maternity and child protection institutions. (Haney, 2002, p 28)

The communist legal tradition treated women in marriage more equally than most Western European countries: the 1918 Marriage Code attempted to establish equality between husbands and wives, to secularise marriage and to make divorce simple (Ferge, 1998, p 218). Benefits and taxation then tended to be attached to women's own employment rather than treating wives as their husbands' dependants, as often happened in the West. Liberal abortion laws appeared to support women's autonomy in relationships. In practice, men and women were not equal partners in marriage because of unequal earnings. Domestic violence has been a common and accepted part of marriage relationships. Lack of contraceptive services and information reduced reproductive autonomy. Housing shortages and allocation policies have made divorce – easy in theory – difficult in practice and escape from domestic violence extremely difficult. Communist marriage, then, was deeply contradictory for women. Marriage and divorce laws appear liberal by western standards, and there seems to be no history or practice under communism of entitlement to benefits through male breadwinners. But there was no women's movement to support women's reproductive autonomy, to challenge the gender division or to challenge men's power over women through domestic violence.

And the constraints of poverty are likely to have made family members deeply interdependent.

Constitutions have been renewed during transition, but the legacy of equal rights remains important: different countries have a very similar legislative base of equal rights, usually incorporated in the constitution: for example, the Estonian constitution has provided protection for women's rights since the first period of Estonian independence and the current constitution, dating from 1992, forbids discrimination on the basis of nationality, race, religion, social status, culture and sex (Haas et al, 2003).

Significant consequences flow from these constitutional commitments, which reflect the official position of states on gender issues, and set the environment for social policies including family policies, family law and property rights in marriage and divorce. In some respects and in some countries the gap between official declarations and the reality of unequal relations between partners may be large (see Chapter Three for Poland) and reflected in levels of acceptance of domestic violence. Men and women in marriage have different access to resources despite the equality legislation, and economic trends may be making women more dependent upon relationships, especially because of unemployment. Privatisation of housing may make escape from violent relationships more difficult. These markets in work and housing may be increasing the gap between constitutional equality and real inequality in family relationships.

The changing social constitution of cohabitation, marriage and parenthood is similar in most respects to patterns in Western Europe, with marriage relationships increasingly separated from sexual relationships, and from child-bearing (Lewis, 2001b). Thus through the 1990s marriage declined (Figure 1.8) and divorce increased (Figure 1.9) while the proportion of births outside marriage increased (Figure 1.10). These trends tend to be strongest in the Baltic states, and weakest in Poland.

Detailed data show the development of these processes in Poland more distinctively. From 1982 the rate of marriages contracted has been diminishing steadily. In 1981, the rate per 1,000 of population at the age of 15 and over was 9.0, in 1993 it was 5.4 and in 2002 it was 5.0 (Central Statistical Office, 2003c, p XXXI). From 1993, more marriages are being dissolved by death and divorce than are being contracted.

The divorce rate in Poland is low in comparative terms. In 2001 and 2002 it was 1.2 for every 1,000 of population but in 2003 it rose to 1.3 (Central Statistical Office, 2004a, p 31). In relation to contracted

Figure 1.8: Age-specific marriage rate

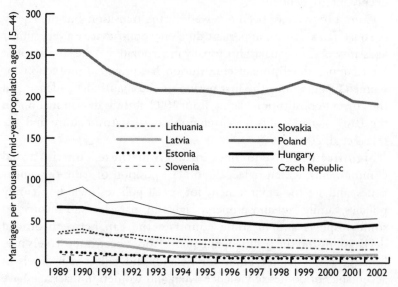

Source: TransMONEE database, www.unicef-icdc.org/resources

Figure 1.9: General divorce rate

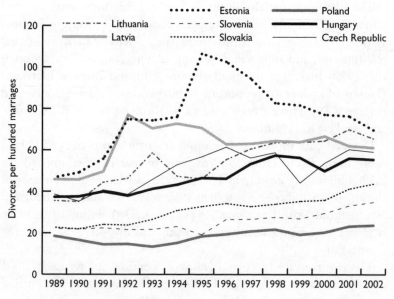

Source: TransMONEE database, www.unicef-icdc.org/resources

Figure 1.10: Share of non-marital births

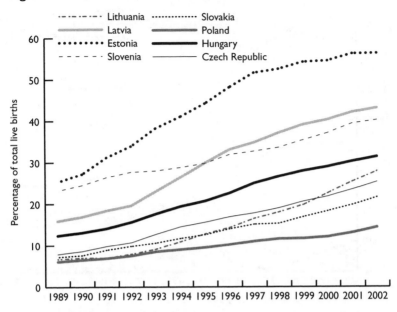

Source: TransMONEE database, www.unicef-icdc.org/resources

marriages, a high rate – between 19.54% and 19.66% – was maintained through the years 1986-88. This decreased in the years 1992-93 to a low of 13.43%. The rate rose again to reach 24.88% in 2003 in relation to the number of marriages.

A comparative study of 14 states (Austria, Finland, France, Germany East and West, Hungary, Italy, Latvia, Lithuania, Norway, Poland, Spain, Sweden, Switzerland) conducted in the first half of 1990s, shows Poland with the highest rate of marriage contracted directly, without prior cohabitation. For women aged 25-29 this rate was 95%, and for women aged 35-39 it was 96% (while in Latvia for the same age groups it was 50% and 67%). The rate of cohabitation in Poland was 2% for women aged 25-29 and 1% for those aged 35-39 (Kiernan, 2000, pp 50-51). In 2002, for the first time, the demographic statistics in the national population census defined 'cohabiting unions', described as 'partners without children' and 'partners with children'. Previously, cohabiting unions were included among marriages with children and without children (Central Statistical Office, 2003b, p 19). In 2002, as a proportion of households, partners with children numbered 1.1% and without children 0.8% (Central Statistical Office, 2003b, p 28).

Abortions have decreased across CEE countries, but again in Poland the severe restrictions on legal abortion have brought it down from

Figure 1.11: Abortion rate (per population)

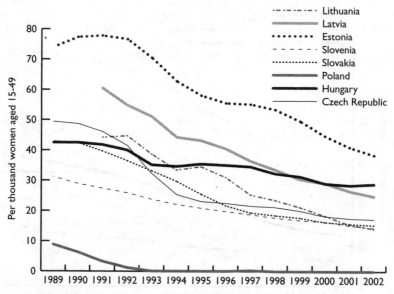

Source: TransMONEE database, www.unicef-icdc.org/resources

15 per 100 live births to zero, amid great debates about women's rights (Figure 1.11).

Cultural identities are emerging, with ethnic, linguistic and religious diversity within and between the new regimes, and differences in families and family policy. The predominantly Lutheran Estonia and Roman Catholic Poland bring differences in families as well as governments. While many trends are shared between these countries – and indeed between the countries of Eastern and Western Europe – the conformity of the communist era has been replaced by a broader spread. Births outside marriage are a clear example of this, low in Poland at transition, rising from 6% after transformation, but remaining well below the other countries. In the first half of 1980s the figure oscillated between 4.5% and 5.0% of total live births. In the 1990s it increased to 9.2% and has gone on increasing, in 2003 reaching 15.8% (Central Statistical Office, 2004a, p 298). But total fertility has declined everywhere in the new CEE member states, with the rate of reproduction now well below replacement level. Poland, which had a total fertility of 2.08 in 1989 has had a particularly steep decline, reaching 1.22 in 2003 (Central Statistical Office, 2004a). Now all the new CEE member states have a total fertility of between 1.17 and 1.37, and have converged in this respect, with Poland ranking just above the middle of the range (TransMONEE data and Chapter Two).

What then is the impact of family and social policy on women as partners in the former communist countries? The position in the post-communist period seems as deeply contradictory as during the soviet era. Equalities of family law, taxation and benefits coexist with domestic violence and with growing inequalities in access to resources. There are significant changes in the new environment, including the room for social action, and voices for change developing with the establishment of women's crisis centres and other political groups. However, the literature reports ideological pressure towards reviving traditional family roles, with Makkai describing a "concerted attack on reproductive rights" (Makkai, 1994, p 197). In Poland the religious establishment is an important political force and has backed changes restricting abortion (Ferge, 1998; Kwak, 1998), which is likely to reduce women's autonomy in relationships.

But despite this, and despite the widespread feeling from every publication that the ideological climate is pushing women into traditional relationships, there is little evidence, beyond Poland's abortion legislation, of social policies designed to do this. In most countries, the constitutional position of women is a significant defence against policies reducing women's rights. The constitutional position and the social legislation are real strengths for women. Broadly, the period since 1989 has seen these instruments little changed. Their embedding in international conventions is an important anchorage, as has been the aspiration to European Union membership and the latter part of the accession process (see Chapter Seven).

Conclusion

The economic turbulence of the transition period has brought serious problems for the systems of social welfare that supported mothers' labour market participation. GDPs fell dramatically at the beginning of the transition period and, in most countries, public expenditure as a proportion of GDP also fell. Increasing inequality and insecurity – especially unemployment – have made it more difficult for people to keep themselves out of poverty or to compensate for losses of public services. While economic growth has been re-established, the new CEE member states are far below the European Union average in individual purchasing power. In 2002, Poland's living standards were around 40% of the EU15 average. Decreases in marriage and increases in divorce and cohabitation meant that marriage became – as in Western Europe – increasingly separated from sexual relationships and from childbearing. These trends were common to all countries, although less extreme in Poland. Total fertility has declined in all the new CEE member states, from around 2 at transition to 1.2 or 1.3 in 2002, figures which may reflect the economic uncertainties as well as the changes in the context of parenthood.

An important question to ask is the extent to which the development of social policies in the post-communist era has brought diversity in assumptions about gender. Soviet domination was never complete, and economic, cultural, religious and ethnic differences played their various parts in the absorption and implementation of soviet ideology and law in practice. The differences are now more apparent with the re-emergence of religious and cultural identities that only ever went partly underground. The end of the communist era has brought new possibilities for diverging welfare states. So, important questions to be asked in Chapter Two relate to how much the new CEE member states carry forward their common history, and where Poland is located among them.

Note
[1] Bulgaria (candidate), Cyprus, Czech Republic, Estonia, Hungary, Latvia, Lithuania, Malta, Poland, Romania (candidate), Slovakia, Slovenia, Turkey (candidate).

TWO

Gender regimes in Central and Eastern Europe

Introduction

How can we best understand the differences and similarities between welfare states, in particular the gender assumptions of governments and households? There is a wealth of literature on the question of how to compare welfare states and how to compare gender regimes as an aspect of welfare states, but little that deals directly with Central Europe and less with the impact on gender in these countries. The enlargement of the European Union in 2004 is primarily an enlargement to the east to include the countries of Central and Eastern Europe that have had very different social policy regimes from those in the west. How are the gender assumptions underlying social policies of former communist countries and households developing now? What light do theoretical debates about gender and welfare regimes throw on the countries that have recently joined Europe? What light do statistical data about social change in the new CEE member states of the European Union cast on these changing gender regimes: data on public expenditure and welfare spending; employment, especially women's employment, working conditions and preferences and working time; kindergartens and care?

It is important to examine Poland's situation amid the new CEE member states of the European Union and how Poland compares, in key dimensions, with countries of Western Europe. Our qualitative data explore the experience of gender in transition – in particular of key aspects of state responsibility for parenting, children and childcare – from the point of view of mothers in Poland. As noted in Chapter One, Poland is particularly important because its people form nearly half the population in the newly expanded European Union. But is Poland also typical of the other countries or is the trajectory of the emerging regimes different in important respects? To what extent has transition from communism brought common conditions and experiences and common responses from national governments? Has the 15 years since the end of communism and their accession to the European Union brought CEE countries nearer to western regimes? Should we think of the CEE countries as having a common experience in relation to gender or as going in diverse directions, towards different gender models? This chapter situates Poland within theoretical debates about welfare regimes and gender, and examines quantitative comparative data about the new CEE member states and the wider European Union.

Gender in comparative frameworks

Typologies of welfare regimes have been many and varied in academic debates (Abrahamson, 1999), but few have centred on former communist countries, and there has been little discussion of the ways that gender shapes the social policies of former communist countries. In the context of the wider European Union, now numbering eight former communist countries among its members, this seems a major gap. How can the tools that have been developed to compare welfare states be used to understand former communist countries and their gender character? Can these countries be understood within existing frameworks, or does their distinctive history in the latter part of the 20th century bring distinctive characteristics into the 21st?

Discussion of welfare regimes tends to start with Esping-Andersen's *The three worlds of welfare capitalism* (1990) and his argument that welfare states' development diverges in three basic political economies: the social democracies of Scandinavia; the corporatist model of Germany; and the liberal residualist welfare state characteristic of the US and Canada, and to some extent the UK. The enormous influence of this work makes this difficult to avoid, despite its focus on western models and its problematic approach to gender. Esping-Andersen's typology of welfare regimes draws from social democracy and political economy, using the concepts of 'de-commodification' to describe the relationship of paid workers to the labour market, and 'stratification' to describe class inequality. Esping-Andersen developed the concept of welfare regimes to mean "the institutional arrangements, rules and understandings that guide and shape concurrent policy decisions, expenditure developments, problem definitions, and even the respond-and-demand structure of citizens and welfare consumers" (Esping-Andersen, 1990, p 80). *The three worlds of welfare capitalism* did not carry through the project announced in its first chapter: "to take into account how state activities are interlocked with the market's and the family's role in social provision" (Esping-Andersen, 1990, p 21). Since then, Esping-Andersen has taken his regime analysis into Central and Eastern Europe (Esping-Andersen and Micklewright, 1991) and has compensated – to some extent – in later publications for the neglect of gender in his original book (Esping-Andersen et al, 2001, 2002). But nowhere in his 'new architecture for Europe' is there room for the new CEE member states. We still need an approach to welfare regimes that can accommodate the regimes of the post-communist world, as well as one that can accommodate gender. The role, valuation and division of unpaid work are in the foreground of most feminist critiques of Esping-Andersen and similar typologies. Jane Lewis argues the need to centre paid and unpaid work and ask how welfare policies relate to the structures of family and paid employment. She offers the best-known alternative strategy, in identifying a continuum based on how welfare states relate to unpaid work. At one end are male breadwinner regimes, such as in the UK and Ireland, whose underpinning assumptions have been of women as dependent housewives supported by male breadwinners. In the UK, policies such as the Beveridgean national insurance system and low levels of state support for childcare supported this model of the family from the post-Second World War period to nearly the end of the 20th century. By contrast, Sweden's weak male breadwinner regime developed in the late 1960s and early 1970s, encouraging a rapid rise of women's labour market participation through changes in taxation policy, childcare provision and support for parental leave. These are ideal types, with no male breadwinner or dual earner system existing in pure form, but rather in different degrees underpinning the gender workings of welfare states (Lewis, 1992, 2002).

The characterisation of gender regimes based on the male breadwinner/dual earner spectrum has the great advantage that it puts gender at the centre of comparative analysis. We therefore begin with the male breadwinner/dual earner approach for an understanding of the gender assumptions that underpin regimes, and develop it for the purpose of analysing the post-communist countries of Central and Eastern Europe. Gender regimes can be seen as systems through which paid work is connected to unpaid, state services and benefits are delivered to individuals or households, costs are allocated, and time is shared between men and women in households as well as between households and employment: the decline of the male breadwinner model has widespread implications (Creighton, 1999; Crompton, 1999; Lewis, 2001a, 2000b). So, of course, does the decline of state support for dual earner arrangements in the new CEE member states, although too little attention has been paid to this (Hantrais, 2002a; Pascall and Lewis, 2004).

Here we analyse gender models on the male breadwinner/dual earner spectrum into component parts: paid work, care work, income, time and voice, asking to what extent they can be seen as systems of gender equality or as systems of traditional gender roles in each of these parts. For western welfare states, Daly and Rake's (2003) complex and nuanced account of gender relations in care, work and household resources gives a deep understanding of the contradictions and complexities in welfare state provision, and many of the arguments and measures developed in their comparisons of western welfare states are relevant to CEE countries. Our account shares with them a concern with welfare states and gender relations as systems of power, with the relations between them, and the ways these are worked out in the key domains of care, employment and income. We ask whether the gender policies of the new CEE member states are moving away from the dual earner assumptions of the communist era, 're-traditionalising' (see Chapter One) towards more divided gender roles and resources in work, care, time, income and voice, with CEE countries rejecting the communist past, and the gender model that went with it, at economic, political and social levels. On the other hand we may see the gender equality models that are emerging in CEE countries as being deeply rooted, with very high expectations of women's position in the labour market, a revolution and transition away from the male breadwinner model.

The levels of policy intervention form our second mode of analysis. As Gornick and Meyers (2003) argue, the regimes of the Esping-Andersen categories are closely associated with gender models in practice:

> The welfare state principles underlying these (Esping-Andersen) clusters are highly correlated with those that shape family policy. In the Nordic countries, the social-democratic principles that guide policy design are generally paired with a commitment to gender equality; the market-replicating principles in the continental countries are often embedded in socially conservative ideas about family and gender roles; in the English-speaking countries the principles of the market nearly always take precedence. (Gornick and Meyers, 2003, p 23)

There is a clear association between high levels of social spending in the social democratic model and measures supporting care and gender equality (Bambra, 2004). The transition in CEE countries has been a transition from strongly collectivist communist states. We need to investigate and map the extent to which collectivist ideals have been transformed into individualist ones bringing more market choice but lower levels of state spending to support dual earner households. We also ask about the extent to which care responsibilities have been pushed towards households. The development of civil society is a key element of the transition from communism and is also important in terms of developing gender ideas and ideals.

While high social spending may be a condition for achieving gender equality, the nature and quality of provisions comes first: so this chapter's sections start from gender, but each asks about changes in the level of intervention and the consequences for gender equality.

Gender equality policies are mapped in Figure 2.1, across the essential elements of gender systems: their allocations of paid work, income, care work, time and voice between men and women, as well as between households, civil society and collective levels. Many gender equality policies are aimed primarily at individuals in order to change individual women's ability to compete with men at work. The literature and the policy environment show a growing awareness of the need to intervene at the household level, with policies to enable households to manage care and particularly to encourage men to engage in care, for example, non-transferable 'Daddy leave'. This idea underpins the Netherlands' Combination Scenario, set out in a White Paper in 1997, to encourage men and women to be equally able to combine paid and unpaid work, thus bringing men into unpaid work, as well as bringing women into paid, with policies addressed mainly at the household level (Plantenga et al, 1999; Knijn, 2001; Knijn and Selten, 2002; Plantenga, 2002). The Resolution of the Council and Ministers for Employment and Social Policy on the balanced participation of women and men in family and working life agreed a 'new social contract on gender' proposing that gender equality in employment requires gender equality in parenting, marking an important shift from preoccupation with individual equal opportunities to equality of care within households. It also proposes more broadly based systems of regulating time, for example, to enable this (Council of the European Union, 2000). Civil society is a crucial source of political change in CEE countries and also an important provider of care in some western countries. Fraser's 'post-industrial thought experiment' offers a similar approach to the Netherlands' Combination Scenario with the proposal of a 'universal caregiver' model, although aimed mainly at the level of civil society (Fraser, 1997). Policies at the collective level allow resources to be

Figure 2.1: Map of gender equality policies and models

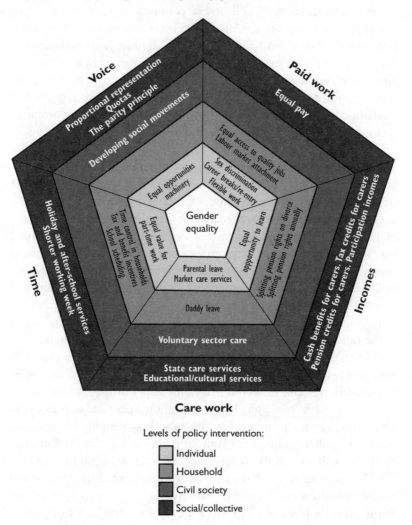

Care work

Levels of policy intervention:

- Individual
- Household
- Civil society
- Social/collective

shared between households as well as within them. We will argue that the evidence of gender equality policies, so far, is that countries with policies involving state level, collective provision – in care services for example – have produced the greatest degree of gender equality in comparison with countries which have relied on individual-level policies, such as sex discrimination legislation, or on household-level policies, as in the Netherlands' Combination Scenario, or indeed provision in civil society (Pascall and Lewis, 2004).

We are therefore using a framework analysing the impact of regimes on gender relations in paid work, income, care work, time and voice.

But we also examine the impact of changes away from the collective social level of provision towards individualised solutions based on markets that may undermine the dual earner systems of CEE countries. Intermediate action and provision in civil society, whose development is one of the core changes in the aftermath of communism, is also explored. We also ask about the extent to which the new CEE member states have policies encouraging gender equality at the household level.

Some commentators on the emerging post-communist states have argued that their gender assumptions are now becoming so divergent that they should be seen as distinctive regime types, with Hungary and Poland now representing contrasting trajectories. The argument is based on differences in family policy in particular, with welfare provisions supporting women's labour market position more strongly and universally in Hungary than in Poland (Fodor et al, 2002). Alternatively, Haney uses Esping-Andersen categories to suggest that Hungary is liberal, concentrating on free markets, Poland is corporatist because of its reliance on church and family, and the Czech Republic is social democratic, with citizenship-based rights and low unemployment rates (Haney, 2002, p 174). But from the point of view of gender there are also many factors in common; for example the common history of soviet domination and soviet law and the development of a dual earner model from the 1950s. If, as Korpi (2000) argues, differences between gender regimes can be partly understood in terms of differences in the dominance of political landscape over time, then the four decades of Communist Party government might be expected to produce some similarities in the gender assumptions of CEE countries, even after communist domination. *The social situation in the European Union (2004)* (European Commission, 2004a) comments on the similarities of the gender experience in the new member states:

> Gender equality in the new CEE member states is particularly marked by both the policies of the former regimes as well as the socioeconomic implications of the transition period. The socioeconomic situation of women in these countries witnessed severe degradation during the transition period, in terms of employment participation and income. The collapse of social policies in support of working women and families has increased the burden on women, and contributed to the depression of fertility rates. (European Commission, 2004a, p 108)

Other developments in common are the freedoms to develop civil society and the economic upheavals of the transition period. So another task of this chapter is to ask about difference. Are the emerging states so different as to identify them as different gender regimes? Or does the common heritage bring a distinctive cluster of gender regimes? And where does Poland sit among the regimes emerging in Central and Eastern Europe in terms of the gender assumptions underlying policies and their outcome in terms of gender equality?

These questions will be addressed in the following sections through statistical indicators developed in the literature around gender and western welfare states, in particular focusing on gender gaps. Not all the statistical data are available in the same form for new member states as for old ones, but the development of European Union structural indicators is an important step to being able to compare CEE gender regimes with each other as well as with Western Europe. With European Union indicators designed to enable member states to reach the same goals by means of their own choice, we now have comparative outcome data by gender on many key dimensions. We are not able here to offer comparative data on the distribution of resources within households, but we have data on employment, care, household income, time and political participation. These are used to compare new CEE member states with each other as well as with the EU15 and particular welfare states, representing particular models: Sweden to represent the dual earner in Western Europe; France for its modified breadwinner counterpart, and Ireland and Malta (a new member) which have a strong male breadwinner tradition (Camilleri-Cassar, 2005). The UK, while maintaining its expectations of women as mothers until the 1990s, has made significant changes in assumptions and practices about women's employment since 1997, and is therefore not used in most of the comparisons here as a male breadwinner state.

Gender in paid work

Gender equality under communism, even more than in other regimes, was about women's place in the labour market, which was supported by social investment in childcare and other services. High labour participation was achieved, at a much earlier period than in the West, with women spending most of their adult lives in paid work. By 1980 half the labour force of Eastern Europe consisted of women, compared with 32% in Western Europe, and they were crossing some gender barriers (Molyneux, 1990, pp 26-7). The basis of gender equality at work was collective support for children and childcare needs, in contrast, for example, to the individual rights approach in the UK from the 1960s. As in the West, employment was segregated and women's earnings were lower than men's, but gender equality at work under communism was more nearly approached than in most of Western Europe. We shall be asking about the extent to which the practices and ideals around women's place in the labour market have survived the transition from communism, and – in so far as they do survive – how well communist practices work in a capitalist marketplace.

Women's employment participation was supported by entitlements through work, with occupational welfare a key source of provision. Participation was high by international standards: at the point of transition from communism in 1989, it was over 80% in the Baltic states and Czechoslovakia, and around 70% in Hungary and Poland – well above the labour market participation rate for women in France or the UK. The gender gap in employment was 11% in Hungary and 13% in Poland and again low by Western European standards, when only Swedish women's labour market participation nearly matched men's (UNICEF, 1999, p 24). State policies were not the only factor in patterns of employment: the importance of cultural aspects is suggested by the lower participation of women in Poland even under communism. But women's earnings were also nearer to men's than in most Western European countries: in 1997, women's monthly earnings were around 80% of men's in the Czech Republic, Slovakia, Hungary and Poland (UNICEF, 1999, p 33). The broad picture of women's participation at the point of transition is of well-established dual earner households, with women in full-time employment and with earnings not far below men's. To what extent now can women in CEE countries participate in employment and earn enough to bring independence in access to income? To what extent have different states brought differences to the regulation of work, welfare and patterns of paid employment and, in particular, what is Poland's position among the new member CEE states? And how do these societies compare on key dimensions with the countries of Western Europe?

Here we use several indicators of women's ability to sustain themselves and their families through high-quality employment, and of their position compared with men, and compared with countries of Western Europe. The literature suggests several ways to make cross-national comparisons in gender differences in employment in order to illuminate differences in welfare regimes (especially Korpi, 2000; Daly and Rake, 2003) and we draw mainly on Eurostat structural indicators and European Commission data from *The social situation in the European Union (2004)* (European Commission, 2004a). Women's employment participation is a key measure of access to independent resources. But we also look at some measures of job security (unemployment) and of job quality (the gender pay gap and part-time work, discussed later under 'Time') as well as measures supporting work, such as parental leave (discussed later under 'Care'). We are particularly concerned with the gaps between men and women, whether in employment, unemployment, pay or part-time work, as these may help to unravel the extent to which changes in transition countries have been about a generally increasing experience of insecurity, or about a re-traditionalisation, in which women's employment is being marginalised in favour of men's (Table 2.1).

Women's employment has certainly fallen across the new CEE member states. It is particularly low, and is still falling, in Poland at 46% (2003), while the highest figure is in Estonia at 59%. The figures are also compared with male employment rates, with the gap between women's and men's employment shown in the final column. The Czech

Table 2.1: Male and female employment rates, as a percentage of men and women aged 15-64, and difference between male and female (2003)[a]

	Employment rate (%)		
	Male	Female	Difference male – female
Czech Republic	73.1	56.3	16.8
Estonia	67.2	59	8.2
Latvia	66.1	57.9	8.2
Lithuania	64	58.4	5.6
Hungary	63.5	50.9	12.6
Poland	56.5	46	10.5
Slovenia	67.4	57.6	9.8
Slovakia	63.3	52.2	11.1
Sweden	74.2	71.5	2.7
France	69.4	57.2	12.2
Ireland	75	55.8	19.2
Malta	74.5	33.6	40.9
EU15	72.7	56.1	16.6
EU25	70.9	55.1	15.8

Note: [a] The employment rates are calculated by dividing the number of women and men aged 15-64 in employment by the total female and male populations of the same age group. The indicator is based on the EU Labour Force Survey. The survey covers the entire population living in private households and excludes those in collective households such as boarding houses, halls of residence and hospitals. The employed population consists of those persons who during the reference week did any work for pay or profit for at least one hour, or were not working but had jobs from which they were temporarily absent.

Source: Eurostat structural indicators Europa NewCronos website 2005 (epp.eurostat.cec.eu.int) and authors' calculations

Republic is the only country to have a gender employment gap above the average for the EU15. Most CEE countries have much lower gender employment gaps: even Poland, where women's employment is at its lowest, has a gap between women and men of 10.5%. This is well above Sweden's (2.7%), but below the gender employment gap in France (12.2%), Ireland (19.2%) and Malta (40.9%). This suggests that in this respect the dual earner model is alive and well in CEE countries, with more equal participation in employment between men and women than in the EU15, and a much lower gap than in countries such as Ireland and Malta, which have been associated with the male breadwinner model.

Data on unemployment for 2004 (Table 2.2) suggest that the changing economic landscape is one in which both men and women are vulnerable to losing their jobs. Polish women suffer particularly high unemployment at 19.7%, but Polish men's rate of unemployment is not much better, at 18.0%. Across the EU25, unemployment rates

Table 2.2: Female and male unemployment rates, as a percentage of the labour force, and difference between female and male (2004)[a]

	Unemployment rate (%)		
	Female	**Male**	**Difference female – male**
Czech Republic	9.9	7.1	2.8
Estonia	8.1	10.3	−2.2
Latvia	10.3	9.2	1.1
Lithuania	11.3	10.3	1.0
Hungary	6.0	5.8	0.2
Poland	19.7	18.0	1.7
Slovenia	6.5	5.6	0.9
Slovakia	19.3	17.0	2.3
Sweden	6.1	6.5	0.4
France	10.7	8.8	1.9
Ireland	3.9	4.9	−1.0
Malta	8.3	6.9	1.4
EU15	9.2	7.1	2.1
EU25	10.2	8.0	2.2

Note: [a]Unemployment rates representing unemployed persons as a percentage of the labour force = active population. The labour force is the total number of people employed and unemployed. Unemployed persons comprise persons aged 15-74 who were: (i) without work during the reference week; (ii) currently available for work, ie were available for paid employment or self-employment before the end of the two weeks following the reference week; (iii) actively seeing work, ie had taken specific steps in the four-week period ending with the reference week to seek paid employment or self-employment or who found a job to start later, ie within a period of, at most, three months.

Source: Eurostat structural indicators Europa NewCronos website 2005 (epp.eurostat.cec.eu.int) and authors' calculations.

for women are 10.2%, which is 2.2% higher than for men, suggesting more insecurity in paid work for women. But while unemployment itself varies greatly between CEE countries, the gender gap in unemployment does not. The proportion of women in work across accession countries is still marginally higher than in the EU15, despite major job losses, with 46% in employment, compared with 42% in the EU15 (Paoli and Parent-Thirion, 2003, pp 15-17).

The quality of jobs matters as well as their quantity and security. Table 2.3 measures women's position in the labour market through a comparison of gender pay gaps in 2004. Recent Eurostat comparisons show a 15% gap in the hourly earnings between men and women across the EU25. Figures in Central Europe range from 24% in Estonia to 9% in Slovenia, with Poland at 11%. The gap has been narrowing in most CEE countries, for example from 14% in Slovenia and 15% in Poland in 1999. The pay gap is slightly larger in Western Europe (16% in the EU15), but by this measure East and West are similar, and there is more variation between nation states. This measure is unusual for western countries as well as for CEE new member states: Sweden's pay gap is average for the EU15, and Malta's is the lowest among the countries in the table. Unusually for the measures discussed in this chapter, the gender pay gaps do not reflect the male breadwinner or dual earner histories of the countries in any systematic way.

Table 2.3: Gender pay gap in unadjusted form (2003)[a]

(Difference between men's and women's average gross hourly earnings as a percentage of men's average gross hourly earnings)

	Gender pay gap
Czech Republic	19
Estonia	24
Latvia	16
Lithuania	17
Hungary	14
Poland	11
Slovenia	9 (2002)
Slovakia	23
Sweden	16
France	12
Ireland	14
Malta	4
EU15	16
EU25	15

Note: [a] Gender pay gap is given as the difference between average gross hourly earnings of male paid employees and of female paid employees. The population consists of all paid employees aged 16-64 who are 'at work 15+ hours per week'.

Source: Eurostat structural indicators Europa NewCronos website 2005 (epp.eurostat.cec.eu.int)

Occupational segregation did not disappear under communism, despite rhetoric about equality, but there is a less-segregated labour market than in EU15 countries and there are more women in higher-level positions as managers, and in technical occupations and as skilled workers, and fewer in service and sales jobs. Overall, there is "a more balanced distribution between men and women within each sector in the acceding and candidate countries than in the EU" (Paoli and Parent-Thirion, 2003, pp 15-17). There is also a higher proportion of women in higher-paid jobs: 41% of women full-time workers in the then accession or candidate countries, compared with 20% of full-time women in the EU15 (Paoli and Parent-Thirion, 2003, pp 73-4).

What is the impact of women's labour market position on the ability to sustain themselves as individuals and on their relationship with their families? Some factors may enhance women's independence and enhance their status within marriage and their ability to live outside it. High levels of participation established over decades may make women less dependent on family relationships (Ferge, 1998, p 220). But there are counterbalancing factors: housing access under soviet regimes was a serious constraint to separation and divorce, and it remains so with marketisation; the gender pay gap may be low in some countries, but incomes are also low; too low to afford independent housing, and too low for lone mothers to escape poverty – they are a major group in poverty now. Living outside marriage, even to escape violence, is not in general a realistic option. It is possible that women's labour market status enhances their position within family relationships but is not strong enough to support life outside family relationships.

To what extent women now want state support for paid employment is disputed. This kind of 'equality' was state imposed, gave women insupportable double burdens and denied the value and privacy of family life. But there is a powerful case showing that women need and value paid employment: their weakened market position may be about constraints rather than choices – the "economic, institutional and social framework" (Kotowska, 1995, p 87) – rather than a preference for becoming housewives. Paid work has become more crucial to the survival of women and children during the transition period. Social supports that enabled women to be paid and unpaid workers have been reduced and the double burden now may well be higher than under communism or in the West. Poverty often makes family life less cosy than western images portray. Women value the independence and social support of the workplace (Łobodzińska, 1995, 1996, 2000; Ferge, 1998). A UNECE report argues:

For younger and well-educated generations of women in transition countries, 'housewife' as a career model has no appeal for similar reasons as in other countries. They want independence and financial security coming from paid work, which includes pensions, important under market conditions and eroding of a cradle-to-grave state protection. They also want satisfaction and social position that come with a professional career. (Ruminska-Zimny, 2002, p 7)

We discussed the issues around this area of the male breadwinner versus dual earner regime with our Polish respondents, asking about their sense of need for employment and their ideas about the proper role of women (see Chapters Four to Six).

The comparative data on women's position at work suggest that women in the new CEE member states are holding on – just – to their position as earners in dual earner households. In each country, women's employment levels are lower than men's, but the gap is by no means equivalent to the gap in countries with a long male breadwinner tradition such as Ireland and Malta. Labour markets are rather less segregated than in EU15 countries. Women's level of education compares favourably with men's (European Commission, 2004a) and gender pay gaps are a little lower on average. The need for women's employment is strong, with low incomes compared with the West, widespread insecurity of work, and increasing insecurity of marriage. There are differences in the experience of work in different countries: women's employment, unemployment and the gender pay gap show serious variations. But the gender gap in employment and unemployment is consistent, suggesting that the main differences are in the wider economy, rather than different experiences of gender at work. Experience of part-time work (discussed later) is clearly different from that in the West: it is a much less common form of work and much less a form of women's work. In each dimension there are outliers: Lithuania has a gender ratio in part-time work more similar to Western Europe; the Czech Republic's employment gap resembles the West; and Estonia and Slovakia have high gender pay gaps – but there is no country where all of these experiences of employment conspire together to disadvantage women. Poland holds a middle position among the new CEE member states in terms of gender gaps in employment and unemployment and the gender pay gap. Where Poland does stand out is in its very high levels of unemployment among both women and men, and relatively high levels of part-time work, again among both women and men.

Care

To what extent do the new CEE member states still treat children as a collective good, and childcare as a collective obligation as well as a parental one? We ask about the extent of changes involving individual and household responsibility for children and childcare, and more conditional and stringent support. Many similar issues are raised by care for elderly and disabled people, and western literature has increasingly framed the issues of care more widely than childcare and parenting (McLaughlin and Glendinning, 1994; Lewis, 1997, 1998). Here, we are more centrally concerned with parenting. So, we look briefly at the broader provision of services that support family work such as health and education and draw attention to the impact of transition on the level of family work. We examine in more detail the provisions for care of young children: nurseries, kindergartens and arrangements for maternity and childcare leave.

> Before the transition, family law accorded women and men equal rights, and families received considerable public support through cash and non-cash benefits. Women's family commitments and functions were influenced by these policies, but also by public health and education services which were widely accessible and which were offered free or at low cost. However, this seemingly strong network of family supports was particularly vulnerable to the forces of transition because it was financed and operated by the state and because many of the benefits and services were delivered through the workplace. (UNICEF, 1999, p 49)

This section investigates these 'vulnerable' structures, and to what extent they have been sustained in CEE countries in the 15 years since the end of the communism. How healthy now are the family support programmes that, at the turn of the 1990s, "were delivered through multiple agents, were widely available and tended to be generous and comprehensive ... and represented a heritage that in many ways was seen as an achievement in both East and West" (Fajth, 1996, p 1). To what extent do the collective social policies of the communist era survive and support gender equality in the regimes of the 21st century? What are the similarities and differences between governments? And what is happening in households, in terms of the impact of changes in social policy, and in terms of changes generated from civil society and from households themselves?

While social policies in the male breadwinner countries of Western Europe have often been seen as keeping women at home, social policies in transition countries have played a major role in sustaining mothers as workers. Under communism, family allowances, childcare leave, and nursery and kindergarten provision were used to compensate parents for the costs of child rearing, to reconcile paid employment with unpaid care work and to enhance children's social and educational development. All were relatively generous. Some former communist countries offered workplace nurseries for 0- to 3-year-olds, while schemes of childcare leave became established in CEE countries. Kindergarten enrolment rates for 3- to 6-year-olds were especially high in Central Europe (Fajth, 1996; UNICEF, 1998, 1999). While the achievement of gender equality in employment was greater than in most western countries, the model of parental care in CEE regimes under communism was of mothering rather than fathering. It was state-supported mothering but nevertheless a traditional model of gender roles in households. While relatively generous employment protection, childcare services and high employment levels enabled mothers to keep their place in the labour market, women still bore significant costs for their motherhood in terms of lower pay and higher workloads (UNICEF, 1999; Gershuny, 2000).

Childcare leave to enable parents to care for nursery-age children has been a strong feature of the systems throughout Central and Eastern Europe, with maternity and childcare leave entitlements adding up to approximately three years (Paci, 2002, p 34; Wolchik, 2003, p 591). Childcare leave was introduced in Hungary in 1969, with compensation at 75% of previous earnings, and in Czechoslovakia in 1987. Fathers were included in Hungary in 1982 where children were over one year old, and in 1985 in Czechoslovakia, although only if the mother was unable to care for the child. By 2002, the Czech Republic had the longest periods of parental leave anywhere, adding maternity to childcare leave, extending until the child is four years old (Kocourkova, 2002). At transition, childcare leave schemes were generally made more attractive and there is some evidence of a shift from nursery to parental care for children under three years of age. Benefits associated with childcare leave have been maintained in the Czech Republic and Slovakia since 1990. In Hungary they were reduced at the end of the 1990s but restored in 2000 to 70% of the parent's previous earnings. There has been some convergence at the end of the 1990s as countries returned to a pro-natalist approach, although "the extent of these measures does not compare with the comprehensiveness of state support prior to the transition" (Kocourkova, 2002). The most recent comparative data on maternity, paternity and childcare leave is shown in Table 2.4.

Table 2.4: Maternity, paternity and childcare leave entitlements and pre-primary enrolments (2001, 2002)

	Maternity leave: days and benefits, 2002	Paternity leave: days and benefits, 2002[a]	Childcare leave benefits, 2002	Pre-primary enrolment[b], 2001 (% of population aged 3–6)
Czech Republic	196 days with maternity benefit		Parental allowance: when caring for child up to age of 4	86.6
Estonia	126 days with maternity benefit		Childcare allowance for parent of child under 3	80.3
Latvia	112 days with maternity benefit	Benefit for 10 days at childbirth	Persons caring for a child under 3	65.6
Lithuania	126 days with maternity benefit		Benefit paid at lower rate until child is 3	52.6
Hungary	168 days with maternity allowance		Childcare benefit until child is 2, Child home care allowance for parents looking after child under 3	86.4
Poland	112 days with allowance (100% earnings) for first child and 126 days for subsequent ones		Childcare benefit for 24 months (36 if more than one child) for lower income families	50.4
Slovenia	365 days with maternity benefit for 105 days	Benefit for 90 days, 15 days during maternity leave and 75 before the child's 8th year[c]	Childcare benefit for 260 days, up to child's 8th year, for mother or father	68.3
Slovakia	Leave until child is 3, of which benefit for 196 days		Parent caring for at least one child up to 3, lower income families	69.5

Notes:

[a] More recent information (ILO, 2005) gives Estonia (14 days) and Hungary (5 days), but not paid.

[b] More detailed information is given in the sources.

[c] Being phased in by 2005

Sources: EISS (2002); UNICEF (2003)

While post-communist governments created a "generous framework for family-related leave" (UNICEF, 1999, p 54) the economic climate makes using these opportunities difficult. Market pressures on firms, job insecurity and fear of losing one's position at work have made women's situation more vulnerable in competitive conditions. These add up to considerable pressures on women in employment to take shorter periods of leave (Erler and Sass, 1997; Firlit-Fesnak, 1997b). Parents in the Czech Republic may have rights to four years' leave, but they also suffer "a gradual erosion in the value of their qualifications and previous work experience, and find it more difficult to return to their jobs after such a long break", while childcare benefit is set at one fifth of average incomes and brings the risk of poverty (Kocourkova, 2002). A review of evidence about parental leave (not including CEE countries) argues that the balance of the evidence favours shorter periods of leave – up to one year – as the best fit between children's need for parental care, the needs of parents to earn, and the requirements of gender equality (Gornick and Meyers, 2003). These issues were also a high priority for our respondents.

Nursery provision for 0- to 3-year-olds has not provided a strong alternative to parental care in CEE countries and has declined with transition as workplace provision diminished. In the late 1990s, 11% of the age group were enrolled in Hungary, and 5% in Poland, and nurseries had nearly disappeared in the Czech Republic and Slovakia (UNICEF, 1999, p 55). For most parents of very young children, then, in most CEE countries, the tensions between earning and caring may be severe.

Kindergarten enrolments have been high in Central Europe (Figure 2.2): around 80% in Slovakia, the Czech Republic and Hungary in 1989, although always lower in Poland, at 49% at transition (UNICEF, 1998, pp 21-2). Enrolments dropped most severely in the Baltic states in the economic turmoil of the early 1990s. Along with economic recovery, there is evidence of recovery and growth to levels above those before 1989. Hungary has sustained high levels throughout.

Changing patterns of demand contribute to this picture, with decreasing paid employment for mothers and other potential carers and a declining population of young children (Figure 2.3). In Hungary, where the highest kindergarten levels have been sustained, the fall in child population was less than elsewhere. In the late 1990s in Hungary, 2% of enrolments were in registered private nurseries, and 3% in Poland (UNICEF, 1999, p 56). But charges by private nurseries are now significant in relation to women's earnings in Poland (Balcerzak-Paradowska (2004a, 2004b).

Figure 2.2: Pre-primary education enrolment

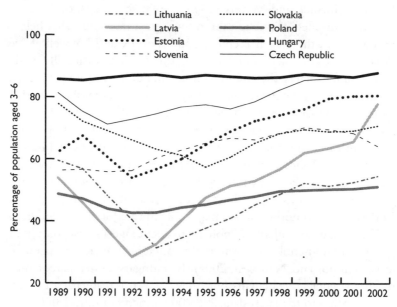

Source: TransMONEE database, www.unicef-icdc.org/resources

Figure 2.3: Population, aged 0–4 at the beginning of the year

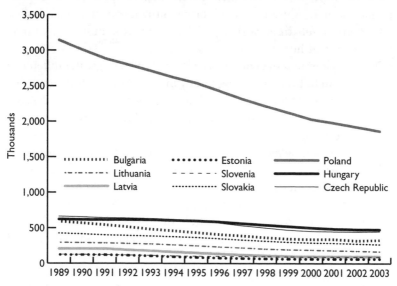

Source: TransMONEE database, www.unicef-icdc.org/resources

How do these measures of care currently compare with Western Europe? Gornick and Meyers (2003, p 318) show 82% of 3- to 5-year-olds enrolled in public care in Sweden, a rate somewhat below Hungary and the Czech Republic, and the UK at 77%, well above Poland. But they also show that in the UK's traditionally male breadwinner society, the children's hours in public care are part-time. Political changes and the desire to bring women into the labour market have brought major developments in the UK, but the established pattern is of a very part-time kindergarten, which contributes little to parents' ability to carry out full-time jobs (Lewis, 2003; Land, 2004). Neither part-time work nor part-time kindergarten is part of the pattern in CEE countries. Poland's rate is distinctly below other new CEE member states in this respect: but its provision is full time and increasing. In Poland, grandmothers play a major role in care for young children.

There is a little evidence of policies to encourage a redistribution of care within households, for example encouraging men to take parental leave (Choluj and Neusuess, 2004). In Hungary either parent may receive parental leave benefits, but "they are seen as maternal subsidies. ... According to the latest data, 296,000 women but only 1,000 men were absent from the labour market due to their parental obligations" (Nagy, 2003, p 286). Slovenia and Latvia have introduced paternity benefit, with Slovenia's provision of 90 days, phased in from 2002, allowing fathers to be involved in care around childbirth and up the child's eighth birthday. But the gender assumptions of communist and most of these post-communist governments appear to be similar: policies should support women's place in the labour market as highly educated and full-time workers, but have no part in influencing men's participation at home.

The development of civil society may have made a greater difference among households than among policy makers. There is little evidence of innovative services for children being developed through local civil action. But the freedom to develop public political organisations and the escape from constraints in academic and policy worlds have all made room for new ideas about gender in households. If the acceptance of traditional gender roles in the home was a core feature of communist societies, the evidence now begins to reflect political change, and to show a population with more radical ideas about mothering and fathering. (These issues are more fully discussed in Chapter Five.)

So while most governments appear to sustain traditional ideas of gender roles, there is some evidence of more radical attitudes to gender roles among the wider population in the new CEE member states. The European Foundation for the Improvement of Living and Working

Conditions produces quality of life surveys that now cover Eastern and Western Europe, with the 25 countries of the new European Union and three candidate countries (Bulgaria, Romania, Turkey). Respondents were asked about their ideas and beliefs about care, in particular whether they think that specific, listed childcare activities should be carried out mainly by the mother, mainly by the father, or by both. This list includes playing, taking children to activities, dealing with nappies, dressing, taking to the doctor, helping with schoolwork, reading, buying toys, punishing, putting to bed, answering important questions. The results are encapsulated in an index, from zero (unshared) to 100 (fully shared) and suggest that beliefs in gender equality in care are widespread in Eastern and Western Europe, with an overall index of 81.8 in the EU15, and 76.6 in the new member countries: "most people of Europe believe that childcare is basically a non-gender-specific task: both mother and father are expected to carry out child rearing" (Fahey and Spéder, 2004, p 60).

Fahey and Spéder discuss whether the long tradition of women's employment in most of the 10 new European Union countries might have been expected to lead to more equal practice at home and more egalitarian ideas, whereas the patterns of belief shown by the data appear to be a little more traditional in the new member countries than in the EU15 (Fahey and Spéder, 2004, p 62). However, the difference between East and West is not large. Furthermore, these data are very much at the level of ideas and ideals rather than of practice: they are about what people think rather than what they do. The political constraints of the communist era – major restrictions on people's access to ideas, and ability to join groups, or develop a public realm of discussion – may have a continuing impact on ideas, particularly among older people. But the dominant evidence of these data is of ideals of gender equality in childcare now widespread, West and East, among women and among men.

There is a serious difference, of course, between what people say about their ideals, and what they do in practice, even what they *say* they do in practice. The evidence of egalitarian ideals is not replicated in the evidence of time diaries, work hours, careers, work flexibility, tendency to take parental leave and so on, where mothers' responsibility for care – East or West – remains imprinted rather than fathers'. However, there is some evidence that men's actual involvement in childcare may now be higher in the new member countries than in the EU15. The report from The European Foundation for the Improvement of Living and Working Conditions on *Working conditions in the acceding and candidate countries* asked about unpaid work as well as paid, care for children as well as care for elderly or disabled relatives. These data, as would be expected, show women more involved than men in raising and caring for children, with 41% spending an hour or more every day raising and caring for children, compared with 31% of men. But these data suggest that the new member countries are the ones with the more egalitarian practices, in comparison with the EU15, where the comparable figures are 41% for women compared with 24% for men (Paoli and Parent-Thirion, 2003, p 78).

How can we understand these patterns in households? The constraints upon households in post-communist countries have been extreme. There has been a loss of state support for childcare while developing markets have put pressure on mothers' older strategies of balancing work and family: taking leave, exiting and entering jobs have all become seriously difficult. CEE countries have a legacy of women's full-time employment but not of part-time. One new strategy may be to reduce family size. One account from the Czech Republic is that "the main adjustment Czech women have made to the problem of the 'double burden' has been to severely reduce the number of children they have" (Ferber and Raabe, 2003, p 139). This is a trend shared between these countries, and with Western Europe, but fertility has declined particularly steeply, and reached lower levels than in western countries, with total fertility now 1.3 in the new CEE member countries, compared with 1.47 in the EU15 (Fahey and Spéder, 2004, p 9).

Figure 2.4: Total fertility rate

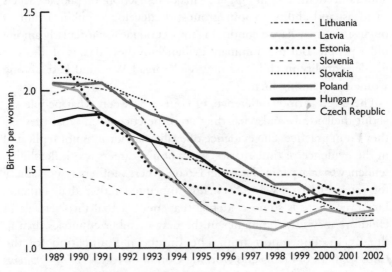

Source: TransMONEE database, www.unicef-icdc.org/resources

Alternatively, Fahey and Spéder (2004) argue that low birth rates stem from increased choice rather than through constraint. But perhaps, in the case of CEE countries in particular, these authors underemphasise the constraints surrounding parenting. The very radical declines in family size after the transition from communism – reducing birth rate levels to among the lowest worldwide – suggest the importance of constraints around income, security, and time to care for children in these countries in particular. Comparison of OECD countries points to the importance of public policy in understanding differences in fertility, especially availability of formal childcare, flexi-time and, less certainly, maternity benefit replacement rates. Women's higher education and access to opportunities also feature in this account (Castles, 2003).

Perhaps the engagement of men in care may be seen as another strategy for balancing work and family in the rather extreme circumstances of the transition. May we be seeing more radical change in the households of CEE countries from the traditional parenting stereotypes, with younger men more involved in caring for children as alternative strategies have become problematic under market conditions? Reductions in social support have led households into making their own solutions. This has meant a very sharp decline in fertility. But it may also have brought new expectations of caring fatherhood and, to some extent, changing practices. And collective solutions have not died with communism. The countries of Central and Eastern Europe have kept systems of childcare leave, which give some social support to parents, and have kept kindergartens for high proportions of 3- to 6-year-olds.

State commitments to health and education services left a legacy of provision of health care and education, of services free at the point of use. Public expenditure on education as a percentage of GDP was high in most countries before transition, and often higher than comparable OECD levels (UNICEF, 1998, fig. 2.9). There is a debate about the quality of services, with little investment in public preventative health, but children scoring favourably on measures of mathematics and science (UNICEF, 2002, p 34). However, social provision represented a commitment to a significant state role in education and care and to the support of women as paid workers.

How has change in this area affected families, and especially how has it affected women in families? What has become of the relative share of states and families in the care and development of children and other dependants? Families are very significant providers of care for the very young and very old. Their role in child development has often been shown to be as crucial as that of formal education systems. Equally important is their role in health making, in terms of nutrition, child safety, health decision making and health care. More collective systems tend to be redistributive between men and women. Where mothers tend to earn less than men, health and education services acknowledge and support women's responsibility for children and other dependants. The World Bank has examined the gender impact of changes in spending during the transition process and argues that "the reform of the family benefit and pensions system has reduced – but not eliminated – women's advantages with respect to returns to paid-in contributions" (World Bank, 2002, p xii).

The countries of Central and Eastern Europe have retained their spending on health and education as proportions of GDP, and have increased it in real terms on the whole. The Czech Republic has the highest spending per child, and has increased it by around one third in real terms since 1989 (UNICEF, 2002, p 15).

Spending on wider aspects of education and health has tended to decline. There has been a withdrawal of social support in schools: in Poland there are reductions in after-school supervision and fewer meals at school (UNICEF, 1998, pp 36-7). Such changes make it harder for mothers to combine paid employment and childcare as well as risking the health and safety of children.

Broadly, the picture is of more fragile support for families and children in a range of areas: family allowance, nursery provision and parental benefits. Policies that shared the cost of parenting, drew women into the labour market and eased the tensions between paid work and motherhood have weakened in most countries. Mothers' employment has become a more pressing necessity, to protect against insecurity, while the systems that support it are under strain. But CEE countries have continued and developed the tradition of high public spending on health services and schools. Kindergartens remain a significant part of the systems of care for pre-school children. There has been a shift from governments to households, and parents face pressures under competitive conditions and gaps in the provision of services. But the level of social support for households with care responsibilities in terms of health, education, as well as leave entitlements and kindergartens enables mothers to participate in the labour market. Polish mothers tend to have fewer rights to leave with pay or benefits than their counterparts in the Czech Republic, Slovakia, or Hungary: they can claim supported childcare leave of up to two years instead of three or four, more targeted benefits, and fewer places in kindergarten for their 3- to 6-year-olds – although these are full-time places.

In Chapters Four to Six we analyse our discussions with mothers about care work, and about their ideas of the role men should play and governments should play in managing the tensions between paid work and care.

Time

Time is integral to gender systems: traditional male breadwinner regimes depended on men's commitment to full-time and lifetime paid employment. The UK pension system in the post-Second World War era, for example, was built on this model of a working life, while it allowed married women to be full-time carers, although dependent on their husbands for pension contributions as well as for income. The working time models that have emerged from the ashes of the male breadwinner model – most often one-and-a-half earner, with mothers in part-time work – have rarely brought gender equality in the use of time (Fagan and Warren, 2001; Lewis 2001a). Even in the weakest male breadwinner states, women tend to do shorter hours of paid work in comparison with men, and much longer hours of unpaid work. On the other hand, the working time regimes of the communist past were of full-time work for men and for women, albeit with parental leave allowing mothers to exit and re-enter work. To what extent does this working time regime survive, and how does it compare with regimes in EU15 countries? Time regulation is increasingly seen among policy strategies: parental leave systems make time to accommodate care work with paid work; a shorter working week may make room to redistribute time between men and women; the regulation of conditions of part-time work to bring it onto equal terms with full-time work may make it more attractive to men and less disadvantageous to women. Policies for reducing and sharing the working week, as in France, or regulating part-time work, as in the EU Working Time Directive and the 1998 Part-time Workers Directive, may be important strategies for sharing work between the employed and unemployed, developing flexibility in managing paid work and family as well as strategies for gender equality (Fagnani and Letablier, 2004).

Working time shows a very distinctive pattern for the new CEE member states, especially their longer working hours overall, but also in their narrow gender gap for full-time workers. The average working week for men and women in the then acceding and candidate countries is 44.4 hours, against 38.2 in the EU15. Slovenia has the lowest number of working hours, and also the lowest gender gap. Lithuania has the highest working hours, and the highest gender gap, with 44.8 and 5.3

respectively. Poland's working hours are on the high side at 45.2 (Paoli and Parent-Thirion, 2003, p 49). The gender gap in weekly working hours is shown in Table 2.5. Poland's gender gap in working hours is among the highest for new CEE member states, at 4.6 hours, but below Malta, included as a traditional male breadwinner state, with a gender gap of 7.6 hours.

Part-time work shows very distinctive differences between East and West. Women's part-time work has been examined in comparative work on gender as one of the ways in which women are marginalised and disadvantaged by caring responsibilities (Rubery et al, 1998, 1999). Very high levels of insecure, low-paid work, with short hours and limited rights: this was one of Jane Lewis' key reasons for describing the UK as a strong male breadwinner model, while Swedish women were likely to do part-time work, but with longer hours and conditions equivalent to full-time employment (Lewis, 1992). While the EU 1998 Part-time Workers Directive has been important in improving the rights attaching to part-time work, in the UK part-time work remains one of the ways in which women bend their employment to their family, and suffer the consequences in terms of lifetime earnings half those of men (Rake, 2000). This pattern is not uncommon in Western Europe, with 33.5% of total employment being women's part-time, over five times the rate for men.

Part-time work in CEE countries is much less common for men or women, has longer hours than in the West, and perhaps is more likely to be combined with another job, whether formally counted or not. Poland's women part-timers contribute the highest rate to total employment among CEE countries at 13.4%, but this is much below western countries: in the EU15 women's part-time employment is

Table 2.5: Number of working hours per week for men and women, and the difference between men and women

	Men	Women	Difference men – women
Czech Republic	44.2	40.0	4.2
Estonia	44.2	40.6	3.6
Latvia	46.1	42.6	3.5
Lithuania	47.5	42.2	5.3
Hungary	44.7	40.7	4.0
Poland	47.3	42.7	4.6
Slovenia	40.8	38.6	2.2
Slovakia	44.8	40.8	4.0
Malta	42.7	35.1	7.6
ACC 12[a]	45.4	43.3	2.1

Note: [a]The then 10 accession and 2 candidate countries Bulgaria and Romania. Turkey was not a candidate country at this time.

Source: Paoli and Parent-Thirion (2003, p 49, table 23) and authors' calculations.

around a third of all employment. It is particularly far below the level of countries with a male breadwinner tradition such as the UK and Ireland. Table 2.6 shows how much part-time work is women's work. The ratios of women's part-time employment to men's show women in Western Europe contributing around five times the rate for men, and even Sweden around three times the rate for men, whereas in Poland – in the middle range of CEE countries – the ratio is around one-and-a-half women for every man.

Where people in new CEE member states are described as working part time, they may be working long hours. Among men, 42% of part-time workers are doing more than 40 hours per week while the figure for women is 29%. Part-time work in the new member states is a very different phenomenon from the older members, where part-time workers usually work for fewer than 30 hours (Paoli and Parent-Thirion, 2003, p 50). It is not seen as a strategy for balancing paid work and family (Cousins and Tang, 2004).

The working time traditions in CEE countries have brought women into the labour market on very similar conditions to men. But they have done very little to reduce the hours women spend on household work or care. The notion under communism, that everyone should have time for work and time for leisure was never fulfilled for women, whose double burden under communism was notorious. Writing of Hungary in this period, Haney argues: "While it is questionable whether men enjoyed the regime's gift of 'eight hours of work, eight hours of rest and eight hours of entertainment', it is unimaginable

Table 2.6: Part-time workers as a percentage of total employment (2002)

	Part-time rate		
	Female (%)	Male (%)	Female:male
Czech Republic	8.3	2.2	3.8: 1
Estonia	10.7	4.8	2.2: 1
Latvia	12.8 (2000)	9.7 (2000)	1.3: 1
Lithuania	12.3	2.0	6.1: 1
Hungary	5.1	2.3	2.2: 1
Poland	13.4	8.5	1.6: 1
Slovenia	7.5	4.9	1.5: 1
Slovakia	2.7	1.1	2.4: 1
Sweden	33.1	11.1	3.0: 1
France	29.8	5.2	5.7: 1
Ireland	30.4	6.5	4.7: 1
UK	43.9	9.4	4.7: 1
Malta	18.2	3.9	4.7: 1
EU15	33.5	6.5	5.1: 1
EU25	30.1	6.5	4.6: 1

Sources: European Commission (2004a, annex 2.3, p 178) and authors' calculations

that working women divided up their days in such a humane way" (2002, p 66). The lack of household appliances, the queuing, the lack of men's involvement: these brought very long working hours for women in comparison with the countries of Western Europe in the 1980s. Maternal ideology competed with the duty of labour. Public policies for women's paid employment combined with an unreconstructed domestic division of labour. The evidence of this period is patchy, but it is of women across CEE countries with long paid work time as well as unpaid work time (UNICEF, 1999; Gershuny, 2000). The labour of housework was especially intensive, with the shortages of domestic equipment and the costs of queuing offsetting any socialised domestic services (Molyneux, 1990, p 30). But, under communism, these burdens were eased a little by the flexibility of working conditions and the ability to enter and exit the labour market easily. Now women experience the pressures of a competitive market, inflexibility in labour market conditions, and long hours.

Gershuny, in *Changing times* (2000), draws on time diary data to argue that there is evidence of convergence in time use, between genders, between classes and between countries. There is some evidence here from Central Europe, and this may suggest that the number of paid work hours is reducing, that men are spending more time on unpaid work. There is some evidence of this in the data from the European Foundation for the Improvement of Living and Working Conditions as previously discussed. But the inheritance of communism in this respect may be a harsh climate in which to parent, particularly in which to mother.

Is there any evidence of governments controlling working time in the period after the transition? Here European Union regulation, through the Working Time Directive, must now come into play: but its limits of a 48-hour week will not bring much benefit to parents trying to combine work and care, or to mothers negotiating with their partners/husbands over working time. There is little debate in Poland about working time or making space for women or men to engage in care: employees need full-time incomes for adequate living standards and future pensions. Post-communist countries in Europe appear to have kept to the principles of their communist predecessors in this respect: men and women are expected to be in the labour market, equally in full-time jobs with long full-time hours. But the conditions under which they do this have become in some ways more challenging, as they compete for jobs, find it difficult to use parental leave, or to re-enter the job market after having children. While men appear to be playing a more serious role in care obligations, they are still primarily mothers' obligations, and cause serious difficulties for them in keeping jobs and caring for children and others with needs.

In sum, working time arrangements in CEE countries are distinctive. First, working hours are longer than in the EU15, with an average of 44 hours rather than 38. Second, very long working weeks are more common, with 38% of people working more than 45 hours a week, against 21% in the EU15. Third, there are fewer people working short hours, and fewer part-time workers, and part-time hours are long, at 32 hours a week on average (Paoli and Parent-Thirion, 2003, p 45). Poland has somewhat higher levels of part-time work for men and women, but is in the middle range of CEE countries on most measures we have looked at. It is a long way from the picture of a male breadwinner regime drawn in these data for Malta. There is more gender equality in working time in the new CEE member states than in Malta, but this kind of equality in working time makes work–life balance and parenting – especially mothering – a challenge.

Incomes

A key welfare state role is income redistribution and one way of understanding the differences between regimes is to explore the extent to which they deal with poverty among men and women. Structural indicators allow us (Table 2.7) to compare poverty, before and after

Table 2.7: Risk of poverty, as a percentage before and after transfers, female and male (2003) (or most recent available figures)[a]

	Before transfers			After transfers		
	Female	Male	Difference female – male	Female	Male	Difference female – male
Czech Republic	22	19	3	9	7	2
Estonia	26	23	3	20	17	3
Latvia	25	24	1	16	16	0
Lithuania	25	24	1	17	16	1
Hungary	15	15	0	10	9	1
Poland	31	32	−1	16	17	−1
Slovenia	18	15	3	11	9	2
Slovakia	27	28	−1	21	21	0
Sweden	31	26	5	12	10	2
France	27	26	1	13	12	1
Ireland	32	29	3	23	20	3
Malta	21	20	1	15	15	0
EU15	25	22	3	17	15	2
EU25	25	23	2	17	14	3

Note: [a] The share of women and men with an equivalised disposable income below the risk-of-poverty threshold, which is set at 60% of the national median equivalised disposable income.

Sources: Eurostat structural indicators, Europa NewCronos website 2005 (epp.eurostat.cec.eu.int) and authors' calculations.

social transfers, for new CEE member states as well as for the European Union as a whole, and for representative regimes. These set the threshold at 60% of national equivalised median disposable income showing poverty in relative terms: standards of living in the new member states are well below the European Union average (see Chapter One).

Across the EU25, a high risk of poverty among women and men was as common in countries as different as Sweden, Ireland and Poland, all with over 30% of women at risk of poverty. The risk of poverty before transfers was slightly higher for women than for men. Overall, the impact of social transfers was to reduce poverty from 25% to 17% for women and from 23% to 14% for men. While welfare states reduced the risk of poverty, they did not, overall, reduce the gender gap. The main differences in welfare states are the extent to which they reduce the risk of poverty rather than the extent to which they reduce the gender gap in poverty risk. Sweden's very active welfare state reduced the risk of poverty among women to 12% and among men to 10%, reducing the gender gap in poverty risk as well as poverty itself. More often, welfare states reduced poverty: the Czech Republic and Poland cut women's and men's risk of poverty nearly in half, while Hungary exposed men and women to lower risks of poverty before transfers, and reduced them even further after transfers. Poland exposed women – unusually – to slightly lower risks of poverty than men, but was typical in other respects in reducing the risk of poverty through transfers. Poland exposed women to a high risk of poverty before social transfers, but transfers reduced this much more than in male breadwinner countries such as Ireland.

These data show the great importance of welfare states' role in reducing the risk of poverty through social transfers. The new CEE member states, apart from Estonia and Slovakia, reduced women's risk of poverty to the European Union average of 17% or below, while the Czech Republic and Hungary and Slovenia reduced women's risk of poverty to below Sweden's figure. Among these countries Poland has the highest risk of poverty for women, but also reduces it through transfers to just below the European Union average. The patterns of women's risk of poverty and the success of transfers in reducing it show a greater similarity to the Swedish example than to the Irish.

Family allowances have been a strong feature of social policies in Central Europe, with a tradition of universal coverage, forming a high proportion of family incomes, and spending forming a high percentage of GDP. Pressures on government spending, pressures from international agencies and inflation brought more targeting and lower values in relation to family income during the 1990s. By the end of the 1990s, the typical pattern in Central Europe was for high coverage, but much lower value in relation to household income and GDP than had been usual under communism. For example, in Hungary, family allowances were 8.1% of household income in 1991 and 3.8% in 1999, while in Poland the fall was from 4.2% to 1.2% (UNICEF, 2001, pp 42-4). Means-testing of family allowances in the Czech Republic, Poland and Slovenia, brings a more stringent and contingent system of support, with means-testing of childcare benefits also in Poland (Förster and Tóth, 2001; MISSOC, 2004). But, despite these reductions, the system of protection for children and their parents remains strong by western standards. Comparing the impact of taxes and transfers on the incidence of child poverty shows Poland and Hungary more successful than the UK and the US in using social transfers to keep children out of poverty. In the UK, 36% would have been in poverty without transfers, a figure reduced to 20% by transfers. In Poland, 44% would have been in poverty in the mid-1990s, and in Hungary 38%, whereas in practice 15% and 10% respectively were in poverty (UNICEF, 2001, p 41).

The new CEE member states have certainly reduced the comprehensive coverage of systems that enabled women to keep themselves out of poverty through employment, and that supported children. But, despite having much lower GDPs than in Western Europe, they have contained the risk of poverty for women and children more effectively than many countries with more resources. Poland is unusual in having a slightly higher risk of poverty for men than for women, but otherwise is average for European countries in terms of its reduction of poverty for men and women through transfers. Poland has also a more contingent system of protection for families, with means-testing of childcare allowances as well as family allowances. These add up to a more fragile system of income support for women and children in Poland than in other CEE countries, but not one that treats women less well than it treats men, or leaves them worse off – relative to men in their own countries – than their counterparts in the European Union.

Gender and power

Gender systems are also systems of power in which welfare states affect gender relations, women's autonomy as individuals, their ability to support themselves and their place in public politics. The restriction of social, civil and political action has limited the development of the women's movement and thus limited the challenge to patriarchal families from within. These were defining characteristics of CEE societies under communism (Molyneux, 1990, pp 44-8; Ferge, 1997a). We ask about the developing social, civil and political action and the impact that this may be having on gender relations in households, and also in public politics. To what extent are women sharing new political freedoms? Can a developing women's movement change the climate in households and challenge the division of unpaid work? Are there differences in the development of political participation and civil society development between the new CEE member states?

Quota systems under communism ensured women's position in parliamentary bodies, with around 30% representation in Parliaments in the 1980s. Women's committees in the Communist Party monitored women's issues, while the reality of women's position in decision making was less than the appearance. First, Parliaments themselves were weak, with decision making dominated by the male-dominated Communist Party. Second, the official promotion of gender equality tended to pre-empt grass-roots action. Third, political action was suppressed, so women's participation in grass-roots politics was limited. The end of soviet authority made room for social, civil and political action. But resources of skill and political experience are underdeveloped. Time is limited. Survival needs dominate. The idea of gender equality itself has been contaminated by its adoption within soviet states and promotion by women's committees of the Communist Party. What is women's reaction to the end of authoritarian regimes, which appeared to promote their interests and participation in decision making? How much do new regimes support women's involvement through consultation with groups in civil society, or women's participation in formal politics? One account is that there is a 'patriarchal renaissance'. Women's political participation has been seen as an optional extra in the transition economies and is everywhere downgraded. The discrediting of socialist gender politics has brought a reaction against any kind of gender politics. There is now no serious challenge to male control of political systems. Democratisation – one of the chief gains of the transition – has not been shared by women (Funk and Mueller, 1993; Ferge, 1998, p 231; Choluj and Neusuess, 2004).

Comparative data in Table 2 8 show representation of CEE women in formal politics to be rather weak. The European Union average for women's representation in Parliaments and as senior ministers is 23% in each case, and only one CEE country (Latvia) exceeds this marginally with 24% women among its senior ministers. But most CEE countries cluster near the European Union average in terms of parliamentary representation and only Hungary has a figure below those of Ireland and Malta. While no CEE country exceeds Sweden's representation

Table 2.8: Women in decision making (%)

	Women senior ministers in national government	Women members of single/ lower house Parliaments	Women at one level below the minister	Women at two levels below the minister
Czech Republic	12	16	8	19
Estonia	8	20	18	27
Latvia	24	20	44	39
Lithuania	15	19	2	24
Hungary	12	9	3	23
Poland	6	22	29	31
Slovenia	7	15	41	67
Slovakia	0	17	15	30
Sweden	52	45	40	45
France	18	13	0	18
Ireland	14	13	11	11
UK	27	18	21	18
Malta	15	9	7	12
Average EU25	23	23	16	24

Source: European Commission database on women and men in decision making (2005)

by women in Parliament or as senior ministers, CEE women tend to be doing better in civil service positions, with several countries above the European Union average, and Slovenia exceeding Sweden's representation. As we have shown above, women's employment position in CEE countries is somewhat above the European Union average. Their position in employment appears to give them better access to decision making within government departments than in many western countries, while access to formal political positions is rather more restricted.

New freedoms allow the development of a women's movement that could, for example, challenge men's violence against women and the domestic division of labour. But political freedom is freedom from the obligation to participate as well as freedom to participate. Amid all the priorities of economic upheavals and the development of class differences, gender may take a back seat (Watson, 1997, 2000a; Ferge, 1998). A review of the new CEE member states' progress on the European Union equality *acquis* concludes that: "The culture of CEE countries has not yet institutionalised gender equality as a political norm" (Sloat, 2004, p 78), while Pollert and Fodor (2005) find a 'yawning gap' between policy and practice. But women's action is developing slowly and may be challenging some patriarchal features of families and households. Negotiation over European Union membership has brought gender equality and the development of civil society into the foreground, if only very late in the process (see Chapter Seven).

These requirements have encouraged the development of civic participation. Eurobarometer data show the CEE countries holding a middle ground in membership of organised activities such as voluntary organisations and trades unions: in 2002 more respondents in Slovenia, the Czech Republic and Slovakia were involved in at least one such activity than 51% which was the EU25 average, while the Polish figure was just below that average at 47%. Sweden shows the highest level of activity in the European Union at 85% (European Commission, 2004a). These figures are about general development in civil society, but may also indicate the development of gender politics. The appearance of Slovenia among the countries with higher participation figures may suggest a stronger women's movement here and be related to its stronger position for women in other respects, described previously. But everywhere there is some development of civic participation, with national figures overlapping those for the EU15 countries.

Conclusion

By the end of the communist era, in 1989, the dominant model in Central and Eastern Europe was similar to the dual earner model of Sweden in some key respects. Both supported women in employment, with expectations of women as full-time workers. Both provided high levels of support for childcare, family benefits and parental leave and had high public expenditure on health and education services that supported family work. But there were crucial differences, as the preceding account has helped to illuminate. First, the prevalence of work as a source of welfare entitlement made employment participation more compulsory for women in soviet countries than in Sweden, where entitlements through citizenship are more the norm (Lewis, 1992). Second, while the domestic division of labour everywhere was relatively unreconstructed, the position of women in soviet societies was especially constrained. Without the ability to organise in civil society, with little access to ideas from the women's movement, and with a sense that gender issues were state-imposed, the main sources of challenge to men's power were cut away. Under communism, then, women's employment position was comparable to that of Swedish women, but their position at home was much weaker.

What is the impact of the transition from communism on regimes' assumptions about gender? Is there a re-traditionalisation, with attempts to re-establish men as breadwinners and traditional gender roles at home? Or have the regimes retained support for gender equality at work, while the new freedoms bring more support for gender equality at home? Of course the answers to these questions are complicated, and there are contradictions.

There has been a politics of tradition – most evidently in the politics of abortion in Poland, which will be discussed in the next chapter – and which reasserts Roman Catholic notions of motherhood. But if we return to the models developed at the beginning of this chapter, and the analysis of gender regimes in terms of work, care, income, time and voice we will not find many examples to match this return to traditional gender divisions. The evidence of outcome measures for CEE countries allows comparison on key dimensions with countries representing more traditional male breadwinner models, such as Ireland and Malta, as well as with the European Union average. Women's participation in paid employment has fallen. But in every country except the Czech Republic the gaps between women's and men's employment are below the European Union average, and everywhere they are well below representative male breadwinner countries: so women's participation overall is still higher than the average for EU15 countries. Women's unemployment rates are high, especially in Poland, but only slightly higher than men's, suggesting that the economic problems predominate over the gender problems there. Women's working hours match men's more nearly in CEE new member states than in the new male breadwinner member state of Malta, or the European Union in general. The relative lack of part-time employment in CEE countries also distances them from the EU15, but in particular from the male breadwinner countries in the EU15, where women's part-time work is five times that of men's on average. Political change has exposed the weakness of women's position in formal politics, but has allowed the development of civil society. In turn, this brings a new possibility of gender politics in households, where women's economic position, in terms of their contribution to household incomes, is already above that in EU15 countries, especially those male breadwinner societies where women's part-time work is the key to care. The evidence begins to suggest that developing civil society is beginning to make changes in households as both men and women now widely believe *women's* that men's role in practical childcare is important as well as their role *role in* as breadwinners. There is also some evidence of men's increasing *politics?* contribution to care within households (see Chapter Five), bringing not gender equality but perhaps less gender difference than in the past and in EU15 countries now. For most CEE countries on most measures, these add up to greater gender equality than the EU15 averages regarding employment, unemployment, working time, vulnerability to poverty after transfers, and care in households, and probably –

although somewhat less well documented – power in households, and much greater gender equality than in male breadwinner countries such as Ireland and Malta.

If we turn to the second layer of analysis, examining the changes that have happened in CEE countries in terms of levels of policy intervention, we can see a serious reduction in social support for women's employment as costs have shifted to households, privatisation has brought diversity in provision, and the comprehensive network of social support for motherhood has grown thinner. Markets have weakened women's position at work, bringing unemployment and particular risks to young women in being seen as potential mothers. Mothers have difficulties using their rights to maternity and childcare leave (see also Chapter Four). Working time practices and policies, with their long hours of paid full-time work, put great pressure on parents, and low incomes make these resistant to change. At work, women's position has been weakened, but more through the new competitive context than through changes in social policy affecting them as women. Most measures show similar patterns for men and women in CEE countries: women's position in the labour market and ability to earn are still strong compared with Western Europe. With recovery in GDPs, spending on public services has supported women's care work, and sustained kindergartens for 3- to 6-year-olds. Collective-level provision for very young children has declined, but childcare leave offers entitlements to care and to benefits, and the states' role in supporting children and childcare is still ahead of Western Europe in some respects. If CEE countries are above the EU15 average on most of these measures of gender equality, they are well above the record of male breadwinner societies such as Malta and Ireland: the politics of tradition has not been the dominant direction.

A final question is about whether we should emphasise the similarity or the diversity in these regimes. There are clearly important differences. Slovenia, described by Cousins and Tang (2004) is the "Sweden of the south", emerges on several measures as more gender equal than other CEE countries, in terms of the gender pay gap, representation of women in civil service positions, paternity leave and benefits and working hours. Poland, in some respects, represents the strongest case for a return to the male breadwinner model, with its Roman Catholicism, legislation restricting abortion, high unemployment for women and more contingent benefits supporting parents. But whatever its abortion legislation, Poland has sharply falling fertility rates, along with other CEE countries which retain liberal abortion policies (Pető et al, 2004, p 23). Polish men share high unemployment with women. Poland is more equal than the EU15 average in employment and unemployment figures, and in these respects ranks as a middle-ground CEE country. Women in Poland contribute more part-time employment than in other CEE countries, but the proportion of women part-timers in the workforce is around a third of the EU15 average, and the gender ratio there is much more CEE than EU15. In gender terms these regimes share a significant 40-year history of dual earner households, dating from communist domination in the post-Second World War period. They share a period of economic turmoil, which results in living standards much below the EU15 average. They also share a history of collective provision for services of childcare, health and education, which have supported women's labour market position, and have produced a measure of gender equality more deeply rooted than in most of Western Europe. On few of the gender equality measures that we have looked at do any of the countries match Sweden, but neither do they match the male breadwinner countries of Malta and Ireland. There is some evidence of a developing civil society and of changes in households towards ideals of dual earner/dual carer parents, as parents in households have found ways to compensate for the reduction in state support for motherhood: both of these bring a greater prospect of gender equality than under the communist regimes of the past. We would argue that the emerging regimes in CEE countries should be seen as dual earner regimes, with comparatively strong collective support for women's employment and for parents, and few characteristics of the male breadwinner regimes with which we have compared them. But these dual earner regimes have suffered economic blows, leading to some losses of state support for gender equality, low living standards and unemployment as a new risk. Their dual earner status is thus more challenged than that of Scandinavian countries, and their support for gender equality more fragile.

THREE

Policy and parents in Poland

Introduction

This chapter investigates Polish policy towards the family, in the context of the opposing family models outlined in the previous chapter. To what extent do changes in the post-communist period represent a change from a dual earner, egalitarian model in which both partners have paid employment, to a traditional male breadwinner model, in which the man supports the family and the woman runs the household and cares for the children? Is the egalitarian model more common in rhetoric than in reality? Can women and men balance work and family in Poland, or do women reconcile work and family while men focus on their paid employment? What is the direction of change at state and household levels: a return to tradition in the wake of communism, or a more complicated mixture, affected by developments in civil society and the European Union as well as reaction against the communist past?

The family in Poland has always been highly valued both by individuals and society. This distinctive meaning of the family was bound up with the history and tradition of Polish society. Undeniably, the family was of great importance in transmitting and forming social values. In various periods of Polish history it was the family that was the most important element of cultural and national stability among the Polish people. The position of the family was strengthened by the doctrine of the Roman Catholic Church. This doctrine explicitly emphasised the constancy of marriage and family, the value of the family as a whole, and differentiated gender roles of family members.

In the post-Second World War period, both the Roman Catholic Church and communism reinforced the family and its role in society. The Roman Catholic Church favoured the traditional family form: changes in this form were perceived as indicating a profound crisis. The Church's attitude was submitted to critical examination by the Subcommittee of Episcopal Experts on Women's Priesthood in a report published in the mid-1980s (Siemieńska, 1996, p 22). Communism also reinforced the family, making the family a place of refuge from the pressures of the surrounding world. This was easy and natural because the family had always been important in Polish society (Siemieńska, 1996, p 22). In the 1960s and 1970s, feminist movements started to develop in Western Europe, with new concepts of the family, describing power and economic relationships within the family, exposing domestic violence and opening traditional gender roles to critical scrutiny. But in Poland there were no such movements, because women's organisations were forbidden unless their aims were to enable women to adapt to the authorities. Some organisations remote from the feminist movement were established: the Women Farmers Society, the Polish Women's League, the Women's Cooperative Society. Therefore, in communist times, the role of the family was not undermined and its traditional inner relationships were not subject to criticism (Siemieńska, 1996, p 22).

The end of the Second World War brought a change of borders, destruction and change in economic, political and social systems in Poland. Industrialisation and urbanisation initiated internal migrations, especially from rural areas to cities, bringing together rural and urban traditions and values and bringing changes in previously existing family models. Women's participation in paid employment was stimulated: it added work as a source of income but did not reduce household duties. Family law, codified in 1950, was very progressive. It enabled women's emancipation and allowed divorce. The Polish Constitution of 1952 stated, in Article 79: "Marriage, motherhood and family are under the protection of the Polish Peoples Republic", and this applied particularly to larger families with several children.

The new Constitution of 1997 upheld this family protection as a role of the state:

> Marriage as a relationship between a woman and a man, family, motherhood and parenthood are under protection of the Polish Republic. (Article 18)

> The state takes family well-being into consideration in both social and economic policy. (Article 71)

> Families experiencing poverty, especially large families and lone parent families, have a right to receive special help from the state. (Article 71)

> Both before and after having a child, the mother has a right to receive special help from the state on a scale defined by law. (Article 71)

The Polish Constitution also said and still says that "In the Polish Republic, a woman and a man have equal rights in family, political, social and economic life" (Article 33).

Are those articles of the Constitution carried out in practice? What is the real situation of women and men in the family and economy? Do the law and social policy protect women's well-being or allow discrimination against them?

Policy past and present: policy under communism

Between 1945 and 1989, family policy in Poland was determined by the ideological rules of the system as well as by contemporary political, economic and social processes. Many social policy solutions were introduced that were ahead of those in more developed 'welfare states'. Social policy critics remark that those solutions were less effective than they appeared, as they were not governed by specific rules (Balcerzak-Paradowska, 1995, p 64). Declarations about equal rights and justice were at the root of the Constitution. But family policy was determined by the political and economic premises of state socialism and these prioritised economic and industrial growth. This brought a shortage of labour with 'all hands needed'. This stimulated and accelerated women's participation in paid employment. Regulation of pay set income from work at a very low level with very little differentiation of any kind. An expanded system of social services accompanied the low and undifferentiated pay system and compensated for the low wage level. Workers had preferential access to certain key goods, such as accommodation, which served the same purpose. Living costs were stabilised through price controls as well as earnings policy. Price increases were decided by the administration. Social services, and especially cash benefits, were a form of compensation for higher living costs. The political premises determining family policy came from a desire to win widespread support for the political system (Balcerzak-Paradowska, 1995, pp 52-3).

From a retrospective point of view, it appears that processes of change were noticeable already in the 1970s: a visible growth in the number of divorces in comparison with the 1960s and an increasing tendency among married women with children to take up paid employment. A dominant family model was one with both spouses employed by state-controlled economic sectors. Families were differentiated through the educational background of the male head of household. Mining families were an exception to this general picture, with a more traditional housewife model dependent on the high earnings of miners. In the

1970s, peasant families also kept to the traditional model: state policy changes advantageous towards individual farming, such as raising the compulsory annual supply of livestock and agricultural products for the state at legally fixed prices, or introducing credits in the farmers' interest, were definitely conducive to upholding the traditional model among peasant families (Golinowska, 1995a, p 22).

Economic depression in Poland started in the 1970s and 1980s, along with the beginning of resistance to the authorities: these factors led to martial law being imposed. In the 1980s there were a great number of political and economical émigrés, both women and men. The depression of the 1980s intensified the family orientation in society because women with small children were more likely to stay at home rather than take up paid work. Leave for raising children, introduced in 1981, was certainly important here. In this period, young people were late gaining their independence and young married couples often lived together with the parents of one of the spouses. The main reason was a longstanding shortage of accommodation, intensified by a standstill in the building trade, resulting in a long waiting list for housing and 10- to 20-year waiting periods. The 1980s also brought an intensification of various kinds of help to young couples by their parents. There was also a marked decrease in the number of children born in urban families during this period (Golinowska, 1995a, p 23).

Family policy

Family policy also had its characteristic periods. The years 1970-79, and especially the first half of the 1970s, can be characterised as being focused strongly on new developments: strengthening social protection for families, and a search for solutions adapted to the needs of various categories of families. Important time and cash entitlements and services for women and children can be listed in three main groups.

First were services for mothers, which included lengthening unpaid leave to three years, and crediting pension entitlements during the leave. A maternity lump-sum grant was introduced, with universal entitlement for all women giving birth. Maternity allowances were equalised for women working at different employment levels. Also an alimony fund was introduced for women who did not receive alimony and were in financial need.

Second were services for children. Institutional help included developing new forms of pre-school education, such as pre-school departments at primary schools or pre-school centres. The need for these services grew when compulsory education for six-year-olds (the first level of elementary education) was introduced. Rules about social activities at work were redefined, according to which the financial situation and the structure of the family were the criteria for priority access to social services at half cost.

Third, help for young families included preferential credits allocated to young couples for the purchase of long-term necessities, while workplaces provided help in paying off debts.

The years 1980-89 brought some changes in social policy, designed to protect families from the effects of the increasing economic crisis. Childcare allowances were attached to childcare leaves, which until then had been unpaid. During martial law, and until 1985, workplaces introduced help in paying off debts for young couples. A system of compensation attempted to alleviate rising living costs. From 1984, changes were made in the system of leave: fathers were given the right to paternity leave and an allowance (Balcerzak-Paradowska, 1995, p 55).

Policy past and present: policy during transformation in the 1990s

The period of government transformation changed the governmental, economical, political and social premises which had hitherto shaped family policy. From the point of view of government, this was a change from a protective state to a state 'supporting' the family. Couples starting a family were made responsible for family living conditions while receiving some rights to childcare and education for their children. Institutions outside the family were restricted in their responsibility towards the family, with policies based on decentralisation and privatisation. The period of government transformation brought restrictions in the state's capacity to finance social benefits. The running costs of welfare institutions increased while state financial assistance decreased. Decentralisation of the state's social policy capacity and new methods of financing were introduced: the organisation, functioning and financing of establishments such as nurseries, kindergartens, elementary schools, culture, sport and recreation centres were given over to local authorities. However, these changes often outgrew the organisational and financial capacities of the local authorities: some establishments serving the family, particularly crèches but also kindergartens, were closed, and the financing of sport, culture and recreation facilities was given over to individuals or other bodies. At the same time, parental financing of care and care services, such as kindergartens, increased, as well as public education services. In this period, law and institutional conditions were created for the development of private and voluntary sectors in family services, creating many private institutions and not-for-profit establishments. This also happened in educational services (Balcerzak-Paradowska, 1995, p 57). New regulations were a result of the decreasing state capacities in financing social services, with a crisis in public finances. Budget subsidies for financing public establishments were reduced.

Government changes were also responsible for the reduction in social support at work. First, family services such as nurseries and kindergartens – until now maintained by workplaces – were closed. Recreation and cultural facilities belonging to workplaces were given to other authorities. New social entitlements focused on the economic situation of families, with entitlements being based on means tests. Transformation processes have affected the living standards of many families and led to economic stratification, increasing income inequalities and poverty. The process has also led to the development of unemployment, a phenomenon hitherto unknown in Poland (Balcerzak-Paradowska, 1995).

Despite these changes, the state is still the main maker of family social policy. It takes responsibility for conducting policy, while regulating for decentralisation of responsibility, and pluralism. Decentralisation assumes that the state may give part of its tasks and powers over to local authorities. Pluralism allows the state to create laws and conditions beneficial to various new ways of organising social life. This allows the creation of various institutions and organisations, social or private, directly and indirectly helping the family. The family's responsibility is to take control of its own life, to take its own initiatives or organise the solution of its own problems. This does not exempt the state from conducting family policy, creating optimal conditions for family development and helping to support the family in all aspects of its life (*Report on the situation of Polish families*, 1995, p 112). Has this proved, in subsequent years, to be a comprehensive policy with a clear programme?

Evaluating family policy

Some social policy commentators argue that in 1990s the programme of family policy was not adapted to the conditions arising from the change to the new market economy (Golinowska, 1995b; Balcerzak-Paradowska, 1995; Kurzynowski, 1995a, 1995b). Some regulations and policies were taken over from the previous political system but did not take into consideration the situation of families in the new and difficult socioeconomic situation. A comprehensive political concept for the family was not formed. Some policy ideas had more to do with pressure groups than with any realistic evaluation of what they might achieve. For example, after the anti-abortion law in 1993, regulations were made to introduce allowances for pregnant women and mothers raising small children. But the state budget had no resources to pay these allowances. Regulations relating to pregnant women in 1994 should have provided 314,291 women with these allowances; at the end of 1994, however, 69,442 women who should have received them did not (Semenowicz and Antoszkiewicz, 1996, p 23).

Family allowances had been a significant part of the family income, paid to all families with children. During the transformation, the real value of family allowances depreciated, means tests were introduced and entitlements narrowed. At the beginning of the 1990s, a unified level of allowance for each child was established. Within one year, between 1992 and 1993, the real value of the family allowance fell by 20% (Golinowska, 1995b). The decreasing value of the family allowance is very evident when compared with the late 1980s: between 1989 and 1993 the fall was 60%. The source of financing also changed, from the social insurance fund to the state budget. From March 1995, the family allowance has been means tested, allocated only to families whose income per person is less than 50% of national average pay. The numbers entitled to family allowances increased because of the rising number of the unemployed and students having children, but the value decreased. Whereas family allowances had previously been paid up to the age of 24 if the child continued their education, and even to the age of 25 if they were a final-year student, the entitlements were restricted to children in education up to the age of 20 (besides disabled children). So, after a decade of transformation, family allowances became a much smaller part of family budgets, and were paid to a much smaller group of families.

A more consistent policy kept childcare allowances in line with incomes from work. The criteria of allocation did not change, while the amount was linked to the pay index and re-calculated every four months. At first, the value of this allowance rose – in 1990 it almost doubled, and in 1991 it increased by about 30% – while later it stabilised. Now the childcare allowance is the main form of help for families with small children and is paid during childcare leave for 24 months. However, this allowance is means tested. In 1994, a special allowance for families with both parents unemployed was introduced, and is paid until one of the parents finds work (Golinowska, 1995b, p 253).

Consequences of transformation for family and family policy

In the short and long term, what are the consequences for family and for family policy of Poland's transformation to a free-market economy? Decentralisation brings changing relationships between central and local authorities. The new concept is that local authorities and a variety of new social organisations must conduct social policy and solve the problems of women and families. The speed of economic reform introduced changes in employment, bringing a high level of unemployment especially among those of parenting age. A *Report on the situation of Polish families* (1995) noted that 62.5% of the registered unemployed were between the ages of 18 and 34, the same age as those starting families and having parental responsibilities. Among this age group, more than half of the unemployed (54.8%) are women. Among the unemployed, 70% have children, and are usually families with two children (42%). The subsequent *Report on the situation of Polish families* (1998) quotes an increase to 60% in the proportion of women of this age group among the unemployed.

Among this age group, the proportion of unemployed women at the beginning of the 1990s was 20% higher than for unemployed men. From the family income point of view, women's employment is crucial, with one person's earnings not enough to support the family. Women's unemployment often leads to family poverty. The earning model of the previous period is still valid: this obliges two partners to do paid work to support the family. The incomes in families with one unemployed person were lower by 40% in 1992 than in other families (Beskid, 1996, pp 102-3).

Among families with children in Poland, two-parent families are in the majority. However, there is an increase in one-parent families; these are primarily lone mothers. Between the years 1988 and 2002 one-parent families increased by 28.9%. The percentage of families who were lone mothers was 13.7% in 1988 and lone fathers, 1.7%, growing to 17.2% lone mothers and 2.2% lone fathers in 2002. A decided majority of one-parent families (68.7%) live in towns or cities (Central Statistical Office, 2003b, p 30). Changes in the labour market touch women and their families: the effects of unemployment are particularly painful for lone mothers bringing up children. Legal protection for their employment was suspended and affected lone mothers and their children very harshly. Their families experienced deep financial deprivation (Beskid, 1996, p 103). Among the long-term unemployed, namely those who have been seeking employment for over 12 months, the number of women is higher than men. Official European Union data for 2004 show women's long-term unemployment at 10.9% and men's at 9.5%, both having just fallen from their peak in 2002 and 2003 respectively (Eurostat NewCronos website: epp.eurostat.eec.eu.int).

The transformation of the socioeconomic system has disadvantaged families, particularly in terms of incomes and poverty. In 1994, the proportions of poor families were: 38.8% of large families (with four or more children); 19.7% rural families; 19.3% families headed by a young parent, under 34 years of age; 20.8% families headed by a parent with only primary education (Fudała, 1996, pp 10-11). The Central Statistical Office states that in 1996 almost half all families (49%) were living below the minimum social standard, clearly a regression since the 1980s. In 2002 almost every fifth single parent (19%) with a child under 24 years of age, was unemployed. In the incomes of lone-parent families, benefits have become more important than income from work (Balcerzak-Paradowska, 2004b, p 125). In the literature, a term 'the new poor' has appeared to describe families who, because of loss of work and/or low income, cannot adjust to the expectations of the job market (Balcerzak-Paradowska, 2004b, p 116).

The survey of household budgets (Central Statistical Office, 2003a, p 69) shows that in 2001 most respondents (51%) with children under 24 years of age (for whom families provide), described their financial situation as 'average', a response shared by families of all sizes. The number of families with two or more children perceiving their financial situation as 'poor' has increased. In the case of families with two children the increase was from 19% in 1997 to 22% in 2001. In the case of families with four or more children, the increase ranged from 29.57% in 1997 to 32.3% in 2001. Generally, a third of the families taking part in the survey in 2001 were not afraid of poverty, yet were worried that their financial situation might get worse, this proportion growing by 3%. One fifth of the families were certain that they could face poverty; however, they also believed they could handle this situation, with this response increasing by 2% between 1997 and 2001. Every tenth family was not afraid of poverty and was not worried about their financial situation: but the percentage of families perceiving their situation this way decreased by 1.5 percentage points. Over half (59%) of families providing for children under 24 years of age found that their standard of living grew worse between 1997 and 2001. Most families (70%) with four or more children thought that their living standards had definitely worsened (Central Statistical Office, 2003a, p 70).

The change in relations between central and local social policy brings a shift of responsibilities for social services, including nurseries and kindergartens, to local authorities. But the limited financial capabilities of local authorities resulted in closing some establishments and raising fees, burdening the parents. Between 1990 and 1993 the number of nurseries decreased by 50% and kindergartens by 20%. These closures reflected a fall in the need for these services, as well as local authorities' financial problems. Demographic and economic factors played their part, with declining fertility, parents' unemployment and increased costs of childcare. Increasing fees became a problem for family budgets. The number of children attending nurseries between the years 1990–93 decreased by 50% and the number of children attending kindergartens decreased by 10% (*Report on the situation of Polish families*, 1995, p 125). As shown in Chapter Two, Figure 2.2, pre-primary enrolment in Poland fell from 48.7% of 3- to 6-year-olds in 1989 to 42.6% in 1992. There has since been a steady increase to 51.1% of the age group.

Nurseries and kindergartens covered a third of their costs by fees to parents. The fees in crèches were lower than those in kindergartens. For every fifth family, payments for kindergartens were a great burden and led them to remove their children. The level of fees is really important when compared with women's wages. In 2001, a kindergarten fee for one child was 38% of the minimum net wage and 19% of the average woman's wage; for two children the cost rose to 76% of the minimum wage and 37% of women's average earnings. Even for women living on an average wage with two children, these expenses were significant. However, for women living on a minimum wage, paying these fees was impossible (Balcerzak-Paradowska, 1997, p 59; 2004b, pp 260-1).

As elsewhere in the then CEE accession countries, the following years brought a diminishing number of nurseries, of nursery vacancies and of children who could attend them (see Chapter Two). In 1990 there were 1.7 million children aged 0-2, while in 2001 this had fallen to 1.2 million. A similar situation applied to 3- to 6-year-olds, whose number fell from 2.6 million in 1990 to 1.6 million in 2001 (Balcerzak-Paradowska, 2004b, p 262). While the number of kindergartens decreased, there are still more vacancies than parents wanting places for their children (Central Statistical Office, 2003a, p 25). Unemployment, affecting women or other members of the family, has also caused a fall in demand for both nurseries and kindergartens. Besides public kindergartens there is also a private sector serving 5% of children in kindergartens (Balcerzak-Paradowska, 2004b, p 263).

The fall in childcare and educational provision takes away opportunities from children whose family environments are of poverty or neglect. They lose their chance of catching up with their peers. The change from a public to a family environment represents a regression in childcare: around a third of children below school age (34% of those under three and 37% of those between three and six years of age) are taken care of by their mothers, partly because their mothers are on childcare leave but often because the mothers are unemployed. Another third are cared for by other members of the family, in particular grandmothers, grandfathers and siblings (38% of children under three and 37% of those aged between three and six). According to surveys in the 1990s, mothers were the most likely to care, even when employed, with little involvement from fathers: 40% of fathers had time for their children only on Sundays (spending it on playing together or going for a walk), and 20% of fathers never had time even for that (Balcerzak-Paradowska, 1997, pp 60, 65). But there are indications from comparative data – and from our own interviews – that these expectations and practices may be changing (see Chapter Five).

The changes in social and economic conditions affect women's choices about taking the leave to which they are entitled. The system of maternity and childcare leave dates from the communist period and can give mothers leave from work until their children are four years old, with 16-18 weeks of maternity leave and a maximum of three years of childcare leave, of which two years are covered by childcare benefits (See Chapter Two, Table 2.4). Widespread unemployment, the difficulties of finding a job in a market economy, the fear of losing a job, and the financial situation of families in poverty, or at risk of poverty, are just some factors responsible for recent changes in women's choices about their jobs. In 1988, 83% of mothers took childcare leave after maternity leave. Even in the first period of transformation, this declined to 72% in 1991, and to 60% in 1994. When making a decision about whether or not to take childcare leave, the most essential factor was the level of income the woman had had before the birth, and her educational level. Those with lower wages and lower educational levels were more likely to take leave (Kurzynowski, 1995b, p 66). This process goes further: in 1993, 336,100 mothers decided to take parental leave and in 2000 only 138,600 did so. These were mainly young women, without professional qualification or women with low-status jobs (Balcerzak-Paradowska, 2004b, p 252).

Maternity leave and benefits also date from the communist period, from legislation in 1970. Some regulations to lengthen and improve entitlements were introduced in 1999 and 2001 but have since been reversed: these changes were aimed at making it easier for women to combine work and family, but prolonged maternity leave can be an obstacle to finding employment. Employers fear financial and organisational consequences for the company as a result of women's entitlements. This means that – as in the communist period – maternity leave now lasts 16 weeks after the first birth, 18 weeks after the second and subsequent child, and 26 weeks when the pregnancy is multiple. One change made in January 2001 and retained, is that fathers are entitled to share maternity leave with mothers. The mother is entitled to give up part of the leave, providing she has used at least 14 weeks and then the father may use the rest of her leave (Balcerzak-Paradowska et al, 2003b, p 140).

Changing legislation relating to lone parenthood illustrates the assumptions of the Polish state about the responsibility of those parents not living with their children, mainly fathers. Family law gave lone parents (mainly mothers) rights to alimony through court decisions, and – until very recently – insisted on this as an obligation of non-resident parents, thus making fathers, in principle, responsible for the maintenance of their children. But the difficulty for lone parents in collecting this alimony, and their consequent poverty, led to the development in 1974, of a child-maintenance fund for lone parents. Polish citizens entitled to alimony through a court decision but with no chance of receiving it in practice could apply for this allowance until the child was 18 years old or a full-time student. The amount was defined by the court and could not be higher than 30% of the national average monthly wage of employees during the previous four months. In principle, the allowances were returnable, with the responsible parent obliged to pay the fund back. But only 16% were returned in practice (Semenowicz and Antoszkiewicz, 1996, p 23). From the beginning of 2004, new legislation replaced the maintenance fund with a means-tested family allowance for lone parents. This is based on one criterion: family income should be no more than 504 zloties (approximately £83 or €121) per person in the family (or 583 zloties (approximately £96 or €140) in the case of a disabled child). The amount of this allowance does not depend on the court decision, but is standardised at 170 zloties (approximately £28 or €41) for each child, or 250 zloties (approximately £41 or €60) for a disabled child. But there is a maximum of 504 Polish zloties (approximately £83 or €121) per month per person, even if the child is disabled. The new legislation is advantageous for some groups: one-parent families who lost the right to unemployment allowance and who are bringing up a child under seven years old; lone-parent families who had not previously been entitled to maintenance. However, the new legislation is disadvantageous for one-parent families who were entitled by a court decision to maintenance higher than the supplementary allowance. It is also disadvantageous for those families experiencing problems with receiving the maintenance when they do not have a court order. These issues are contentious because they represent key changes in fathers' responsibility for their children. Some perceive the closing of the maintenance fund negatively because it decreases alimony responsibilities: non-resident parents are no longer 'debtors of the state' (Balcerzak-Paradowska, 2004b, pp 233, 273-4). These changes represent the state accepting responsibility for children, but only if they are in poverty. As in Hungary, need has become the criterion for state assistance (Haney, 2002).

Equality of rights and duties for parents?

Polish family law assumes that spouses have equal rights and duties in marriage. This, however, does not mean performing the same roles in a marriage. The division of roles and the range of tasks depend on the relationship within the marriage. The rights and the duties are of a mutual character but this does not mean that equivalent rules are applied. It is often one person who is burdened with all the tasks. As a commentator on family law argues:

> The division of various functions fulfilled by spouses is defined by a special predestination of a woman to fulfil the tasks connected with motherhood and childcare and therefore most of the burden of providing for the family in an average Polish home to be on the man's shoulders. (Ignatowicz, 2000, p 126)

The legislator equates women's work with running the household and men's with paid employment. A wife has the right to work for pay, as well as the right to give it up in order to focus on caring for her children (Ignatowicz, 2000).

What do these 'equal rights' mean in practice? The right to receive care during pregnancy and after giving birth, the right to go on sick leave and maternity leave – these traditionally belonged to women. Since the beginning of the 1980s, some rights have been given to men. From 1981, the father of a child was also entitled to go on childcare leave, but under certain conditions:

- when the mother did not use the leave and agreed that the father of the child could use it;
- when the mother was no longer alive or was unable to take care of the child through sickness; and
- when the mother had restricted parental rights or they were entirely taken away from her.

Policy thus long prioritised mothers' care over fathers' care. Policies aiming to make it easier for women to reconcile work and family cannot be dismissed. They are connected with the biological functions of motherhood: special rights during pregnancy, birth and breast-feeding (Balcerzak-Paradowska, 2004a, 2004b). But now these laws weaken women's position in employment. Employers have not been eager to employ young women, afraid they would use their rights.

More inclusive policies to include fathers in childcare leave date from 1995 when women and men were given equal rights to take leave to care for a sick child under four years of age. The same leave applies in other circumstances; for example when a nursery or kindergarten is closed suddenly and the child is under eight years of age (Balcerzak-Paradowska, 1997, p 57). In 1996 the Labour Code was amended, widening some entitlements to include men, especially when the man is the only guardian of the child. Where two parents work, only one can use the entitlements, with the decision left to those involved.

Childcare leave lasts 36 months and can be taken until the child turns four years of age. People living on low incomes are entitled to an allowance of up to 25% of an average market wage for 24 months (see Chapter Two, Table 2.4). In 1996 the above principles were modified. At present, when parents or guardians both work, only one of them can take childcare leave at a time. This decision rests with the parents. The second parent is to declare in writing that he or she is not taking leave.

But to what extent do fathers use these rights or undertake responsibility for childcare? Balcerzak-Paradowska (1997, p 58) argues that the exercise of those rights will be limited for some time to come. Unequal pay for women and men is a factor, reducing the incentives for men to take childcare leave or leave to care for a sick child. Decisions are constrained by the need to safeguard the family income. In 2002, only 1.4% of men took childcare leave (Kotowska, 2003, in Balcerzak-Paradowska, 2004b, p 250). Traditional perceptions of childcare tasks are still common, although there is some evidence that these may be changing (see Chapter Five). Changes in practices are taking place even more slowly than changes in perceptions and ideals: childcare is still more likely to be a woman's domain than a man's. So, while there have been some policy changes towards more equal rights to time to care for children, equal practices in the family are some distance away (Balcerzak-Paradowska, 2004a, 2004b).

Women's rights

Present policy should also be examined from the point of view of gender equality. Communism in Poland accelerated the process of women entering public life. In the years between 1946 and 1964, laws discriminating against women at work or in the family were annulled. Legal regulation gave women equal rights with men in all spheres of governmental, political, civil, economic, social and cultural life. However, of great importance were the rights to take up paid employment, take leave from work, have social insurance, be employed in public posts and receive distinctions. But the legislation contained contradictions: it emphasised gender equality but it also referred to gender differences based on biology. Privileges for women based on fulfilling maternal functions were intended to equalise women's position with men in employment. Analysis of these policies gives rise to the question: "Was the true intention of the legislator who limited women's right to choose work freely an attempt to protect their health, or was it rather a desire to make their access to some well-paid occupations simply impossible?" (Zielińska, 2002, pp 88-9).

Those regulations of the Labour Code apparently intended to enable women to combine paid employment with childcare are, according to Zielińska (2002), the symptoms of inequality and exclusion of women from public life. Whatever the legislative intentions in the period of communism, now – with new regulations about private ownership – the increase in unemployment, changes in the job market and the rules of employment, these regulations have become discriminatory in their impact on women. They have noticeably reduced women's competitiveness on the job market and allowed their exclusion from employment.

In the 1990s changes were made towards equal distribution of rights in childcare shared between the parents, to combine paid employment with parental duties. Yet, according to Zielińska:

> the law and social policy both underline the outstanding importance of women's role in bringing up the children and taking care of them in person and law and social policy

> enable women to combine the duties mentioned above
> with paid employment. Neither the law nor the policy
> however, expects the man to perform both paid work and
> parental duties. (Zielińska, 2002, p 90)

Another example of discrimination comes from the legislation relating
to retirement. Retirement regulations differentiating the entitlement
age for women (60 years old) and for men (65 years old) were perceived
as a special privilege for women. The earlier retirement age for women
was seen as compensating for their double burden of employment and
family. The transformation period makes this not a privilege. Employers
dismiss women from work after they reach retirement age. This situation
originates from high unemployment levels: women's entitlement to
earlier retirement became compulsory in practice and brought serious
financial consequences. In 1999, the system of social insurance was
changed and brought a decrease in retirement pensions. It has been
estimated that women's retirement pensions may be 30% lower on
average than men's (Zielińska, 2002, p 91). The question of making the
retirement age equal for women and men became the subject of wide
public debate. Many women want to retain the previous regulations
on retirement age, allowing them to retire at 60. They mention their
tiredness from working 'two full-time jobs', the unattractiveness of
paid employment and family needs such as childcare for grandchildren.
Counter-arguments centre on retirement incomes for women, with a
low retirement age for women bringing lower retirements pensions
within the current regulations. Differences in pay, working lives shorter
by five years, and longer life expectancy already mean lower retirement
pensions than for men. Even at the same pay level, women's pensions
are now around 62% of those of men (*Gospodarka*, 2004).

The Citizens' Rights Spokesman has often drawn attention to ways
in which the economic and social transformation in Poland has changed
the impact of legal entitlements, turning some guaranteed rights against
women's interests. The existing system for protecting women's
employment, maternity and families was created, for the most part, for
different socioeconomic conditions: a labour-intensive system of
employment without unemployment or mass redundancies and
dominated by state employers that operated a widespread system of
social services. However, the present situation encourages the
elimination from the labour market of groups which are not flexible
and have the weakest resistance: "Gender discrimination is, on the
one hand, women's elimination from paid employment and, on the
other, a lack of options which would alleviate difficult living conditions

resulting from the family situation" (Zielińska, 2002, p 93). The intervention of the Citizens' Rights Spokesman resulted in changes to the two days' paid leave for care of a child up to the age of 14 and childcare allowance, allowances which were mainly for women and only exceptionally for men when they were the child's only guardian (Zielińska, 2002). These small changes made the entitlements more equal between men and women, which should make women and men more equal on the competitive labour market.

The economic restructuring, developing a market economy based on competitiveness and economic profitability, brought increased mobility of employment. The private sector retained young women with vocational training while the public sector employed more highly educated women. There was an increase in female employment in stereotypically male areas: the building industry, transport and communications. According to the Centre for Women's Rights (2000, quoted by Balcerzak-Paradowska et al, 2003b, p 95), the public sector does make redundancies, but is more concerned than the private sector with protecting women's employment and stability. While private sector employment increases, it is more high-risk and more male orientated. The public sector provides older women with longer-term employment security. In the state sector there are more highly qualified/specialised employees. About 29% of women employed in this sector have received higher education, whereas in the private sector the figure is only 10%. As the private sector has developed, problems with implementing employees' rights have increased. This can be seen in the pattern of employees' complaints upheld. The most frequent problems are connected with pay: the pay level is lowered, or payments entirely missed. There is evidence that such incidents are increasing and the reason is very often the difficult financial situation of the business. Private employers do not fully respect employee rights concerning holiday leave and very often the length of these holidays is reduced. Another example is enforced overtime, working on free days and restricting the employment of necessary extra personnel (Balcerzak-Paradowska et al, 2003a, pp 91-2).

Research shows that, during interviews, private sector employers more often than public sector ones ask questions about prospective employees' private and family lives, and more often to women than to men, suggesting that qualifications were less important to employers than the family situation. These data support those from the Centre for Women's Rights, which also showed differences in interviews according to the sex of the candidate. Women were asked additional questions: their age, family situation, number and age of children, marriage plans, maternity plans, the possibility of working overtime, business trips. Employers rarely cited family responsibilities or children as the reason for rejecting a candidate. However, respondents themselves believed that family responsibilities, especially those connected with having children, were the real reason for rejection. This was the opinion of 93% of women, usually young, having children of pre-school and school age (Kołaczek, 2001b, pp 123, 128). Private employers prefer employees to be free of responsibilities and mobile. Gender, age and childlessness have become important criteria in the new Polish economy for employers seeking workers. Questions about children were asked twice as often of women as men. Employers asked women about pregnancies more often in the age group from 20 to 29 years old and less often in the age group from 30 to 34 (Kołaczek, 2001b). Less formal conversations with women seeking employment have uncovered even more serious hurdles. Besides asking questions about family planning, employers asked women to do a pregnancy test, whose result decided whether to employ them or not. There were also expectations that women should give a written statement that they would not become pregnant over a specified period of time.

As mentioned earlier, in 2001 the campaign to help women carry out their family duties resulted in the lengthening of statutory maternity leave. What did women think of this solution? Research suggests they were not happy with it: over half the women respondents (56.8%) considered the former periods of leave and childcare leave sufficient. They feared that a lengthier maternity leave would exclude them from the labour market altogether. Among women asked if they would take advantage of a longer maternity leave, less than half (46.9%) said yes. They also perceived the full length of leave as being for mothers, with only 2% considering the possibility of the father using part of it. Some older women (41.9%) said that maternity leave should be longer than at present. Younger women more often (66.6-77.8%) preferred to leave it as it was. As suggested by Balcerzak-Paradowska (2004a, 2004b), the main motive for extending maternity leave was ascribing a particular meaning to motherhood. Also important is the allowance accompanying the leave: the maternity allowance. Post-maternity childcare leave is a different matter, with the allowance for absence from work calculated on different premises. Maternity leave is available to all female employees with full compensation for lost earnings. The associated problems are: returning to work after leave, the fear of missing promotion, that it restricts access to good professional positions, or causes difficulties with finding re-employment. Various studies suggest a relationship between attitudes towards the system of childcare leave and women's level of education. Women with a lower education level favour prolonging the leave periods. With a rise in the level of education, the percentage of women who consider the leave adequate as it is also rises (Balcerzak-Paradowska, 2003, pp 311, 314).

In Poland, debates and policy around the right to abortion offer an important indication of the state's assumptions about women as mothers and workers, and of changing models of the family reflected in government policy. A long period of discussion in the post-Second World War period brought legislation permitting abortion in 1956. This legislation was justified as protecting women's health, in the context of damaging abortions carried out in unsanitary conditions or by unqualified practitioners. The law of 1956 did not give the women the right to decide for themselves about motherhood. It permitted abortion for so-called 'social reasons', which meant, in practice, difficult living conditions. Abortions could be carried out only by doctors: in general, 'medical' as well as 'social' conditions could be decided by one doctor alone. However, in a criminal case, of pregnancy due to rape, it was necessary also to have a statement from the public prosecutor. Abortions could be refused on the grounds of a lack of medical support, or justifying social conditions, as well as, in the case of a minor, lack of consent of the parents, guardians or guardian court. It took four years to carry the law into effect, partly because the executive regulations were not of great precision. The resistance of doctors, especially gynaecologists, was also significant. Doctors, for ethical reasons and because of their outlook on life, were simply refusing to implement the legislation. At the same time, illegal abortions were still taking place. In 1959 a new executive regulation made abortion a matter of the woman's decision without the necessity to verify her social or medical condition by the doctor who would do the abortion. This made matters much easier in reality and allowed women to make this decision of their own free will (Zielińska, 1990, pp 54-5).

The law was accompanied by much debate involving the Roman Catholic Church and Circle. The 'protection of the unborn' movement began. In the 1970s the first surge of discussion on the abortion law was linked with some pro-natal policies, including prolonged maternity leave and unpaid childcare leave. Already in this period, the decrease and ageing of the population were noticed, although no connection was demonstrated between the abortion law and these changes. In the years 1976-78, the family model of 'two plus three' was promoted in the context of the ageing population (although an increase in the fertility rate was noticed). The Council of Family Matters was established in 1978, and a law giving motherhood protection was added to the 1952 Constitution. These constitutional amendments gave support to the fight against the abortion law. Defenders of the abortion law argued that the duty to protect motherhood should be understood only as the duty to provide, when necessary, a woman who chooses to have a child with help and/or protection, and this should not be misinterpreted as compulsory motherhood or the state forcing reproduction (Zielińska, 1990, pp 55-61).

Debates about a 'moral revival' came with the development of the Roman Catholic Circle movement at the beginning of the 1980s. The movement warned against the moral and health consequences of abortions and offered practical help to single pregnant women (Zielińska, 1990, p 61). This was the beginning of stricter controls on abortion, with a new regulation passed in 1990 by the Minister of Health and Social Care. From then on, abortions would require permission from two doctors (one a gynaecologist/obstetrician and the other an internist) and discussion with a psychologist about the wish, circumstances and motives for abortion (Zielińska, 1990, p 132).

More stringent legislation was approved at the beginning of 1993 relating to planning a family, protection of the human foetus and the circumstances allowing abortion. This law brought a ban on abortion, except for extreme circumstances where a woman's life or health was threatened, or when she had been raped, or when a baby with congenital abnormality was expected. Severe penalties were attached to the law and anyone helping to carry out an abortion in circumstances other than these could be imprisoned for up to two years. In 1996, the abortion law was amended and a new circumstance, 'poor social situation', added to those in which abortion would be permitted. But the following year, the Constitutional Tribunal found the new 'social circumstances' unconstitutional and disallowed them. A doctor, or anyone helping a woman to receive an abortion, may be held responsible if it is found that the intervention is illegal; this carries a sentence of up to three years' imprisonment. But the Penal Code does not allow prosecution of a woman who decides on an abortion.

Debates about changing abortion law have taken place in the context of debates about women as mothers, and attempts to 're-traditionalise' the family. Right-wing parties (ZCHN, UPR, Solidarność [Solidarity]) favour restrictions on abortion laws and perceive women's roles as maternal and domestic. Some more extreme representatives argue for restrictions of women's public roles in politics and for their exclusion from paid employment. They argue that a married man should earn a 'family wage', supporting a wife who is not employed. These ideas have emerged in the context of rising unemployment, and the idea of a 'family wage' is to enable women's retreat from the job market. Left-wing and some centre parties have defended a more liberal law allowing abortion, in the context of women's rights to employment and involvement in politics (Siemieńska, 1996, p 25). Zielińska argues that the current legislation resulting from the Constitutional Tribunal decision, has omitted the needs of women, and 'protection of the mother'. The Tribunal's opinion presents in a broad way the father's right to be included in making a decision about having a child. Parliamentary discussions have focused on protecting the foetus, while women's rights seem to be forgotten (Zielińska, 2002, pp 96-7).

What are the consequences of the current legal position on abortion? The restrictions in Poland have encouraged some previously existing abortion tendencies and sponsored some new ones. These are 'the abortion underworld', with illegal abortion intervention and 'abortion tourism' to countries where abortion interventions are legal. There are no data on these trends. Legal abortion is difficult to obtain: some media report that doctors are refusing to perform abortions, even where there is a legal foundation, because they say it is discordant with their professional code of ethics. Most recently, there have been reports of 'internet abortion': "500 women from all around Poland have had an abortion using early-miscarriage pills they bought online" (*Gazeta Wyborcza*, 10 September 2004).

Women, work and family

Introducing and overthrowing communism have been the most significant factors in women's changing situation in Poland. In the first years after the Second World War, women started to migrate to cities with developing industry and found work there. Movement to the cities increased in the 1960s, and in the 1970s and 1980s women were the majority of migrants. Women's educational achievements were also increasing: at the beginning of the 1980s over half of university students were women. Women are less likely to have technical qualifications than men, having more often entered the arts, medicine, law and economics faculties.

In the early post-Second World War years the communist system quickly engaged women's labour: they were needed as part of the large workforce employed under communism when the economy was working at low levels of efficiency. Women were a cheaper workforce than men and were mainly employed in female sectors of the national economy such as education, health and administration. Although they were well educated and experienced, women were rarely appointed to higher posts. Legislation strengthened the constitutional equality of women and men: women's rights were strengthened with creation of new policy solutions. Attempts were made to enable women with small children to take up paid employment through increased provision of nurseries, kindergartens and childcare leave, discussed above. In 1946, a divorce law was introduced allowing women to end unsatisfactory relationships, and in 1956 an abortion law allowed women to decide on the number of children they wanted. Abortion intervention was very often a contraceptive 'device' as there was no adequate information on contraception (Siemieńska, 1996, pp 11-14).

Even before the Second World War, many women in Poland were employed in the consumer goods industry or as domestic servants. According to the census, in 1931 only three in 100 married women had employment, but by 1950 the number had doubled. The participation rate grew significantly in the years 1960-70. This tendency continued strongly until the end of 1970s. The important feature of women's activity between the years 1945 and 1989 was an increase in the number of women employed in sectors besides agriculture. By 1960, 42% of married women had employment, in 1970 it was 68%, and in 1989 about 74%. Research carried out across Poland in 1968 and 1988 shows that economic reasons dominated the motives for taking up employment, with 56% citing these. However, a considerable percentage of women (44%) declared the non-financial rewards as important (Kurzynowski, 1995a, p 41).

Poland's transformation into a market economy has changed the situation of women again. The job market was restructured: some workplaces disappeared and new ones with a new profile were established. The demand for workers with women's qualifications has decreased. Women in older age groups in particular experience problems with keeping employment. Private sector workplaces bring redundancies. The changes also affect the nature of many posts: those of an executive character become more independent and involve decision making and long hours. Employers prefer men, because of the extended entitlements for working mothers. Women's lack of experience as managers makes it more difficult for them to find employment. Employers underline the need for managerial experience in their job specifications. Men with managerial experience often decide to set up their own businesses, but few women do so (Siemieńska, 1996, pp 13-14).

How does women's employment situation relate to their higher levels of education in the new market situation in Poland? Over half of women (58%) have an educational background above secondary school level, compared with around 40% of men. Among the employed, in 1998 there were 54% of women and 34% of men with this level of education. Despite these superior levels of education, women fill only 10% of all managerial posts. Women with higher educational levels fill a little over a quarter (28.5%) of all managerial posts. Young female graduates as well as middle-aged women have problems in finding employment. Women who do the same job as men, or a job of similar value, are paid less. Research on unemployment shows that in the case of group redundancies, women are made redundant more often than men. Unemployed women are then discriminated against when it comes to job offers (Janowska, 2000, p 15).

The transition period brought a severe reduction in women's labour market participation, which declined faster than men's. In 1992, women's economic activity was at 53.7% and fell to 47.9% by 2003. In 2003, for every 1,000 economically active men there were 603 economically inactive. Yet, for every 1,000 economically active women, there were 1,088 inactive: the inactive population is therefore over two thirds women (Central Statistical Office, 2004b). The highest level of economic activity is among women with higher and/or above secondary school education among whom economic activity is as high as for men. On the whole, however, the female employment rate is a quarter lower than the male. The majority of employed women have at least secondary education: but they rarely fill managerial posts, especially at higher grades. Among managers and professionals, in 2003 there were 35% women. Only 29% of employers are women (Central Statistical Office, 2004b).

The labour market situation of Polish women can be compared with the European Union as a whole, and with other CEE new member countries:

- The gender pay gap for employees working at least 15 hours per week was 11% in 2003, a little below the European Union average of 15%, and more favourable to women than in other then CEE accession countries such as the Czech Republic (19%) and Hungary (14%), although greater than in Slovenia (9%) (see Chapter Two, Table 2.3).
- Polish women's employment rate in 2003 was 46%, well below the EU25 average of 55.1% and below the other then CEE accession countries such as the Czech Republic with 56.3% and Hungary with 50.9% (see Chapter Two, Table 2.1).
- Polish women's unemployment rate in 2004 was 19.7%, nearly twice the EU25 average of 10.2% and above the other CEE new

member states such as the Czech Republic at 9.8% and Hungary at 6.0% (see Chapter Two, Table 2.2).

• Women's unemployment rate was higher than men's in 2004 (19.7% for women and 18.0% for men) as in other European Union countries. But the threat of prolonged unemployment touched more Polish women than men (10.9% for women and 9.5% for men) (Europa NewCronos website: epp.eurostat.cec.eu.int).

Employers tend to prefer male employees to female ones, seeing men as more committed to their jobs, while women are perceived as more committed to childcare and household duties (Leszkowicz-Baczyńska, 2002). Research shows clearly that economic factors are important motivating factors for female employees: asked "would you give up your job if the financial situation of your family allowed this", 36% of women interviewed answered yes, 38% no, while 26% did not offer a view. These researchers argue that "financial means make a great impact, if taken together with other factors, inducing a temporary or permanent departure from the labour market". These factors are the time of active motherhood, the need to provide a child with care, low professional qualifications, restricted work abilities because of poor health, large families and/or unemployment (Graniewska and Balcerzak-Paradowska, 2003, p 296).

Motherhood is a key reason for women leaving their jobs. The systems developed under communism have left women exposed under market conditions. Maternity and childcare leave periods, which once protected women's employment, now expose them to the risk of unemployment. As shown earlier, taking childcare leave has become less common and a decreasing number of women take them. A very important factor is the limited eligibility for childcare allowance. Women were asked if they would take childcare leave "if they were entitled to an allowance when they gave up their job in order to care for their child". Only 23% said they would take leave; over a third (38%) said it depended how much of their previous earnings it would cover; 7% did not find childcare allowance a reason to take the leave ("no matter how much the allowance"). Younger respondents, aged 20-29, were more likely to say they would take leave if there were an allowance to compensate for lost earnings (52%), than women aged 30-39 (45%) (Graniewska and Balcerzak-Paradowska, 2003, pp 291-2).

But, despite the increasing precariousness of women's employment, quantitative evidence suggests that there is an increasing sense among Polish women of the importance of employment to their economic situation as well as to their sense of identity. The main motive in taking up paid employment is their desire to improve the family's financial situation (CBOS, 1993). But over half of the women interviewed in 1993 and in 1996 said they would not give up their job even if their husband's earnings allowed their families a satisfactory living standard. Women also said that paid employment gave them economic independence, future financial security, improved self-esteem, allowed self-development and enabled social contacts. Continuing employment goes together with higher education and a satisfactory financial situation, with these responses most often made by women who were in managerial and intellectual occupations. The desire to give up employment was expressed by women who were discontented with their jobs. But social perceptions of women's paid employment changed between the studies in 1993 and in 1996: there was an increase in women who found employed women more admirable than those with household duties only, from 48% of women who said that women's paid employment was worthy of respect in 1993 to 71% of women in 1996 (CBOS, 1993, 1996).

In 1989, 96.7% of women employees were in the public sector. Of course, the transition from communism has reduced this, and in 2001 the proportion had declined to 51%. The change in the political system brought new private sector workplaces. The number of women employed in the private sector grew from 3.3% in 1989 to 49.2% in 2001. But these changes were more dramatic for men than for women, with most men now being employed in the private sector. The characteristics of women employed in the private sector differ from those in the public sector. Women in the private sector are younger. The 2001 data show 33.3% under 30 years of age, while in the public sector only 15.5% are under 30. The different age patterns suggest that greater mobility may be more important in the private sector. The level of education among those employed in the private sector is lower than in the public: 29% of women working in the public sector have higher education, compared with one in ten of those in the private sector. Permanent employment is the major form of employment in both sectors, but women private sector employees are three times more often in seasonal and temporary work than public sector employees (Balcerzak-Paradowska et al, 2003b, pp 93-5).

Working hours and wages

Regulation of working hours in Poland began in 1974. Gradually the number of Saturdays off grew, and by 1981 a working week of 42 hours was established. Changes followed in the years 2000-03, with legislation in 2003 shortening the working week to 40 hours. There are only small differences between Poland and the European Union as a whole in the weekly hours for people with full-time permanent employment (see Chapter Two). In 1993 in Poland, the average working week for full-time workers was 1.3 hours longer than the European Union average, with the difference falling below one hour in 2000. In the same year, the average working week for men in Poland was 1.9 hours longer than in the European Union as a whole, while women worked shorter hours than the European Union average. There is a difference between women's and men's working hours in Poland, with men working 5.6 hours longer per week than women, a gender difference greater than the European Union average (Gładzicka-Janowska, 2003).

Part-time jobs are not as common among Polish employed women and men as elsewhere in the EU25, although a little higher than in other new CEE member states (see Chapter Two, Table 2.6). In Poland, part-time workers were 11.1% of the workforce, and more often these were women. International comparisons showed part-time work among Polish women at 9.7% below Greece, where women's part-time employment was the lowest among EU15 countries. International comparisons also show that in Poland the reasons for part-time employment are quite rarely connected with the family situation: only in 12.7% of cases. By contrast, in Austria, Belgium and Spain, family reasons account for 60% of people in part-time work. In EU15 countries besides Belgium and Portugal, taking a part-time job meant that people did not want a full-time job (most often respondents were German, Dutch, British, French and Irish). In Poland, however, 43% of part-time employment is explained by low pensions, several part-/full-time jobs at a time, political activity and work in social organisations. These reasons were least frequent in Belgium and Portugal (Gładzicka-Janowska, 2003, p 35). Part-time employment may also be a result of structural problems in workplaces.

The private sector offers part-time employment to 20% of women and 10% of men, while the public sector has less than 5% part-time jobs for men or women (Siemieńska, 1996, p 42). The dynamic growth of female part-time employment in EU15 countries arises from the development of the service sector, flexible working hours offered by employers, coupled with low wages for unskilled workers (Gładzicka-Janowska, 2003, pp 35-6). In Poland, the demand for part-time employment is not great, and part-time jobs are taken up for many different reasons such as studies, gaining new qualifications, to supplement low pensions. The low living standards of Polish people make them averse to part-time employment: it provides low earnings and reduces the level of future pensions. While interest in part-time employment is growing, it is hardly noticeable compared with Western Europe. In Poland, 13% of the workforce consists of part-time women workers, while in Hungary this figure is 5.1% and in Slovakia 2.7% (See Chapter Two, Table 2.6). Company owners find the cost too high and the taxation system discouraging to part-time employment (Kołaczek, 2001a, pp 13-14). A new phenomenon occurred in the 1990s: 'under the counter' jobs. The grey zone employs seasonally every 10th man and every 20th woman of working age but usually these have a low level of education. Most often, this form of employment is an extra job, and not the sole one. The main reason for taking up 'under the counter' work is the need to protect the family budget because incomes are too low (Kołaczek, 2001c, pp 69-71).

Under communism, the Polish Constitution guaranteed the right to work for people of productive age. It also guaranteed the right to equal wages for men and women doing the same jobs. There was no unemployment, with no limit to jobs in the public sector. In the state-controlled economy, the authorities set wages at a low level, which meant that both men and women had to undertake paid employment. Women's employment was supported by family allowances and services such as fully paid maternity and childcare leave, public nurseries and kindergartens, free/subsidised summer holidays for children, and family expenses partly covered by the workplace. Women worked full time for their entire working life. Big public workplaces in Poland had their nurseries, kindergartens and medical centres. Unofficially, women would leave work during working hours, cope with family problems or shop: it was difficult to get some goods and queues were enormous. The transition to a market economy changes the rules. The state does not provide work: each individual has to try and find it. The decrease in women's employment is visible in all age groups: for younger women, reasons include an extended period of gaining education, the need to take care of children as childcare establishments are harder to access, and limited prospects of finding a job. Many women retire at the age of 55 and take care of their grandchildren (Kołaczek, 2001a, pp 10-12).

Women more often work in lower-paid economic sectors and occupations, which is one of the reasons for the gender pay gap (Kołaczek, 2001a, p 14). The most feminised sectors of the national economy in 2003 were: health and social services (412 women per 100 men), education (337 women per 100 men), financial brokerage (243 women per 100 men), office workers (235 women per 100 men)

(Central Statistical Office, 2004b). Women's hourly earnings are around 11% less than men's (see Chapter Two and Table 2.3). Gender pay gaps are smaller in the private sector than the public sector (Balcerzak-Paradowska, 2004a, p 21) Three quarters of women (74%) and a little over half of men (56%) are paid below the national average wage (Kołaczek, 2001c, p 65). According to the Central Statistical Office, in 2001, women with higher education were paid 68% of the earnings of men at the same educational level. The smallest difference was among people with secondary school education: the pay for this group of women was 83% of men's pay. The European Commission, in its report for the year 2000, stated that among candidate countries at that time, Poland showed least respect for equal rights for women and men. A year later, in 2001, it noticed a significant change, as provisions for equal treatment were introduced in the Labour Code (*Gospodarka*, 2004, p 65).

Conclusion

All political parties (besides radical liberals) declare the need for state support for the family, but there has been no programme for a family policy that was coherent and accepted by the various political forces (Szatur-Jaworska, 2001, p 54; Balcerzak-Paradowska, 2004b). Family policies are underpinned by contrasting ideological propositions. The first assumes a traditional understanding of indissoluble marriage, allows natural regulation of births, and favours large families. The woman's role derives from her maternal tasks and care for the family. The second underlines the equality of spouses, with both combining employment and family. Divorces are perceived as permissible and contraception a part of planning the number and timing of children. Szatur-Jaworska (2001, p 55) argues that the underlying aims of contemporary Polish family policy are closer to the traditional model than to the modern one. But contemporary policies and values in Poland are a contradictory mix, blending traditional male breadwinner ideals with the practices of dual earner regimes under communism, which were similar in some ways to the Scandinavian model. Equally contradictory is the mixture of market liberalism with some more collective solutions remaining from the communist period.

Contemporary debates are about work–life balance, reconciling work and family. This demands solutions that would not discriminate against women and would enable equal access to the job market, public activity and social life. Women's labour market participation helps family budgets and keeps families out of poverty. Paid employment is also valued for itself in terms of satisfaction and personal identity. Work competes with family but does not exclude family: it may mean later marriage, later childbearing and limiting family size. The transformation to a competitive market economy has brought sharp conflicts for women, who experience discrimination because of their entitlements as mothers: policy needs to ensure that guaranteed rights do not disable women in the labour market. In families, reconciling employment and family responsibilities means leaving traditional models – whether Roman Catholic or communist – and turning to a new partnership model of the family. Policies could underpin family partnership, sharing both paid work and care work. New social values are needed, particularly in governments, where traditional expectations of women persist.

Poland has ratified international laws obliging it to comply with equal rights for women and men. Accession to the European Union brings new commitments, including a 'new social contract on gender' in the work–life balance resolution. The end of communism has brought new developments in civil society, with freedom to organise, and a wide range of influences on social values. Membership of the European Union has brought some defence of policies for gender equality (see Chapter Seven). The Polish Constitution declares equal rights, the Labour Code regulates work relations and the Citizens' Rights Spokesman intervenes when the law is violated. But women still experience a worse position in the labour market and at home. Cases of discrimination are hard to prove. Often women are afraid or not aware of their rights. The development of new machineries to protect women's rights is important, but only a step on the way to a partnership model supporting gender equality at work and in the family.

doesn't answer the question * in the introduction

Re return to traditional communist system

FOUR

Mothers and the state

Introduction

This chapter investigates women and the Polish state, in the context of debates around gender in post-communist societies. The political questions of the post-communist era have tended to focus on issues of participation and identity, especially feminist identity, or the lack of it. But the state under communism was a major provider of services whether directly or through state-owned companies. How do mothers perceive the changes towards a liberal state, preoccupied with marketisation and with reducing public expenditure? Does the lack of participation reflect a lack of trust and interest in the state and a disjunction between public politics and women in households? And does a lack of feminist identity in Poland and other post-communist societies mean that women do not associate themselves with movements to develop policies for equality in work and the family?

Issues of participation and identity are crucial. The development of liberal democracy in Poland is a development from which women have been largely excluded, with low representation in the new institutions and little voice. Compared with the communist era, when it was regulated by quotas, women's representation has radically diminished (Pető et al, 2004). However, women's movements have developed in civil society in Poland in the space created since the transition from soviet domination and from martial law. In the period since 1989, women's groups have been developing to defend abortion rights, freedom from violence, and equality in legislation (Fuszara, 1997, 2000a, 2000b, 2000c, 2000d). But "optimism about women's participation in politics should be tempered by the reality that most decisions that affect women, and that shape women's situations and opportunities, continue to be made in traditionally defined, male-dominated political bodies" (Fuszara, 2000b, p 261). In Poland, 94% of senior government ministers are male, as are 78% Members of Parliament (see Chapter Two and Table 2.8). Governments in the region lack a true commitment to gender equality politics and, in Poland in particular, efforts to enact equal opportunity legislation have been unsuccessful (Jalusic and Antic, 2000a, 2000b; Siemieńska, 2000). Liberalisation in practice has brought men into positions of power through democratic processes but it has not brought many women into key decision-making positions (Regulska, 1998, 2001). Decisions about reducing support for families, including changes to the basic infrastructure of services that supported adult earner families, have been made by mainly male politicians in the context of pressures from international agencies, and with little input from those most affected.

Feminist identity, and its development – or lack of development in the post-communist era – is another concern of the literature about gender in post-communist societies (Siemieńska, 2002). The lack of freedom to organise in civil society was one of the gravest oppressions of the communist era, and women expected the new freedoms to be expressed through development in civil society of a feminist movement. While some commentators acknowledge the development of processes of democratic participation (Szalai, 2002), most are concerned about their weakness: "One of the puzzling facts about the new democracies is that women do not appear keen to use the new freedoms to improve their position" (Ferge, 1998, p 231). Women's higher level of education compared with men's, and their widespread participation in paid work might lead us to expect a strong identification with feminist politics. Women's organisations are indeed developing but these new organisations are reluctant to identify themselves as feminist (Fuszara, 1997, 2000a, 2000b, 2000c, 2000d). For example, in Poland the phenomenon of self-organisation, to solve actual problems or improve the local environment, is manifesting as protests against closing down a school or constructing a motorway. Non-governmental organisations working for the interests of the family, children and young people are also developing strongly (Głogosz, 1997). But these organisations mainly identify themselves with an agenda about the family rather than one about feminism.

A number of explanations have been offered for the relative lack of organisations with a feminist agenda. One is the experience of women's organisations during the communist era which were "inauthentic organisations imposed from above" (Fuszara, 1997). Another is the extreme double burden created for women under communism, which led to the feeling that they could have "too much equality" (Siemieńska, 1998, p 127). Perhaps most important here, however, is the argument that the family was a refuge under communism and "a locus of resistance against the omnipotence of the state". In these circumstances, suspicion of egalitarian movements and western feminist ideas became a core part of people's identity (Heinen, 1997, p 579; see also Heinen and

Portet, 2002; Jalusic, 2002). Ferge argues that rhetoric of the "politics of the personal" alienated women living under totalitarian systems, who were fearful of the encroachment of the state on the family: "Totalitarianism was about invading every sphere including the private, and women and men had the utmost difficulty in retaining some freedom, which was possible only in the family" (Ferge, 1998, p 232). Similarly, Peggy Watson argues that under communism, society as a whole was against the state: people saw themselves as families and households, rather than as men and women. Since the collapse of communism the primary change is the development of class differences, with spreading unemployment and poverty. Gender equality issues have taken a lower place in women's priorities in the context of these social and economic upheavals (Watson, 1997, 2000a, 2000b). Finally, Haney suggests that state retrenchment brings about "a retrenchment in women's opportunities for social citizenship" (Haney, 2002, p 174).

These discussions help us to understand the development of women's identity within the new post-communist societies, but there has been little comment about the implications for women's relation to policies for social welfare and the way that these interact with gender equality. The transition from communism may have been first about political and economic transformation and the development of markets and of civil society, but the implications for women as mothers have also been a major consequence (see Chapter Two). State socialist policies sought women's labour for economic development. They enabled it through education systems oriented to producing highly qualified women and men (UNICEF, 1998), through workplace social provision and through state-guaranteed entitlements such as childcare leave and benefits, kindergartens and nurseries (Fajth, 1996). These societies retained an unreconstructed domestic division of labour that left women with a very heavy double burden of paid and unpaid work. However, changes in the state have brought radical changes to households and particularly to mothers of young children. Economic upheaval, a changing labour market, changes in the generation and collection of resources for state services, as well as the international agencies, have brought reductions in the value of benefits such as family allowances, and charging for previously free or low-cost services, such as pre-school and nursery care and holiday provision (UNICEF, 1999; World Bank, 2002). They have also brought aggressive markets into employment, generating income inequality and insecurity, and into services, making them more accessible to better-paid workers than to people who are lower paid or unemployed. There has been some academic commentary on the "peril of the welfare state's withdrawal" (Ferge, 1997a, 1997c, 2001a, 2001b), but it has been a small voice against a liberal orthodoxy.

In Poland, during the first years of transformation, the state withdrew help for the family under the slogan that individuals who decide to have children are responsible for their own existence and that of their family members. The scope of social protection has been limited and changes in the field of social services became connected with their commercialisation. The transformation period brought a distinct decrease in family income, rising poverty, unemployment and at the same time a complete lack of mechanisms of adjustment to the changes taking place. Decentralisation of the competencies of the state was intended to develop the "independence, self-government and responsibility of local communities", and "reforms of social areas were intended to increase participation of families in the realisation of social and family policy" (Balcerzak-Paradowska, 2004b, p 104). How does this cooperation with local authorities work in practice? Only 19.9% of respondents described cooperation between local authorities and inhabitants as existing, while 30.2% said there was a lack of cooperation, and almost half (49.9%) had no opinion on the subject. On the other hand, a national survey of 2,000 respondents shows that only 7.9% work for their local authority and 92.1% did not do any such work (Balcerzak-Paradowska, 2004b, p 105). This is a rather minimal level of cooperation.

In Poland, women's rights during the communist era were framed by two contradictory ideologies of women: as equal independent workers under communism and as mothers in the Roman Catholic Church (see Chapter Three). The first was entrenched by communist law, the second by cultural tradition and practice (Fuszara, 1994, pp 79-81). The requirement to fulfil both roles was underpinned by legislation that supported women as workers and mothers. The framework of rights was generous by international standards and remains (to some extent) although the value of the benefits has tended to fall. The rights now include maternity benefits, leave to care for sick children, the right to up to three years' childcare leave to care for a small child up to the age of four, and – for those on low incomes and for two years – benefits to compensate for loss of earnings during leave (see Chapter Two, Table 2.4 and Chapter Three). These rights belonged at first to mothers, and could be transferred to fathers only in particular circumstances, and policy thus prioritised maternal care. Legislation in 1995 and 1996 widened entitlements for men, and parents can now choose for fathers or mothers to use childcare leave. But, as shown in Chapter Three, these are still seen as mothers' entitlements, and only a tiny minority of fathers take childcare leave.

The economic conditions within which these rights developed minimised the competitive disadvantage with men. But the competitive conditions of a liberal economy bring different consequences for women who now suffer discrimination and do not take up their rights (Siemieńska, 1998, p 131, 1999). At the same time the costs of childcare have increased and many nurseries have closed as neither businesses nor local authorities could support them. Heinen argues that social policy measures that would be regarded as progressive in western countries were seen as "integral parts of the authoritarian system based on an obligation to work. ... The core of mistrust towards anything that looked like state intervention masked the possibility of any positive appreciation of these social advantages" (Heinen, 1997, p 583).

There are some suggestions in recent literature that, in the wake of the loss of collective social support, women have come to regret their loss and to "resent the sacrifice of programs" (Ferber and Kuiper, 2004, p 83). The 'statist feminist' period may have offered a flawed emancipation to women. But as the legacies of the 'statist feminist' period recede, bringing East nearer to West, women's employment and participation in public life decline and justify the perception of these as losses (Pető, 2004, p 102). But what are mothers' views of the social policies that enabled women to be brought into the labour market through the state's support of care work? And what are their views of the decline of these systems? Men and women may have been opposed to the state under communism but what do they think of it now? Clearly, the overthrow of communism involved a popular rejection of one kind of state, and the development of markets involves developing alternatives to state domination of welfare structures. In her rather critical review of the implications of transition for women, Ferge argues that "the neo-conservative and neo-liberal ideologies, which are in the ascendance throughout the world, have had a particular appeal in the transition countries where formerly only one ideology was recognised as legitimate" (Ferge, 1998, p 222). Transition from communism has brought an ideological resistance to the public sector, which now challenges the political basis of support for state services, while problems with public expenditure undermine its economic base: "After years of communism, and in common with the dominant new-liberal, market-oriented ideology in Western countries during the 1990s, the preference for a 'small state' was often expressed" (Redmond et al, 2002, p 7). More particularly, gender equality and equal opportunity policies have a problem of legitimisation "encumbered by the socialist past and ... the structural-historical context of anti-politics, anti-feminism and liberal-market discourse" (Jalusic and Antic, 2000b, p 3). New gender policies exist in other countries in the region, but there is "a lack of true commitment to gender equality policies at the government level" (Jalusic and Antic, 2000b, p 10).

But how deep and wide are these reactions? Do people share the views of their political leaders? While the transition from communism has brought a swing towards neo-liberal and neo-conservative ideologies and governments, a highly critical view of the state and these developments is emerging from Poland. Respondents to the national report on the social costs of transition were more likely to have experienced bad (40%) than good (14%) events in their households in the previous three years, and no respondents mentioned changes in the social sector as positive elements of the transition. Their evaluations of the new regime in comparison with the communist one tipped in favour of the new, but only just, with 43% of respondents assessing the new system as being better than the previous one, and 38% finding it worse. Respondents expressed a wish for stronger state control of public life, especially in primary education, health care and conditions of living for disabled people, but also in secondary and higher education and care for children under six years of age (Milic-Cerniak, 1995).

Parallel debates elsewhere have challenged the legitimacy of states in general and welfare states in particular, through economics, proclaiming preferences for markets, and politics, doubting the trust of modern citizens in their political leaders. The implication from both these sources has been that the basis of welfare state funding has been undermined by new citizens' preference for making choices as individuals, their mistrust of politicians and their unwillingness to contribute to the collective good through taxation. These have had particular salience in the UK, with its Thatcherite legacy of low welfare funding and a concurrent desire for 'world class' services (Taylor-Gooby and Hastie, 2003). But the issues are clearly salient in CEE countries too, as international organisations and national politicians have fostered liberalisation policies involving major reductions in state involvement in welfare. The UK evidence is of wary politicians who are fearful that voters may give different answers in polling booths from those they give in social surveys. But there is also widespread support for spending more on social services across social divisions. There is little evidence that mistrust of government connects to resistance to social spending (Taylor-Gooby and Hastie, 2003).

In CEE countries the sense of state responsibility may be deeper than in Western Europe. Haney argues that growing up under communism has brought powerful expectations of the state: the majority of Hungarians still look to the state to ensure their overall well-being: "They expected the state to provide decent work and affordable basic necessities but instead received a bit of poor relief. They expected stable housing but instead received meagre funds for flat upkeep" (Haney, 2002, p 222). The European Foundation for the Improvement of Living and Working Conditions, in their quality of life survey found that more respondents in the then accession and candidate countries held social injustice to be responsible for social exclusion and the primary cause of poverty, and more respondents in these countries agreed that social welfare cuts were determinants of social exclusion (Alber and Fahey, 2004, pp 25-7).

In research on the meaning of transition in Poland, Pine argues that people's experience is very diverse, with economic restructuring having very different effects in different regions. In the highlands, dissatisfaction with the state was "often a reiteration of their historical resistance to and animosity towards the state, while for many villagers in central Poland it reflected not only the severe hardship resulting from unemployment but also a very deep sense of loss after the collapse of the socialist system" (Pine, 1995, p 53). In a village in central Poland:

> The post-socialist governments are viewed with deep distrust; they are seen as betraying their country and their people by selling the nation's industry, by eroding the rights to employment, health and welfare that the socialist government had developed. ... These are serious moral judgments about the meaning and obligation of government, which are being made within the context of what is perceived as a forced move from a completely secure interconnection of work, family and state, to a vacuum in which such proper and indeed moral connections are fragmented and no option exists to replace them. (Pine, 1995, pp 555-6)

Our research discussed these issues with mothers of young children in two locations in Poland, in the provincial town of Skierniewice and in the capital, Warsaw. We interviewed mothers of young children, primarily because they seem likely to have felt the effects of the gender policies of transition and we wanted to understand their reaction to the transition and to the current situation. We discussed their views of the state and the state's obligations as well as their ideas about the division of caring responsibility in households, and of particular social policies. In the following account names have been changed to protect confidentiality.

Comparing past and present

Some things have improved or stayed the same. The end of communism was experienced as a removal of authority and an opening up of choice and opportunity. Thinking of themselves as women rather than as mothers, some respondents commented on developing rights: "Women have more rights than before" (Agnieszka) and freedoms. "Women have many opportunities for self-development: there are no barriers, women are everywhere, if they wish to realise themselves in their careers they can. In the past they did not have such possibilities" (Halina). "A woman's situation is easier, because she can study, evolve, work. She is not limited, she can make choices" (Janina).

Some respondents emphasised the changes brought about by improved living standards. In comparison with her mother, Gabriela argued that "everything is on a higher level, better; for example, nurseries and pre-schools ... I live in a more predatory system but my mother (a lone parent) was not able to secure a proper level of existence for my brother and me". Marianna balanced living standards, which were getting better, with time constraints, which were getting worse: "Material living standards are better fulfilled now. However, in general, children have less contact with their parents". Justina emphasised improvements and upheld the contribution of technology to these changes: "Technology ensured that everything went forward. I have an automatic washing machine, gas stove, central heating, comfortable conditions in the house ... I have a car ... my mother had to bring in water in a pail". The freedom and ability to buy for themselves and their children brought obvious improvements to many mothers' lives: "There are so many facilities, one can buy ready-made things, there are no queues in shops, no problems with buying things for children. It is rather easier" (Marzanna).

The free market provided obvious advantages to those able to buy. But these better-off mothers often noted the increasing divisions between themselves and others, between rich and poor. One mother commented on these widening disparities:

> "For some families it was perhaps easier [in the past]. They had no problems with jobs, people worked until 4pm, pre-schools stayed open until 5pm, so it was easier to fetch a

child. Now, because I work, I must hire someone to fetch my child from pre-school." (Liliana)

Now access to earnings is everything, and makes the difference between those who can pay for help and those who cannot:

"A pre-school, school, a job for parents were guaranteed, but on the other hand it was difficult to buy anything needed for life and the children's development. People who are able to adjust to a market economy live better but others perhaps are worse off now" (Klaudia)

Comparing past and present: most things are a lot worse

The difficulty of keeping jobs and earning enough were commonly noted. In particular, women commented on the fragility of their position in paid work in the context of motherhood: "No one could say [under communism], well, you have a baby so you cannot work, or you are pregnant so thank you and goodbye. That is why children are born later now; women just have to make a career and money" (Anna).

Most of all they commented on the lack of material resources needed to support children. When they thought of themselves as mothers or parents rather than as individual women, the restrictions of the new system came to the fore: "Parents are not in a better situation" (Barbara).

In each aspect of parenting, and policy supporting the combination of paid work and motherhood, respondents elaborated problems. These involved problems in taking maternity and childcare leave; problems with working hours; the costs of essential services, such as pre-school care; the risks involved in having children while being unable to support them. Services and policies existed on paper, which were not dissimilar to the system of support under communism, but under the current regime the system was full of holes, with services inaccessible in practice.

Maternity and childcare leave exists in theory but there has been a dramatic decline in use, as described above. Our respondents described the stress of going back to work early after the birth of their children, and the stress of fear of losing jobs if they did not. Stefania went back to work after maternity leave and had experienced the beginning of motherhood as a stressful period:

"Women have many more opportunities to undertake personal development. However, the woman-mother is in a much more difficult situation because sometimes she has to give up being with her child in order to keep her job."

Maternity and childcare leave under communism were seen as benefits which could be taken up without risk. But Magdalena noted a change in access, in the context of competition and unemployment: "Mothers could take childcare leave without fear of loss of work". Dorota gave a similar account of this change, and the risks for mothers now: "For my mother it was easier, going on maternity leave she was sure of being able to return to her job. Now, times are different: every pregnancy, every child brings the risk of losing your job".

Charges for services, and the high costs of services – and essential 'extras' such as text-books – were another theme. Some respondents had been unable to afford to send their children to pre-school, while others were concerned by the increasing charges for the whole range of services, which mean that many poorer parents could not afford them: "There used to be much more support: pre-schools were available, vacation and winter camps for children, the state paid for more. Now one can't use it" (Dorota).

> "Services that formerly were free, now have to be paid for, I mean health and school services. ... When a woman gives birth to a child she is told in the hospital that the child should be breast-fed for as long as possible. How can the mother breast-feed if maternity leave lasts [only] three months?" (Hanna)

Working time and the lack of control over it were also barriers to combining work and motherhood which have become much more extreme under the current regime: "My mother was able to organise her work so that she could work six hours a day. Organisation of my work demands a 10-hour workday" (Alicja). Respondents also commented on their partners' long hours, which sometimes included second jobs, and made it difficult to share the responsibility for children in some households. Katarzyna described both her parents as working shorter hours than herself and her partner:

> "My mother did not work for so many hours as I do. ... She was a doctor and worked six hours a day and came home at 2pm. So we could have dinner together. Now I have no chance. ... My father worked in a bank from 8am

to 3pm. About a quarter past three he was back at home. If my husband returns at 7pm we are happy."

Isabela thought that "work time should be reduced, especially in the case of women, because the care of children mainly falls to them, but it should also be reduced for men so that they could be good fathers".

The systematic and comprehensive nature of the state's support for the family under communism were compared favourably with its fragmentary nature now. As children, our respondents had experienced a system of support, which they saw as covering not only the full day but also the whole year, with holiday support: "When I was pre-school and school age, so-called kindergartens were organised during vacations. Care of children was guaranteed from morning to dinnertime. At present there is no such form of care for children" (Hanna). "When I was a child, we could go to school for the whole day for two weeks of vacations, the care was secure, play, meals ... the vacations were free – nice vacations. At present the state has no funds for similar institutions" (Stefania).

These services amounted to a system that supported mothers' employment effectively, without the costs and the pressures that characterise mothers' lives now. Halina's mother had told her that "formerly it was easier, it [state support] was less expensive and more available" (Halina). But this support also represented something our respondents valued in state responsibility for crucial areas of life. Barbara described the greater care expressed in these arrangements: "I remember that holidays and festivities were organised. Greater care was taken of the family; for instance pre-schools were attached to an institution, food parcels, organised holidays and summer camps for children". Danuta compared the difficulties of life under communism with those now:

> "It was positively easier to raise children, to plan and think of their future. It was more difficult to get food – just ordinary things such as juices for children or some varieties of clothes were difficult to get – but planning for the future, arranging pre-school, nursery or other forms of day care were easier. Paid meals were guaranteed ... [social support] was positively better, in all respects, than at present." (Danuta)

Respondents did not want to hand responsibility for their children over to the state, but they did want their own responsibility acknowledged and to feel that the state was behind them. As Dorota put it: "Social policy is going in the wrong direction. Parents should be responsible for their children but the state should support the parents".

Consequences of the current situation

Accounts of the consequences of the state's withdrawal from family support were deeply critical. Respondents commented on their own sense of neglect, their fears for their children and on the pressures leading to one-child families.

There was a strong undercurrent among our respondents of feeling that the state had a responsibility to society to support the family. They referred often to government claims about support for the family and to their feeling that these were empty of content in relation to themselves as parents of young children. "It's rather lame, this pro-family policy" was the comment of Adriana from Warsaw. Renata contrasted the rhetoric with her experience of being in trouble, and her feeling of neglect: "I do not see any support. There are only promises and debates ... I have small children, work and I am in trouble. In spite of that nobody tries to help me. There is more bureaucracy than help".

This experience is broadened in Agnieszka's comment into an explicit rejection of the contemporary minimal state: "The state does not play a sufficient role in relation to the family. It cares for the most affluent but not for the poorest. I do not accept this role of the state because I feel neglected and even forgotten".

The consequences for children – sometimes respondents' own children – were another theme, with anxiety about their current care and safety: "My children spend their vacation practically without any guardianship" (Grażyna). Others emphasised the problems of supporting them and meeting their needs in the long term: "Having three children I am afraid for their future. I am not certain if my husband and I will be able to ensure their start in life, on our own" (Eleanora).

But there were also wider anxieties about young people with the decline in sports, educational and cultural services:

> "We get more and more removed from the ideal of a state that is able to support the family and help a mother with the care of her children. Institutions which formerly cared for children and developed their talents became fee-paying, so a child is left on its own and pushed on the street to smoke cigarettes and drink alcohol because there are not

the same alternatives as before, such as sports clubs or cultural centres." (Alicja)

Insecurity among mothers – and consequently their children – was another theme, with many respondents referring to the ease with which their own mothers had returned to their jobs after maternity/childcare leave, while they themselves had to look for new work or returned quickly after leave, and lived in fear of family ill-health and unemployment: "It was easier to get and keep a job [then]. Now, you are afraid that if your child gets ill and you have to go on leave, they would not take you back in the job again" (Marianna). "It was easier to reconcile paid work with rearing children ... to get leave if a child was sick. ... Formerly, grandmothers could retire earlier and take care of grandchildren" (Patrycja). "When my mother gave birth to my sister she had to give up her job after maternity leave, but on the other hand when she wanted to come back to the job, there was no problem, she just went back to the same job" (Mirosława). "Questions about children were always the first ones I had to answer to my prospective employer" (Eugenia). "Parents could take up childcare leave without fear of loss of work" (Magdalena).

Reducing family size, evident in data from across the new CEE member states, was another theme. Hanna commented on the many difficulties facing parents, including "lack of assistance on the part of the state in many fields of life" and concluded: "No wonder that most couples have only one child because they cannot afford to support a family"; while Bożena described deepening financial problems and the lack of time and concluded that "the model of the family in Poland becomes two plus one" (two parents and one child).

Government to be feared?

There were very few respondents who argued for the minimal state. Among our Skierniewice respondents, Grażyna came nearest to this argument with her claim that "there should be no obligatory payments for social insurance, and everyone should care for themselves. If one does not work anything out it is his business ... local authorities should not poke their noses into other people's business". But she went on to argue for a considerable level of support for families with young children in terms of income and leave: "The state should guarantee children and parents a social minimum at least" and to argue for parental allowances to be raised "to enable a mother to be with her child for up to four years at least".

Among our Warsaw respondents there were a few adherents to the free market philosophy. Perhaps the strongest advocate of market solutions to the family problems was Elwira, who argued for the flexibility of markets in comparison to legislation:

> "Does it mean that the state should buy a woman a washing machine? It would be not bad, but no, no, no ... I do not feel any state [influence] in my family ... it does not disturb me that I have nothing to do with any state. ... Shops are full, people buy things they need and can devote more time to their children, but it has nothing to do with social policy. ... All legislation is absurd because it does not keep up with life, there are always cases that do not fit. ... Law does not fit to life and that is all. ..."

Elwira was not quite alone in her criticism of government solutions. But other respondents tended to hedge their critical attitudes with the need for intervention. Mirosława's argument was that "parents should secure the living standard of their children". But she made exceptions for large families and unemployed ones. Marianna, too, argued for the responsibilities of parents: "I believe it is a decision of every parent. Everyone who decides to have children should foresee the consequences". But she also argued for legal regulation of working time, state intervention to reduce unemployment, and more support for nurseries and pre-schools.

Arguments supporting the free market approach – and the Polish government's approach – to children were very few. Most respondents, in both locations, argued in support of a more active government involvement in providing services, regulating the economy and working time, and regulating companies and services.

Government to be used? The case for social welfare

Respondents took a strong critical stance about the contemporary state in Poland, arguing that it was failing its citizens, in particular its poorer citizens, and that it should do more to support families as the core element in society. Many expressed outrage on their own behalf, and for their children, at the neglect of family needs, and many more expressed this on behalf of the wider society, describing the neglect of those in poverty, disabled people and young people left without activity or supervision. Families were seen as having responsibility themselves, "because it is a natural responsibility of everyone who decides to start a family". But only the state could do the job of providing a context of "employment, pre-school and everything that makes it possible to live in peace of mind" (Anna). These were widely seen as problems which families could not solve by themselves and which only the state could address. These respondents were often passionate in their advocacy of the needs of parents and children, and expansive about the situation of families: they took a principled stance about unmet social needs, not only unmet personal needs. They also took a principled stance about the meaning of democratic citizenship and the role of the state. Elżbieta encapsulated these themes:

> "First of all, financing in greater degree pre-schools, schools and, of course paid childcare leave ... at present the state only talks a lot about help for family, even those poorest, but in reality there is either no help at all or it is minimal. ... We live in a democratic state. The family is a primary element of each society, so its situation should be of interest to every state, and in particular the situation of children in the most disadvantaged families. ... I believe that the problem of the care of children should be organised both by local authorities and by parents. It is their duty. It should be done by organisation of care in various types of community centres, clubs and so on."

[handwritten margin note: lack of civil society for these clubs. women are not socially for public life.]

Some responses focused on respondents' own problems as mothers with young children. Adriana compared her situation to her own childhood: "Every child went to pre-school, they were free or very cheap, so my parents could afford to send two daughters to pre-school. Now it is different ... I cannot afford to send all the children to pre-school". Małgorzata felt she was standing alone with her parental responsibility: "I do not feel there is any help. I have an impression that I can count only on myself". Ursula argued that motherhood should be better supported: "The state does not support mothers at all. ... A woman who gives birth to a child should be favoured, and this does not take place. On the contrary, she is persecuted".

> "They say that there is pro-family policy but it is only words. We are not aware of it. An average family does not feel it. The state should also take some responsibility for children. We are frightened when we think that the children will have to go to college and we will not be able to afford it. We are not certain about having enough to live on, we

do not know if we will be able to give our children what they need." (Zuzanna)

Several respondents commented on the duties of the state in relation to families poorer than themselves, in terms of the educational and cultural needs of children, and the problems brought about by charges:

"I do not like the situation that more and more things must be paid for by parents because children from poorer families do not get an equal start in life. At present the state guarantees free vaccinations, rather low-cost elementary and secondary schooling. But there is little support for families with small children in particular." (Alicja)

"The state is obliged to take responsibility for the development of the younger generation, to render knowledge accessible, to make children and young people equal. Worse-off parents cannot secure the development of a child by themselves." (Eleanora)

"Not everyone can afford everything and children should not be refused ... they [the state] should not interfere, but should help." (Zofia)

Respondents also commented critically on the need for better state provision and regulation in a wide range of services. Maria noted the particular needs of "mothers with disabled children or children having problems with alcoholism, narcotics", and "dealing with discrimination against women", while Karolina raged against the bureaucracy and cost in getting medical help: "At present there is so much trouble with these 'illness funds'. It is difficult to get medical examinations. When I go to a doctor with my child *I* also get a high temperature. In every place one has to have the right form, with the first one you must go and collect another and so on all day long. Working women have no time for all this". Edyta saw it as the state's "duty to support parents as well as all citizens through a good free health service, free schools for those who want it, or supplements for private schools, organisation of cultural centres. All those services are going down". Wanda argued for a secure quality of care at school: "not only parents, but a school too, when a child is at school. The school should provide such care that we can depend on it". Justification for the role of the state came in comments about human need and dignity, social resources and citizenship:"Social policy constitutes one great mistake … if politicians are supposed to be ordinary people why do they not understand that the social minimum is not enough for dignified living which is deserved by every human being and by children in particular?" (Danuta). "There are a lot of problems that only the authorities with their means can solve" (Anna). "Parents, school, pre-school, cultural centres; the state is responsible for its citizens" (Eleanora). "I think society is all of us, parents should be responsible and the state should help" (Violetta).

Variations within Poland

We rather expected to find major differences between respondents in Warsaw and in Skierniewice. There are clearly differences of experience between people living in the capital compared with other areas: in Warsaw, capitalism is most dynamic, opportunities are most open, and the benefits of transition most likely to be felt. Elsewhere, in towns such as Skierniewice, there may be fewer opportunities, more experience of insecurity, and a greater sense of loss.

There were indeed differences between respondents in the two locations but they were differences of degree rather than of kind. Respondents from Skierniewice were more likely to emphasise the losses of state support for families rather than the gains of opportunity. Respondents from Warsaw were more likely to balance their accounts of the state's inaction with accounts of their new ability to buy and to choose, the greater problems of a life one has to put together oneself against the greater resources available in the post-communist era. Warsaw respondents, such as Klaudia, spoke of "pluses and minuses" in changes from communism:

> "There used to be easier access to state support. Now one has to earn [enough to pay for it]. There was easier access to health service and other things, pre-schools, nurseries, vacation camps for children. Organisation of spare time was easier too, many things were funded. Now everything falls on the parents' shoulders." (Klaudia)

Urszula framed her account of a more secure past and an irresponsible present within a reference to the authoritarian nature of government:

> "I think it was easier despite the fact that the system was more authoritarian. It was easier to provide a decent standard of living, housing, most people had a job, services were an

> entitlement. At present no one is interested whether people
> have a job, whether they have the means to live." (Urszula)

There was a more powerful sense of neglect, exhaustion and isolation
among our Skierniewice respondents than those in Warsaw, feeling
left alone with their responsibility for children, overworked and fearful
for their children's well-being: "I do not accept this role of the state
because I feel neglected and even forgotten" (Agnieszka). "Too much
hard work and an overabundance of responsibilities make us exhausted
psychologically so we forget our children" (Ania). "Children certainly
feel isolated, pushed into second place, and parents are not able to
help it" (Bożena).

There were differences of emphasis between respondents from
Skierniewice and those from Warsaw, but the broad picture from both
areas was that the government was failing families through its lack of
support.

Conclusion

Post-communism clearly represents a major reaction against the state
as an authoritarian government and the restriction of individual and
civil liberties. The space created in politics has admitted the extreme
Right wing, as Ferge (1998) remarks. It has also admitted a liberal
economics in government policies, unpicking the welfare role of the
state as well as its restrictive apparatus. In post-communist Poland,
governments have also been strongly male dominated. Along with a
lack of women's participation, there has been a lack of an explicit
feminist identity developing in post-communist countries. Women's
organisations have developed quite strongly in Polish civil society but
are said to be wary of identifying themselves as feminist. These
arguments have led us to ask about mothers' views of the loss of state
services.

Should we be surprised that our respondents from Warsaw and
Skierniewice criticise their government, expressing bitter feelings about
its failure to support them? After a period of 'empty shelves' in the
shops there are shelves full of goods. But while, earlier, shopping took
much time and competitive strategies for essential products, now many
people are just not able to afford essentials. Cash has become central
and incomes decide families' life style. Transition from communism
has brought quite distinct differentiation in the material situations of
families, with increasing numbers of families in poverty and at risk of
poverty. Families have to try to cut their costs and increase their

economic activities. The security of constantly available work ceases to exist in a market economy. A job is easy to lose; unemployment becomes a constant element in the labour market. Developing individualist values and ideas in government and society stress the need for people to fend for themselves, making them responsible in the competition for an adequate standard of living for themselves and their families. Slogans about 'taking matters into their own hands', the necessity of 'shifting for oneself' are common. The problem is that the slogans are addressed to individuals and families, including those who are not able to fend for themselves in the changing reality. Those who have problems with employment and poverty, or have lost the income and benefits from their places of their work are now lost to themselves.

There is very little in the accounts of mothers in Skierniewice or in Warsaw that could be interpreted as critical, or even wary, about the state's role in supporting the family. The system that supported mothers in employment under communism was regarded almost wholly positively, and its loss almost wholly negatively, among these mothers. Our respondents spoke from the experience of being children under communism and being mothers in post-communism, mothers of young children, with jobs, or – in a few cases – on maternity or childcare leave. They may have romanticised the past, but in the present they were doing paid and unpaid work, stretched and stressed, lacking time and money, in a struggle to meet the needs of their children. The overriding sense of these mothers was that they could not achieve a safe or good quality of life without a context of more accessible and comprehensive services. Their sense of the state's duty to be involved in supporting parents and children was very strong. If they were not expressly feminist, our respondents nevertheless shared a major part of the international feminist agenda about their rights to paid work and to share the responsibility for their children with the state as well as with their partners. They were not individualists who wanted above all to make money and buy and make choices; they, on the contrary, thought that these areas of life required a strong government responsibility. On all these subjects, respondents were eloquent and passionate advocates of their rights as mothers to more support than their state currently gives them. The tenor of our respondents' attitudes to the state fitted with Pine's account of respondents' replies in central Poland, making "serious moral judgments about the meaning and obligation of government" (Pine, 1995, p 55).

FIVE

Mothers and their households

Introduction

This chapter looks at relations between mothers and their households in the context of the many pressures on parents in contemporary Poland. There are pressures from the Roman Catholic Church for women to go back to a pre-soviet traditional motherhood. There are pressures from the demands of children in the context of the withdrawal or reduction of state support for women's employment in the areas of pre-schools, paid childcare leave and children's holidays in particular. There are also pressures arising from unemployment and poverty that make paid work difficult but necessary for many mothers. What is happening inside households in terms of caring practices and in terms of working and caring mentalities? Is women's unemployment, together with the Roman Catholic Church, bringing back male breadwinner families? Or are the needs of families bringing men into caring for their children?

If the transition has meant a radical upheaval in the economic and political institutions of CEE countries, it has also brought a radical transformation in households. The loss of security means not only a rising risk of poverty but also more room for decision in the place of tradition (Beck and Beck-Gernsheim, 2002). Decisions about family size have led to one of the most radical changes, namely the reduction in childbearing, leading to a reduction of around a third in the pre-school population of the region: the average fall in the population of young children in the region is of 31% (UNICEF, 2002, p 18). In Poland – despite the Roman Catholic Church – this means a decline in the total fertility rate from 2.05 to 1.30 between 1989 and 2000 (UNICEF, 2002, p 107). By 2003 the total fertility rate was 1.249, and lower in towns (1.107) than in the country (1.421) (Central Statistical Office, 2004a, pp 53-7) (see also Chapter Two, Figure 2.4). The room for negotiation in households around issues of money, care and time must surely have enlarged as the certainties of socialism – secure work and secure state services – slipped away.

All over Europe, birth rates have declined to the point where there is concern about developing welfare structures that will support children (Esping-Andersen et al, 2002). But the change in CEE countries is more extreme than elsewhere. Comparable data from the UK, which was typical of Western Europe, show a decline in the total fertility rate from 1990 to 2000 from 1.83 to 1.64 children. Total fertility in Poland fell from 2.04 to 1.34 and declined to 1.24 by 2002, well below the EU25 average of 1.46, though comparable with other new CEE member states (European Commission 2004a, p 176).

Inside the household: the male breadwinner family?

Traditional attitudes are generally held to prevail: household work is done by women (Plakwicz, 1992, p 81; Lobodzińska, 1995, p 166). Men's idea of partnership is that women should do both paid work and housework (Firlit-Fesnak, 1997b, p 153). The state, under communism, offered little support to women doing domestic work, or to men sharing it: "State institutions, therefore, could not (and would not) significantly lighten women's burdens, and men were certainly not about to change their domestic habits"; the evidence of the early transition period was of little change in this regard (Fodor, 2002, p 371). The change from a centrally planned economy has brought unemployment and discriminatory practices, conveniently meshing with a call for women to recover their traditional role in the family (Kotowska, 1995, p 86). Women experience conflict between the necessity of paid employment and the ideology promoted through the Roman Catholic Church that the family should be their prime responsibility (Plakwicz, 1992). The ideals of Polish motherhood, *Matka Polka*, are rooted in Polish culture and history and support women's identification of themselves as mothers above all. In the communist era, identification with the family was a refuge against the authoritarian regime. Furthermore, the Solidarity Party joined the Church in promoting traditional ideals of motherhood (Heinen, 1995, pp 91-6). Social policy since the transition has restricted abortion rights and reduced women's control over their home and working lives (Fuszara, 1993, 2000a, 2000b, 2000c, 2000d; Zielińska, 2000, see also Chapter Three). Men's relatively higher earnings, overtime and second jobs militate against sharing household work (Erler and Sass, 1997; Sass and Jaeckel, 1997). Traditional methods of time and money management predominated in a qualitative study of households in poverty, a picture supported, according to its author, by quantitative data:

The last available study of time-budgets of Poles in 1996
showed deep gender inequalities both in work time as well
as in leisure time. Women spend half as much time as men
in paid work but they use three times more time for home
and family obligations. Men more often than women
exercise and watch TV. (Budżet, 1998, p 41, quoted in
Tarkowska, 2002, p 429)

Under communism, households were insulated from outside influences.
Ferge argues that this hindered development and change in gender
relations. A system that looked, in formal respects, like a Scandinavian
model of gender relations was not so inside households:

Because of the impossibility of free public discourse, gender
relations never became a public issue. In public life, work,
studies, culture and politics, women had become (almost)
equal, and they may have felt (almost) equal. But in the
private sphere, in partner relations, within the family and
the interpersonal arena, traditional ways of constructing
men and women's roles remained, by and large, untouched.
(Ferge, 1998, p 221)

In the post-communist period there have been constraints on the
development of a feminist identity: in the context of the economic
upheavals and the development of class differences, gender is not a
priority (Ferge, 1998; Watson, 1997, 2000a, 2000b). Survey research
has reported that traditional attitudes within households may be
changing only slightly, held by 85% of respondents in 1992, reducing
to 79% in 1995. But there is also evidence that "almost all Poles are
convinced that both the husband and wife should support the family
financially" (Siemieńska, 1998, p 147).

Changes in state support for parents

As was shown in Chapter One, the gender regimes of CEE countries
had a distinctive character under communism. They were dual earner
systems with social policies designed to sustain motherhood as well as
employment. Soviet working motherhood had high costs in terms of
women's time, with full-time paid work and long hours of unpaid
work and an unreconstructed gender division of labour in the
household. They achieved high levels of participation and low gender
pay gaps by the standards of Western Europe, using education systems

to produce highly qualified women, workplace social provision, childcare leave and benefit entitlements, kindergartens and nurseries (Fajth, 1996; UNICEF, 1998, 1999). These systems involved high levels of public expenditure.

Transition from communism brought losses in GDP throughout the region and reduced capacity for government social spending. Poland took the strongest medicine in reaction against the communist regime and recovered sooner than others, recovering in terms of GDP per capita, by 1999. But the economic medicine has involved reducing public expenditure on social policy, the very radical restructuring of social spending, and diversification of welfare provision. In Central Europe the proportion of GDP spent by government went down from 55% to 45% during the 1990s (UNICEF, 2001, p 16). Poland is typical of Central Europe in this respect (see Chapter Two). This has clearly come with changes in spending on families: the change in policy in Poland has been towards reducing eligibility for services, especially by stringent means testing. Family allowances in 1991 were 2.7% of GDP, while in 1999 they were 0.6%, their value per child halved during the same period, and their contribution to household income went down from 4.2% to 1.2% (UNICEF, 2001, p 43). Educational enrolments have been sustained at a high level: pre-primary enrolments (3- to 6-year-olds), which dipped after transition, have begun to climb back – although at 50% of the age group they are well below Hungary (87%) and the Czech Republic (86%) (UNICEF, 2002, p 75). But public support for education has been reduced by increasing charges. Likewise, spending on childcare leave has been reduced by the narrowing of eligibility (Fodor et al, 2002). Childcare leave is now means tested (see Chapters Two and Three).

In particular the transition has shifted the burden of cost of having children. Since employment-based welfare has ceased to be a feature of the region there has been a shift from employers' responsibilities (Fodor, 2002). But there has also been a shift away from the state. The cumulative effect has been to move the burden onto households and to raise the costs sharply (Ruminska-Zimny, 2002). Even the World Bank acknowledges that in transition countries "the burden of nurturing activities has shifted increasingly away from the state and into the household" and that this has serious implications for gender equality in the region (World Bank, 2002, p 12).

Mothers in employment?

Economic medicine and recovery – even in Poland where these are strongest – have not translated into jobs. Women's jobs have been lost across the region: "The relatively favourable position of women in the labour market, which had made the region comparable to Sweden, the leader in the West in this regard, is now a phenomenon of the past in most transition countries" (UNICEF, 2002, p 14). Does this mean a return of male breadwinner families as men's employment is given priority?

The experience of risk and insecurity around employment has been a consequence of transition for men as well as for women, and in most CEE countries unemployment rates have been high for both (see Chapter Two). A review of changes in gender inequality in the first five years, focusing on issues of employment and unemployment, found the situation of men and women less divergent than expected, with women retaining their occupational status and not withdrawing to become full-time housewives, as often predicted (van der Lippe and Fodor 1998, p 146). Fodor argues that women are not simply resourceless victims of the 'velvet revolutions': their high levels of education and experience in the service sector have become more valuable in the period since transition (Fodor, 1997).

However, there is growing diversity in unemployment patterns between different CEE countries. In 2004, Hungary had the lowest women's unemployment rate among the new member CEE states at 6.0%, while Poland had the highest at 19.7% (see Chapter Two, Table 2.2). Using data from "two major cross-country surveys" in 1993 and 2000, Glass and Kawachi argue that women's unemployment has worsened more than men's, widening the gender gap much more than official figures suggest. The authors argue that such gender differences in unemployment may indicate a tendency to 're-traditionalisation' in Poland, where women's higher education has not protected their jobs, and there is an increase in the proportion who describe themselves as 'keeping house' (Glass and Kawachi, 2001). European structural indicators, discussed in Chapter Two, show great varieties in unemployment between countries, and less gender difference than this account suggests (see Chapter Two and Table 2.2). Divergent statistical accounts of gender and unemployment may reflect a high level of unregistered unemployed women, with perhaps half of those women seeking employment not actually registered, especially among middle-aged women with children (Łobodzinska, 2000). But, as argued in Chapter Two, the gender gaps in unemployment – which are quite similar in CEE countries – also suggest economic problems and differences between the countries rather than radically different gender regimes.

There is also evidence of discrimination against women in the labour market in Poland. Women's monthly average income in 1998 was 81% of men's, while they are more likely than men – as well as more likely than women elsewhere in EU25 countries – to have upper secondary educational qualifications (91.6%, compared with 87.4% of men and 79.1% of women in EU25 countries) (Europa NewCronos website: epp.eurostat.cec.eu.int). It appears that discrimination may be higher in Poland than in comparable countries of the region (Pailhe, 2000, p 514). The data on use of maternity and childcare leave in Poland also show a radical decline: women appear not to be taking up their rights (see Chapter Three).

While Poland's economic recovery has been among the strongest in the region, the rewards of recovery have been unevenly spread. Economic growth has been accompanied by reduced employment, with a decline from almost 75% of the 15-59 age group population in 1989 to 59.8% by 2001. The Gini coefficient for those in work has widened too, while the unemployment rate was 19.7% for women and 18.0% for men by 2004. Women who are raising children have lost ground in the shift to more competitive labour markets (UNICEF, 2002, 2003; Chapters One, Two and Three of this book).

Time and care work in households

Time-budget data from 1965 showed Polish men spending 32 minutes per day on 'core domestic work', while women spent 215 minutes, a pattern that was similar in Hungary and Czechoslovakia (Gershuny, 2000, p 188). During this period, men's contribution to core domestic work was equally low in western and in CEE countries: women in most Western European countries had similar levels of unpaid work but much lower levels of paid work. Women's domestic workload in CEE countries was in addition to a full-time paid workload, and the evidence of gender inequality in the households of CEE countries is very striking in this data.

At the beginning of the 1980s, a dominant picture from research was of unequal relations in families: among married women with children, employed women did about 70% of all housework and those not employed 85%. Employed mothers did 80% of childcare and upbringing while mothers without paid employment did 90%. Fathers' involvement in housework, childcare and upbringing was greater when mothers were employed but stayed low: it was 15% when wives worked and 6% when they did not (Piotrowski, 1980, p 84). Analyses through the 1980s showed a model of the household that was not very flexible with traditional gender differences highly visible. The 1980s also brought recession and empty shelves in shops; running the household became hard, especially for women with jobs:

> In 1984, married mothers were employed three hours fewer per day than their husbands, but housework took them more time: four hours and fourteen minutes longer. In this large group of women, their work time altogether was, in comparison with their husbands, over one and half hours longer on average, and their spare time therefore over one and half hours shorter. (Duch-Krzystoszek, 1996, pp 154-5).

What was the cause of this situation? Increasing women's household labour was connected with the impoverishment of families and problems in the economy. It was a constraint on women rather than a choice.

What was the division of household duties in Polish families in the 1990s? Comparing 1988 and 1992, data "demonstrate that changes have been made. Tasks traditionally perceived as being 'women's work' – cooking, washing the dishes, cleaning, doing homework with children – are more frequently being performed by both husbands and wives" (Siemieńska, 1998, p 132, quoting Central Statistical Office, 1992). In 1994, the average time spent on housework by women was 4.5 hours while men's was 53 minutes, showing diminishing, but persistent gender differences (Firlit-Fesnak, 1997a, p 28). According to married women with children (an all-Poland sample), in families with both parents a traditional model predominated. Employed women did a little less housework than those at home. There were some differences in responsibilities: employed women were more often involved in official issues, arranging services, helping their children with homework, and less often with rubbish disposal, washing up and cleaning, clothes mending, taking care of sick family members or pets. But much everyday housework such as laundry, ironing, household cleaning, shopping and cooking was equally performed by both groups. Employed women were helped a little more often but not entirely released by husbands or children (CBOS, 1997a). There is some evidence during the 1990s of an increasing tendency to share household duties, especially among poorer families, and often with children (CBOS, 1997a).

There is evidence that this division of time and responsibility was not what Polish women wanted. In 1996, only 15% of women preferred the family model in which women had a dual role while men contributed little in the household – the pattern that was most common in practice – while 54% of women favoured a partnership model in which "a husband and a wife spend about the same amount of time on work and both of them share housework and childcare duties to the same extent" (CBOS, 1997b, p 2). A partnership model was preferred by young women up to 24 years of age, by divorcees, single women, those with a higher educational level and office workers below management level. The interim model, in which women combine paid work with family and motherhood, was approved more often by women at management level and by intellectuals, whereas the traditional model was preferred by older women, religious women, those with primary education, those not in paid employment, housewives and pensioners (CBOS, 1997b).

Research on three generations (in the age ranges of 25-44, 45-64, 65-80) of urban families points to changes in ideals about parenting. Asked who should bring up children, the majority of respondents (87%) favoured equal participation of mothers and fathers while only 11% identified these as mothers' duties, with the egalitarian model even more favoured (93%) among the younger generation. But in practice, 62% of mothers were responsible for childcare, and both parents in only 26% of households. Dominant ideals of parental roles were egalitarian, whereas dominant practices were traditional (Doniec, 2001). These findings are supported by research on an all-Poland adult sample (CBOS, 1998): a majority (95%) of respondents declared that both parents should participate equally in bringing up a child. The same research gives parental accounts of everyday practice: two thirds said that bringing up the child until they are three years old was mainly mothers' responsibility. But for school-age children, parents are more likely to see parenthood as a partnership: 46% describe childcare and upbringing as both parents' responsibility (CBOS, 1998, pp 10-11).

The evidence of working time has tended to stress the rigidity of the household division of labour (UNICEF, 1999). The implication is that there is a strong tendency for a return to the male breadwinner model in Poland, a re-traditionalisation in the specific cultural circumstances of the influence of the Roman Catholic Church combined with state policies for privatisation and reducing social services. Interpretations have tended to stress the distance to be travelled before Polish families have equal responsibilities in households.

But there are some signs pointing towards more gender equality in households. Experience of unemployment has given holding down a job a more positive value (Heinen, 1995, p 99). Quantitative evidence tends to show some increase during the 1990s rather than the decrease that re-traditionalisation would lead us to expect in fathers doing childcare: in 1995, in families with small children, fathers spent an average of three hours (per day), compared with six hours for mothers, but they were second, after mothers, in caring for children (Firlit-Fesnak, 1997a, p 29, quoting Polish Society of Household Economics, 1995), a finding supported by the comparative quantitative study carried out early in the transition period (Erler and Sass, 1997, pp 39-40). Fathers' participation in childcare stopped being symbolic. Fathers participate in childcare more than in housework, and by the mid-1990s the rate grew to around 40% of fathers, with both mothers and fathers acknowledging their important role, especially where mothers were employed (Firlit-Fesnak, 1997a, p 29). There is also some evidence about family decision making, suggesting a partnership model in economic decisions (78.5%), arranging family life (72.5%), and bringing up children (64.9%). In the first two, partnership is more likely among younger women and those with higher educational qualifications (Firlit-Fesnak, 1997a, p 29, quoting Central Statistical Office, 1994). Tarkowska's study found a predominance of traditional patterns in the division of labour in poor Polish households (22 characterised this way), but 15 of her respondents stated that such a division did not exist. She identifies a new model, based on equality and partnership, mostly in the younger generation (Tarkowska, 2002, p 427).

So has the transition turned people back to tradition? Or has it forced the pace of change in the gender relations of care? We ask about what is going on inside households as well as outside them, in terms of unpaid care work as well as employment and unemployment. Our interviews address the question of the way care relations are developing in Poland and the identity of men and women as workers and carers and the way that caring practices are developing at home.

Respondents' accounts of tradition and change in the male breadwinner and dual earner traditions in Poland

If the re-traditionalisation thesis held for Poland, one would expect a lot of accounts like those of the Warsaw respondents Adriana and Alicja. Adriana was at home on childcare leave, with four children, and took "more care of my children than my mother did", and her husband often had to take additional paid work. His relationship with the children was good, but he "does not have enough time" to be as close to the children as she does. Comparing her ability to keep her job with her mother's, Adriana "cannot imagine that I could go to work having four children". Pre-school is now too expensive and Adriana is rather stranded at home, although she would "like to come out to people, do something different from only washing the dishes, ironing etc".

Alicja described a dual earner/dual carer arrangement among her parents: her "father had to take a three-month paternal leave from work to take care of me because my mother was taking her final examinations and had to devote all her time to that. Later my mother stayed with me for a year and then took a job". Now, she herself is on maternity leave and her "husband could not take paternal leave from work". Magdalena also described a dual earner pattern among her parents, with a father who had more time for care than her husband. Her account was that "my parents both had jobs, my siblings and I went to pre-school and my children also go to pre-school. My father spent more time with the children, because there was not the same problem of chasing after money. My husband devotes more time to his job". There were, then, several respondents who described households in today's Poland that were more 'traditional' than their parents' households. All of these older generation households involved employed mothers, and in Alicja and Magdalena's case, fathers who took responsibility for care. Their own households were more differentiated into male breadwinner and female carer than their parents' households in their own childhood.

But comparisons made by our women respondents with their own mothers, and their husbands with their fathers, were actually diverse. If these accounts of Magdalena, Alicja and Adriana might suggest a transition from a dual earner pattern to a more traditional one, with male breadwinners now married to women with sole responsibility for care work and less time for jobs, there were accounts of contrasts between domesticated older-generation mothers and respondents with paid jobs. Irena's mother "was mainly busy with home and the household", while she herself has "a job and limited time", while Karolina described her mother who "did not work outside the household", although she had a small farm.

Our respondents were employed and described mothers who were mainly employed. There was, then, some continuity for most women between their own lives and their mothers', both with jobs and children.

The conditions under which they experienced working motherhood were radically different, with major changes in material conditions, security and support, but our respondents were, like their mothers, working mothers. In contrast, their husbands' roles had changed more radically in comparison with their fathers'. Hanna described her mother "as myself now ... up to her eyes in work, so she had little time for us. ... My father often worked in two jobs, he was often out of the home from early morning until night. ... My husband, on the other hand, takes care of our son while I work on shifts". Marlena described her father as "a typical man who is not interested in anything; everything must be cooked for him, put under his nose, and my husband is quite the opposite". Lidia's mother was "burdened with the responsibilities of rearing children. ... It is easier for me because my husband helps me ... is more engaged in the care of our child". And Elżbieta describes a husband who "participates more in raising the children than my father. My father was mostly concerned with his job and with supporting his family". Urszula, too, gives an account of a very stereotypical father: "My father did nothing at home. Those were the times when a woman did everything, and the master of the house came back, sat and read a newspaper. My husband is my partner in the marriage, and my father is very astonished by what he does".

There were, then, diverse accounts of trends in gender models in Poland. These certainly included accounts of more 'traditional' households, with women at home with young children and men working long hours, pre-occupied with their role of breadwinning. But the majority picture was not this. Rather, most respondents described themselves as working mothers, like their own mothers, but their partners as working but caring fathers to a much greater degree than their own fathers.

Paid work: men's role/women's responsibility?

This section investigates the current situation of 'the breadwinner'. Who in households is seen as having responsibility for earning? What is women's experience of combining employment and motherhood, paid and unpaid work, and their sense of themselves and their partners as mothers, fathers and earners. Chapter Six asks what practical policies they would like, and what these amount to in terms of the gender model they hold in their heads as an ideal.

There are accounts of men as providers here, in the assumptions of respondents, the practices of households and sometimes in respondents' accounts of their ideals. Jolanta is a teacher, employed half time, and her account assumes a male breadwinner role: "My mother worked as I do – my husband and my father have had to work to provide". Ela and Patrycja argued for a traditional gender role for mothers. "Unless they want work very much, women should stay at home with children up to 14 years of age" (Ela), and "they should prefer not to work and to be with the children" (Patrycja). Dorota stressed the importance of motherhood and the opportunity to spend time at home with children: "A woman with children should not have a job … she has less strength for herself, for her children and the family". More respondents wanted the ability to put motherhood higher among their priorities, with employment that would adapt to the needs of children: "Women engage in the race for fame and money. They forget that first of all they are mothers" (Danuta).

But most of our respondents see themselves as working mothers: the importance of their jobs shines through their accounts. They describe intense pressures on women in Poland who have to balance work and family under stringent and competitive conditions. If they put family first – as they often did – most still saw paid employment as important in terms of their sense of themselves, and in terms of their need for income. Isabela saw family responsibility has having priority: "First, women should have the possibility of raising their children, and then … they can fulfil themselves professionally. … Paid work strengthens me, mainly financially … I feel useful and that I will be able to give the children something more". Janina was "eager for work after a three-year stay at home", while Kasia saw paid work as bringing a range of benefits: "A woman feels her value, shines; in spite of troubles, we see the world from the other side, it gains colour, a woman gains importance, becomes independent and liberated". Monika argued similarly that "in today's world, finances are very important. Women feel more confident, are independent. They are not 'kept women' of their husbands".

Zofia is a post-office worker on night shifts, with two children aged three and four, whose debate about paid and unpaid work points to the difficulties of a male breadwinner earning enough, as well as mothers' current difficulties with employment:

> "Some people say it is the husband who should maintain a family. But not everyone can afford it. On the one hand it would be good if women stayed at home. But I would be bored being at home all the time with children. I'd rather they go to pre-school and I could go out. Three years is

enough ... there is not much possibility of paid work for women. ... It is hard." (Zofia)

Eugenia had recently returned to paid employment and described the consequence as a more equal partnership:

"I even see it after less than a month in work. My husband must accept that I can be tired too, and that he has to take over some responsibilities, more than while I stayed at home. We must solve problems somehow equally; we are now more equal, my position is strengthened."

Respondents are preoccupied with the risks and difficulties of combining paid work and motherhood, and with the constraints on their choices. There are many comments on insecurity, time pressures, and the difficulty of balancing responsibilities in a context where the responsibilities are shared less with state services, and where the conditions are aggressively capitalist and competitive. Respondents stress the risks to women today in comparison with their mothers' lives. Adriana emphasised the costs of childcare, the risks of unemployment and her sense that as a mother with four children now she feels virtually unemployable:

"When I was a child it was somehow different – better – it was easier to have more children. I do not know if I could keep hold of a job because there were and are redundancies. My sister was 'let go' [made redundant] after three months' leave. If a woman does not devote everything to work, she lags behind. ... Women are thought to be employees of the worst sort, because they need sick leave for children. Formerly it was not so."

Many respondents emphasised the difficulties of getting jobs and keeping them. They were very conscious of the risks to mothers in a market economy in comparison with their own childhood. The insecurity of the market economy exposed them to discrimination and made it very difficult to move between paid work and motherhood:

"I have had to compete for my job and position. The fact that I am a mother and have two small children that might get sick and need much time devoted to them has made my situation more difficult. Questions about children were always the first ones I had to answer for my prospective employer." (Eugenia)

"My mother has always had a job ever since I can remember and she did not have any problem with returning to work whereas I, after childcare leave, was dismissed and looked for a job for a long time. I had to take what I found although it is very hard work. ... An employer who can choose between a man and a woman always takes the man." (Zuzanna)

"My mother had much worse conditions than I have now ... [but] with jobs it was easier before. My mother had four children – if she could not go to work she just did not; her job was never endangered." (Marlena)

Iwona, with three children, and employed in a bank, adds working time to these concerns:

"If I decided to quit my job, as my mother did, for eight years, I could not return to my position. ... At the present level of unemployment women return to work three months after giving birth and stay in work until late at night. ... It was incomparably easier [formerly]. It is connected with the present feeling of the threat of unemployment and its consequences. Who then [under communism] worked 12 hours a day?"

While these respondents emphasised more stringent working conditions in terms of time, employability and risk of unemployment, Zofia spoke of low pay and her more fragile pay-packet in the conditions of competition:

"My mother worked on her farm and was able to care for us ... now if a child goes to hospital or I am sick they would not pay me for those days. ... Now there is everything in the shops, everywhere, but one cannot afford it. They do not raise wages."

Respondents often had better material conditions than their mothers but their comparisons often emphasised the ease with which their mothers could weave in and out of employment, cover holidays, school and pre-school hours. The pressures of their own situation, in contrast, often left them with few choices about work and motherhood, the hours they worked, the hours their partners worked, the length of maternity/childcare leave, the decision to remain at home with the children. They also felt acutely vulnerable to losing their jobs, their position at work, and their income because of pregnancy or children's needs, especially health needs. Zuzanna argued that under current circumstances, damage to job or family was unavoidable: "Paid work interferes with raising children and the care of children causes difficulties in work. ... It is very difficult, something must always be neglected".

So, if there is a trend among Polish governments and other leaders to think of women as mothers rather than as workers, this is not the picture given by most of our respondents of their sense of themselves. Despite the pressures under which they do working motherhood, our respondents mainly retained a strong sense of themselves as mothers and workers, valuing their jobs as well as their families. It seems likely that mothers' unemployment (see Chapter Three) is a constraint rather than a choice, a consequence of the economic conditions rather than a trend among women towards a more traditional motherhood. And those respondents who were employed but said they might prefer to be at home more may be responding to the acute time pressures of doing everything, rather than seeking a more traditional way of life as 'home-birds'.

Care work: women's role/men's responsibility?

There are diverse accounts of the practical division of responsibilities within households, and of the sense of overall responsibility for children. But most respondents took a principled position about men's responsibilities and obligations, even if they expected less than equal shares in practice:

> "Both my husband and I try to be close to our son, to be his parents and friends. ... We both read him books. ... Usually all three of us go for a walk together. It is not a duty of one parent ... a man-father has his share in it and he cannot avoid the responsibility." (Bożena)

Joanna's expression of this sense of duty is very similar:

> "If I am out my husband takes care of our child and plays with her ... prepares meals, keeps the home tidy ... I think

> that childcare does not belong only to a mother, although
> I believe that being a mother is a very important task, but
> both parents should take responsibility for childcare."

In their accounts of these more participating husbands, some respondents described a new moral sense of obligation among their partners. Aleksandra from Warsaw describes her father as "spending all his time on the farm. ... My husband spends more time with the children because he believes that he should help me".

There is very wide agreement among our respondents that men should be involved in childcare: "Men constitute a very important element in bringing up children" (Eleanora), or "Childcare is a problem of a whole family" (Halina), "a man should help too" (Zofia). Eugenia argues: "As far as we can we should share responsibilities and also care of children. It is very important for the children's emotional development". Janina is at home on childcare leave and doing all the childcare, but responds to our question about this as women's role, with "No, certainly not, why only women, and what about the husband, family, the state?". There is a strong and widespread sense that this is both a moral and practical responsibility. Stanisława argues that "education of children is a responsibility of a mother and father and there are no limits – who cares more and who cares less – for the development of the children". Róża puts men's responsibility for their children into their decision to have children: "If parents undertake a decision to conceive a child, then the responsibility for bringing it up rests on both of them".

Responsibility has translated itself into experience and a wider competence in childcare according to Barbara: "My father went for walks with me but was not able to take care of me as my mother did. My husband is more globally able to take care of our son" (Barbara). "My father took very little care of children. My husband cares for the children when he can; he washes them and plays with them" (Grażyna).

Accounts of practical responsibility are of something that is less than equal. A lot of respondents describe partnerships in which both partners have a sense of responsibility, but mothers take a larger share in practice. Zofia, for example, claimed: "We educate the children together, there is no important difference between us", but acknowledged that her shift work made her more available to the children. Gabriela's husband "plays a decisive role in everything relating to our child" but she did leave very "'precise instructions" and prepared clothes when she was leaving the child with other family members. "They have the greatest contact with me except the days when my husband does not work ... in practice I do everything" (Beata). But most accounts are of men much more engaged with the day-to-day of parenting than men of the previous generation. These are not men who play with the children while their partners do all the work. Tatiana describes her husband as organising "his time of work and fetches the children from school. ... We both make decisions"; Wanda's husband "can do everything, even cooking"; and Marlena describes her arrangement as: "We take turns, whoever has time at the moment, everything must be done and there is no talk about the division of work". "As I work on two shifts my husband and I have to split our responsibilities ... of course, he has to [care for the children]" (Dorota). Agata says that her husband's relationship with their children is "perfect ... he spends a lot of time with them ... I spend too little".

Edyta's account of contemporary households summarises this picture neatly: "One can see a much greater role of fathers in raising children". While there are accounts of men as providers here, more evident and more striking are accounts of men whose identity as breadwinners is not threatened by caring for their children. Anna's husband "likes to take care of children and it is no trouble for him, causes no complexes. He manages to reconcile it with his job, he is always willing to help. ... He sings to them, tells stories and fairy-tales".

The phrase "causes no complexes" captures a strong theme in these accounts of men who are different from the men in the previous generation, not only in the time they give, but in their sense of themselves as fathers. Aneta's account was that when she was young "a man did not touch children. ... Now men more readily take care of children ... my father just played with children for an hour or so and later let them play on their own. My husband devotes a lot of time to our daughter. If he could he would feed her". Iwona describes her husband as "a home-bird and if he could he would spend all the time at home. ... When our daughter is ill my husband takes leave and stays home with her. In such situations I can see that our child is his life".

Solutions

Dual earners/dual carers?

Respondents, in general, gave a very positive account of men's responsibility as carers, both in terms of their acceptance of responsibility, and in terms of men's changing identity. But discussions of how the state should support childcare tended to reveal something less than equality of paid work married to equality of care work, in terms of practice or in terms of respondents' mentality as mothers (see also Chapters Two and Six).

Among the respondents there were advocates of a male breadwinner model as well as advocates of a social democratic dual earner system. Both Krystyna and Isabela thought that men should be paid enough so that women could stay at home, although this was a minority prescription. At the other extreme Edyta expressed a commitment to a Swedish system of maternal and paternal leave, because it "motivates fathers to take care of children, and it gives good results in the form of good relations between fathers and children". Maria described her demands of the paid employment side of this equation: "Women should be appreciated in their work positions and their wages and salaries should not be lower than men's. They should be more accepted in management positions".

More commonly, however, discussions of social policies tended to reveal women as valuing their own positions in paid work, expecting input from their husbands, but accepting a greater role in childcare for themselves than they expected from their partners.

Flexible women

Frequently, women proclaimed the responsibility of fathers, praised their partners' contribution, and then accepted the reality of their own greater contribution to childcare in their proposals for support. Inconsistency between ideals and reality – as well as between different accounts of the same ideals – is to be expected. Couples in Jane Lewis' study were often struggling between their ideals of equal partnership and fairness, and their practices of parenting, and "disjuncture between mentalities and behaviour seems to be more common than correspondence" (Lewis, 2001b, p 169). Having asserted their husbands' responsibilities, our respondents often also described a daily practice in which they themselves contributed more to the care of their children. Their sense of policies that would help to get them through was also permeated with the reality of their responsibility for their children being greater than their husbands'.

Most desires for shorter working time or more effective systems of leave seemed aimed especially at women, although they sometimes included men: "Work time should be reduced, especially in the case of women, because the care of children mainly belongs to them, but also for men so that they could be good fathers" (Isabela). "A woman who plays a leading role in bringing up a child should have an opportunity to do paid work at home" (Janina). "Women should have access to shorter hours, more jobs for mothers with hours from 7.30am to 3.30pm and paid childcare leave" (Eleanora). "A woman should be protected in practice, not only in theory, and be able to return to her job" (Kasia). "Shorter work time for mothers of small children, security of work for mothers with small children" (Irena).

Like their UK counterparts, "on the whole, the women were mother-workers, whereas the men were mostly worker-fathers" (Lewis, 2001b, p 152).

Grandmothers

A more traditional division of labour could be sustained, with women associated with care, in the many households shared with grandparents. There were warm accounts of grandmothers as indispensable to the management of childcare and as devoted to the grandchildren:

> "My mother is very important ... she always takes on the childcare when it is needed ... without my mother I would not have been able to do a job ... I can always count on her ... [but long hours mean that] my little son often calls granny his 'mother' and me his 'granny' – parents lose time they should spend with their children." (Hanna)

For most who described their mothers as strongly involved, this was as a successful solution to the very dire problems of bringing up children in post-communist Poland, with little support outside the family. But the grandmother solution was not always available: there were mothers who lived 400 kilometres away and were able to offer childcare only in the summer holidays (Aleksandra). One respondent who grew up in a children's home was not in touch with her mother, had no support from her mother-in-law and "cannot count on any member of my family" (Beata).

Iwona – alone – argued that childcare "in better organised societies is essentially women's responsibility". Otherwise women were forthright about men's obligations: "A man should help too" (Zofia); "Childcare is the responsibility of both parents" (Tatiana); "A whole family, older children, husband, grandmother, grandfather [should be involved]" (Patrycja). The significance of the state's support (see Chapter Four) was also a large part of their concern.

Quantitative evidence

How typical are our surveyed households of the wider Poland and other countries of Central and Eastern Europe? Emerging quantitative data from the European Foundation for the Improvement of Living and Working Conditions, including paid and unpaid work, in the then 12 accession and candidate countries (ACC12[1]), begin to give a much clearer account of CEE countries, offering data which is comparative data with EU15 and other accession/candidate countries. Poland is by far the biggest country, with 38 million of the 105 million workers in the ACC12 and so its figures are likely to be consistent with the trends reported. Broad comparison of the ACC12, and the EU15 offers much that we would expect, with high participation (46%), longer paid working hours, 44.4 hours compared with 38.2 in EU15, less gender differentiation (men 45.4 and women 43.3), and little part-time work (7%). Part-time work is more equally divided but a less satisfactory option in the ACC12 (see also Chapter Two, Table 2.5, Table 2.6). The distribution of men and women in the various income brackets is more equal in the then accession and candidate countries.

But less expected is that unpaid work is now much more equal in the new CEE member states.

> Men in candidate countries are more likely (often significantly so) than their EU member state counterparts to be involved in activities such as caring for and educating children, cooking, doing housework and caring for elderly or disabled relatives. This can be explained at least partly by the fact that the proportion of women at work is higher and part-time work less developed than in EU member states. (Paoli et al, 2002, p 6)

The figures show 31% of men involved in caring for children (24% in EU15), 28% in cooking (13% EU15), 33% in housework (12% in EU15), and 5% caring for elderly/disabled relatives (6% EU15). These figures are all lower than for women, but they result in more equality of the dual workload than in Western Europe: "The dual workload is more balanced between the sexes, although it is still far from being evenly distributed" (Paoli et al, 2002; Paoli and Parent-Thirion, 2003).

Is this emerging evidence that the transition has brought a more rapid convergence of overall working times between men and women in CEE countries than has occurred in western countries? It appears that men in the new CEE member states are now contributing more unpaid work than they were and more than men in Western Europe. This may mean that both men and women are now suffering a heavy dual burden, rather than reducing women's loads, but it does seem to have brought men into caring for children, with 31% of men involved in childcare, compared with 41% of women (respectively 24% and 41% in EU15). While these (European Foundation for the Improvement of Living and Working Condition) authors point to the high working hours of women and the lack of part-time options, we might also point to the loss of state support for childcare. This may well have forced the pace of change in households, compared with the past, and compared with the West (Paoli et al, 2002; Paoli and Parent-Thirion, 2003).

These findings from the European Foundation for the Improvement of Living and Working Conditions appear to support an interpretation of our qualitative data, that men (according to their partners) are more likely to be involved in childcare than their fathers were, that men's identity has changed from the male breadwinner tradition of the past towards an identity in which they are comfortable with parenting practice, and suggest a strong sense of a shared commitment to children and childcare. This does not mean that there were not differences in time committed to children, or in their sense of the responsibilities of childcare, but it does represent a major change from the past, and a transformation of the experience of men in families.

Quantitative comparative data on childcare ideals are also emerging from the European Foundation for the Improvement of Living and Working Conditions:

> The basic finding is that most of the people of Europe believe that childcare is basically a non-gender-specific task: both mother and father are expected to carry out child rearing. The index score on this issue is 81.8 (out of 100) in the EU15 member states and 76.6 in the AC10. (Fahey and Spéder, 2004, p 60)

Poland's index score is around average for the then accession countries. Unlike the data on childcare practices, described previously, in this account of beliefs about shared childcare the accession countries appear to have more traditional ideals. The broad finding of this study is intriguing, but should not tempt us to believe that ideals of shared childcare are about to be turned into equal practice:

The belief that child rearing is a shared responsibility for the mother and the father is the prevalent one in Europe. Much more than half the population in all countries affirm this view. ... Where there are gender-specific views on child rearing, then the mothers are expected to be responsible. ... Considerable differences between the European countries could be identified and these differences correspond strongly to the existence or otherwise of welfare state regimes. In countries where in-kind, universal and employment-related programmes are widespread, there is a much more widespread belief in sharing. (Fahey and Spéder, 2004, p 68)

Conclusion

The transition from communism has brought radical change to economics and politics. Mainly these have been discussed in terms of issues of employment and political participation, and the transition has been seen as bringing re-traditionalisation, especially in Poland, where the Roman Catholic Church is particularly influential. But the transition has had a radical impact on households, too, and in particular on the resources available to households through social policies supporting family work.

This discussion has concerned what is going on inside households. A number of features of life outside households in Poland do indeed suggest a reversion to a tradition of male domination in public life. We are also limited in our accounts to respondents who were in paid employment or on maternity or childcare leave. While the latter group certainly contained mothers whose attachment to the labour market was rather tenuous – with several who expressed fears about the reality of getting back into their jobs – we did not have respondents who were unemployed. However, the evidence our respondents offered of life inside households does suggest a move towards more equal partnerships, in the sense of both partners' responsibility for children and their care, and in the practical management of households, which often depend on men's participation in childcare.

There is no single transition in the lives of households. There are respondents who describe a change towards traditional roles in the household, and there are respondents who describe a change away from them. But more respondents describe something new: these are dual earner households, for the most part, and women are usually following their mothers as earners and carers. But their account of their husbands is of men who take pleasure in their children, see themselves as responsible for childcare and are not embarrassed to sing, play, feed and nurture. The accounts do not amount to an equality of responsibility, but they do describe men engaging in care. These respondents do not describe dual earner/dual carer households, but their accounts suggest a more radical change in Polish households than has happened in the rather more slowly adapting households of Western Europe.

Note

[1] The 10 accession countries, plus Bulgaria and Romania. Turkey was not a candidate country at this stage.

SIX

Mothers and social policy

Introduction

How can we understand the nature of the welfare regime emerging in Poland in terms gender and of social policies relating to gender? In Chapter Two we examined and mapped (Figure 2.1) policies in paid work, income, time, care and voice, examined their implications for women and for gender equality, and asked whether the dual earner system of the communist era has survived the transition or brought a male breadwinner model in Poland? This chapter explores mothers' perceptions of these policies and their ideas about what should happen. How should men and women work in households? How should governments support households?

First, what are the implications of the transition for changes in the assumptions that governments are making about gender? The communist expectation was for dual earner households with women in paid jobs. While in this respect they bore some resemblance to Scandinavian regimes, they were very different in other ways. As Ferge comments, "women did not feel liberated by systems which imposed paid work on them, allowed no freedom in civil society, and burdened women with household work" (Ferge, 1997a, 1998). The lack of individual choice, of feminist organisations and an unreconstructed domestic division of labour made key differences between the Scandinavian and the CEE models. However, these regimes achieved high levels of women's participation in paid work, with parental leave and childcare (especially kindergartens), family allowances, education and health care, and represented a level of state support for families that was high by comparison with Western Europe.

What are the implications of transition from communism for the gender regimes in CEE countries? There is a lot the countries have in common, with a common history of legislation that treated women as individuals rather than as dependent within families, and a common history of women's participation in the labour force. Their continuing core family responsibilities as mothers were supported in some measure by state policies: in CEE countries, this was particularly through kindergartens for pre-school children aged three to six. The lack of political rights to participate as citizens was common across the region, to men as well as to women. There was less gender equality in pay and working experience than appeared on the surface but, nevertheless, there was a tradition of dual earner households in CEE countries stretching back to the post-Second World War period that contrasted with the male breadwinner regimes of the UK and Ireland, for example (Lewis, 1992). CEE countries challenged the Scandinavian countries in terms of women's labour market participation and state support for women's participation. The reaction against communism has brought markets and prices into social services as well as into industry. Public sector values have become more corrupted, de-legitimised, than in western countries (Ferge, 1997b, p 177). A reduction in state revenues has brought lower public spending, inflation has reduced the value of benefits, and legislation has changed entitlements, in particular bringing means testing to most countries. The levels of public support to families and to the dual earner system have fallen everywhere.

But women still need to earn, and in this context the conflict between the need for income and the need for care is growing. While CEE countries have been throwing off this bit of communist past, Western Europe has been trying to encourage women into the labour market and looking for solutions to the problems of reconciling work and family. In Western Europe, low fertility has been connected with the costs of motherhood and its incompatibility with paid employment (Esping-Andersen et al, 2001, pp 79-81, 2002). But the problems identified in developing this new architecture for (Western) Europe are actually now more pressing in CEE countries. Women's "relatively favourable position in the labour market, which had made the region comparable to Sweden, the leader in the West in this regard, is now a phenomenon of the past in most transition countries" (UNICEF, 2001, p 14). The numbers of young children across former communist countries have fallen by an average of 31% (UNICEF, 2001, p 18). But these two solutions bring their problems: diminishing family size is causing concern throughout the East and West (UNICEF, 1999). The alternative solution of withdrawing from the labour market brings risks of poverty to mothers and their children as well as threats to gender equality.

If communist identity meant a strong measure of uniformity, post-communist identity brings emerging differences, sometimes differences rooted in the past, which have been hidden from view and are now allowed to develop. There is still a lot that post-communist countries have in common, but social policy legislation has taken on varying characters. Whether these amount to diverging gender regimes, as Fodor et al suggest (2002), we rather doubt. But if there is any tendency towards a traditional male breadwinner model we would expect to find it in Poland, so this issue to some extent frames our discussion. Have policies in Poland held on to the assumptions of gender equality and women as earners, or has the essentially conservative influence of the Roman Catholic Church put a male breadwinner model into legislation and practice?

In comparison with other CEE countries, Poland emerges on a number of issues as the most strongly affected by a backlash against communist policies relating to women and gender equality. Abortion in particular (see Chapter Three) illustrates the way gender has been politicised in the post-communist era, and is an example of how in Poland women's rights have been reduced (Zielińska, 2000). Hungary has reverted to a more comprehensive and universal system of support for families, with parental leave and kindergartens: most pre-school Hungarian children attend public kindergarten while the number in Poland is around 50% (see Chapter Two). The consequence of all these differences in social policy is that "in Hungary, women have a better chance of combining work and family obligations" (Fodor, 2002, p 488). The evidence of participation rates is that these are indeed lower for Polish women, although men's participation rates are low in Poland too (see Chapter Two and Table 2.1). Unemployment rates also show these differences: in Hungary they were 6% for women and 5.8% for men, while in Poland women's unemployment in 2004 was 19.7% and men's 18%, and these figures in reality may be much worse, if fewer women are registering (see Chapter Two and Tables 2.1 and 2.2; Fodor, 1997).

If the question of 're-traditionalisation' to a male breadwinner model forms one pole of this discussion, gender equality forms the other. International agencies such as the European Union, the United Nations, even the World Bank, acknowledge, in principle at least, gender equality as a goal for former communist countries as well as other nations (Ruminska-Zimny, 2002; World Bank, 2002), while gender equality policy from the European Union has become a standard for new CEE member states from 2004. To what extent has any move to re-traditionalisation contradicted goals of gender equality? What losses have come from the processes of transition and are there any gains? And what model of gender is now available for building into social policy?

In particular, we examine the social policies identified earlier for their impact in Poland on gender inequalities in paid work, care work, income, time and voice. These are the essential elements of gender systems. The allocation of work, income and time between men and women and between households and the state defines the gender system of different welfare regimes. They are also systems of power in which women's voice is suppressed to a greater or lesser extent. Gender equality policies have tended to be directed at aspects of the system of gender inequality and have often failed to deliver their promises. For example, under communism women were promised equality through paid work. Governments supported care to some extent, but they left women with very heavy burdens in households, a continuing sense of unshared responsibilities as mothers, and very little leisure time. If gender equality policies are to be more effective in delivering equal treatment in paid work and welfare they need to address the interconnecting elements of gender regimes as systems, with a logic of gender equality across these elements. This means developing an environment that favours more equal shares between men and women in paid work, care work, income, time and voice, between individuals within households and in paid work and politics.

As the dual earner system of CEE countries is challenged by these trends in economics and policy, we take Poland as the most likely case for re-traditionalisation and ask about aspects of social policy as experienced in households. We ask how equal are policies in legislation and in practice in mothers' experience. We ask about the extent to which mothers in households identify themselves as mothers and their partners as breadwinners, or themselves as paid workers and their partners as carers. We also ask mothers about the social policies they would like for themselves and their children and discuss how social policies might support their ideals in gender relations within and between households, and in relations between the state and the household.

Paid work

Chapter Five looked at women's experience of combining employment and motherhood and about their sense of themselves and their partners as mothers, fathers, and workers. It argued that although some respondents would prefer to be at home, most saw themselves as working mothers, albeit very stretched working mothers, who were very conscious of discrimination, the risks of unemployment, the difficulties of meshing work and motherhood in contemporary Poland in comparison with the experience of their mothers and their own experience as children. This chapter discusses respondents' views of practical social policies, and what these amount to in terms of the gender model they see as ideal.

Paid work was the core duty of men, especially of fathers, in the male breadwinner model. In Poland, women have been very active in the labour market since the middle of the 20th century, and we might expect that their experience of this dual earner model would flavour respondents' assumptions about paid work and motherhood in their ideas about social policies that would support them. On the other hand, transition has brought new opportunities as well as unemployment. In Poland, the situation of the job market and unemployment in particular, submits women's employment to critical examination. Views critical of women's employment were brought to life at the beginning of political transformation (1989) when unemployment occurred in Poland, and sustained through the early 1990s as unemployment increased (Ciechomski and Morawski, 1996, quoted in Balcerzak-Paradowska et al 2003b, p 131).

Research conducted in the beginning of 1990s shows that in families with small children, over two thirds of fathers (69%) agreed that "my wife should have the same chances of a professional career as I do and the duties of running the household and childcare should be shared by both of us". Men's support for women's employment seems strong here but it is also often contingent on traditional expectations of women's continuing responsibility for children's well-being (84% of fathers interviewed); 72% of fathers interviewed also agreed that "in the evening when I get home, I expect my family life to be in order" (Firlit-Fesnak, 1997a, p 24). In such responses home, family and childcare are ascribed to nature and taken for granted as the most important tasks for women, not their paid work.

Research conducted on three generations (age ranges: 25-44, 45-64, 65-80) of an urban family brings some evidence about changing ideals. Men's responsibility for financial provision was agreed by 57% of respondents, while 40% saw this as belonging to both parents. The middle and oldest generations were more traditional, while among the younger generation 52% still saw men as primary providers, with 44% of the opinion that both parents should provide financially for the family. A quite traditional model of male breadwinning dominates expectations, with some changes among the youngest generation (Doniec, 2001). A study in the 1990s showed that a traditional model of family life was often preferred by men, with 46% preferring this ideal, while 29% approved of married women's employment only if wives prioritised household responsibilities. This model did not meet the expectations of women, with only 22% preferring to be housewives if the family could afford it (Firlit–Fesnak, 1997a, p 26). Economic and other motives are mixed, in women's accounts of employment, but related to their level of education: women with higher educational levels are more likely to cite non–financial reasons such as interest in a job, a desire to be promoted, achieving prestige and appreciation, confirming self-esteem and a wish to take part in social life (Balcerzak–Paradowska et al, 2003b). Evidence from the 1990s, then, suggests that women's employment has been questioned in the context of high levels of unemployment; it takes place in a context where men's expectations of women's work may include traditional expectations of motherhood. However, there is some evidence of ideals shifting among younger generations, towards more gender-equal expectations of employment and parenthood.

How important is paid employment in our respondents' perceptions of themselves and of the policies that would support these ideals? Some respondents looked to the male breadwinner model and argued the need for higher earnings for men. For example, Hanna wanted to "be able to be more often at home, which means that a husband should be able to earn more in order to enable a woman to take care of a child". But Hanna's account of paid work for women was that it raised their status: "A woman becomes equal to a man ... a couple live in a more partnership relationship. ... The man must take into account the woman's opinion. ... A woman earns money in the same way as a man for supporting the home, so she gains equal rights with a man". Employment, according to Anna, "positively strengthens her position ... she is conscious that she also adds to the achievements and the position of the family. She is not subdued". Both respondents saw paid work as improving women's position; they appear to be looking for a freedom to make their own priorities between work and family. Perhaps these pleas for more time at home should be seen in the context of the time and money pressures of Polish families now, as argued in Chapter Five.

The dominant position taken by respondents, however, was that women should be able to combine motherhood and paid employment. Their experience as mothers under Poland's unregulated competitive capitalism was of discrimination and anxiety about their jobs. Many respondents noted the problems of changes in the labour market and the need for regulation against discrimination and dismissal and for rights to the flexibility needed in caring for children:

> "I think it is connected with discrimination against women. In relation to work a man more often gets a position than

a woman because there is a risk that she will become pregnant. Often an employer asks if a woman intends to have a family. Women earn 70% of what men earn in the same position. We are wronged ... if a child gets sick it is a miracle to get leave." (Violetta)

"The majority of young mothers, after bringing up small children, want to place them in nursery or pre-school and have a job, but there is no job for them. Nobody wants women with small children." (Klaudia)

Eugenia looked for "guarantees for women with children, that they should not be dismissed", and explained that she "'was told to accept the conditions my employer set or get fired".

It was widely seen as the state's duty to support women's right to work:

"I think that the state should take into account the real situation of women, who on the one hand want to have families and children, and on the other hand have to work and support their families. Security of getting and retaining work after giving birth to children should be guaranteed." (Marlena)

"It is unjust that mothers cannot find a better job because they have children. The state should be happy that a new generation is being born. ... Women who are pregnant should be guaranteed not only their job but opportunities for promotion, the same as every other person." (Marzanna)

If most respondents saw themselves as paid workers, they also saw themselves as mothers, with primary responsibility for children and childcare. Respondents typically wanted work that would adapt, with hours that fitted children's school time: "More jobs for mothers with hours from 7.30am to 3.30pm, and paid maternal leave" (Eleanora). Some wanted work that could be done at home: "A woman, who plays a leading role in bringing up a child, should have an opportunity to do paid work at home. In the West ... more and more companies send out computers, and a woman can work effectively at home" (Janina).

It was much more common for women to ask for adaptable work for themselves than for their husbands. Despite their eloquent accounts of men who were accepting responsibility for childcare, these respondents still saw themselves as needing paid work that they could fit around motherhood, rather than their partners as needing paid work that could be fitted around fatherhood. The difficulty with flexibility of work for women has been evidenced in the UK where flexible part-time jobs are marginalised employment. But the problems are also evident to these Polish respondents, with women who acknowledge that concessions to motherhood make them vulnerable in the competitive conditions of contemporary Poland. Gabriela discusses women's vulnerability to discrimination where they have legal protection to allow them to take leave, and acknowledges that "it is difficult to suggest a solution to this problem".

Income

Mothers raged about the low level of earnings, the low level of financial support for children and benefits for maternity leave, and the high costs of pre-schools, educational and cultural services. "If we have three children, my husband's wages should be high enough to provide for our family. If I have a job too, we should be able to afford much more. We both have jobs and in reality it [our income] is only enough for our basic needs" (Wanda).

These issues were directly connected with parenting, with the need for mothers to be employed and with working hours being determined by their employers, while state support and regulation had been withdrawn: "We earn too little – children are neglected whereas before [under communism] a mother could take care of a child" (Dagmara).

The level of family benefit, according to Bożena, is "just comic", while Joanna rails about the costs of education: "The state guarantees a free education for children, but takes no account of the high prices of textbooks".

> "I do not understand it. In my family we both work, and we have to pay for pre-school. No support. We get no reductions on the part of the state. My husband gets just 75 zlotys [approximately £12 or €18] as a family allowance." (Zofia)

The need for financial support for families and for family services followed from these accounts of low earnings and high costs. Beata was clear that financial support from the state was the most crucial need now, and many respondents argued for better state funding for schools, and more funding for pre-schools and paid parental leave. Ewa commented on the position of women caught between the authorities' promotion of the traditional family and the lack of real support for children:

> "Parents have difficulty with finding jobs: the material situation of these families is really dramatic. There are no one hundred per cent safe contraceptives for women; those available are very expensive. Abortion is forbidden. As a result, successive unwanted children are born. Local and church authorities are against abortion, but at the same time do nothing to help support successive children. Family allowances are symbolic. A woman is in fact deprived of her free choice."

If respondents looked for more material support for their children, they also looked for a stronger regulatory framework "with no discrimination at work. Why do women earn less [than men], for example?" (Anna), while a more tolerant and flexible attitude to them as mothers with children – "the possibility of taking a child with her to work from time to time would certainly not damage anyone" (Danuta) – would enable them to earn enough to support themselves and their children.

The need for financial support, whether through higher levels of family allowance and other benefits or tax credits or through earnings, especially women's earnings, dominated the accounts of their situation as mothers under post-communism, and dominated the demands they made of the system in which they lived. Broadly, although not universally, these women's accounts of themselves were of mothers who needed and expected to earn their living. They felt that motherhood counted against them in the new labour market and that the state could and should do more to guarantee their ability to work and to earn, as well as more to meet their needs and the needs of their children through family allowances, public services, and stronger public support for parental leave and pre-schools.

Time

> "In those times [under communism] work time was more regulated, people had more time for their family. People returned home earlier after work." (Eugenia)

Experience as children under communism suffused our respondents' accounts of post-communism. Their own childhood had been marked by very comprehensive arrangements of parental leave and childcare, in marked contrast to their own situation as parents. They were very demanding of state support, wanting a much more active central and local state to regulate working time and conditions for mothers and their children; for example: "shorter work hours, longer leaves, availability of pre-schools, more free days for care of children" (Ela).

It was rare for respondents to find that time was not a problem. Jolanta remarked on her unusual advantage: "I am in a privileged situation as I work only a few hours a day – on paid parental leave – and have the possibility of returning to work without any trouble". This was indeed contrary to the experience of most respondents who felt very uncertain about their ability to return to their jobs if they took parental leave, and very pressured about working time and fitting it to their children's needs.

Alicja thought this should be down to employers, because "legislation could provoke employers into not giving work to young women. If any official solutions were too radical or too authoritative, employers would just not employ women". She raises a very serious issue about the situation of women, especially mothers, in Poland today, caught between expectations of them as mothers, developed under the Roman Catholic Church and communism, and the prevailing competitive market conditions. State regulation is a habit from the old times, and fits ill with the new. Protecting mothers makes women vulnerable to discrimination. The hazards are evident in women's accounts of their exposure to unemployment, accounts which might be replicated elsewhere, but seem more extreme in Poland now. But more often, despite the hazards, respondents wanted state control in the interests of consistency and reducing exploitation. Anna argued for norms so that "for example, men and women working in shops and supermarkets should not be exploited, as now, when they have no time for private or family life". Wanda argued for "the regulation of working hours, though it is rather unrealistic, because private firms work according to their own rules" and Urszula pressed this as a state responsibility:

> "Rules for working hours should also exist, in particular for mothers with little children, who do not want to take childcare leave. They should be allowed to go home more often during working hours. This should be a decision of the state because employers are inconsistent."

Many respondents argued for shorter working time. Alicja wanted "for example a four-fifths time job which allows for an additional free day a week or a six-hour working day". Klaudia wanted the "opportunity for women to have three-quarter time work, or half-time work. The majority, however, have to work full time or not at all; it is a tragedy". Urszula argued that "six hours should be the maximum for mothers with little children". Olga reflected the despair of many respondents about their current situation, but also about the difficulties of addressing this in the present context:

> "I have some ideas, but I think they are unrealistic. I think that our work should be organised in a different way in order to give us more time bringing up children ... I have to be at work for 10 or 12 hours and my son misses me and cries; he does not want me to go to work and asks if I will come back late again at night. He asks why daddy left again and why he is out for days. I think that it should not be so."

Most respondents agreed with Violetta that "present times force us to devote little time to our family". They needed more time. But they also needed more control over time. The need to be able to respond to children in illness or other problems brought many comments about the need for flexible work, over which mothers had some control. Wanda shared Olga's despair about the difficulty of finding 'realistic' solutions: "I can think only of impossible solutions, as for example, deciding on the working hours as a woman needs ... the possibility of flexible times of work".

Urszula, too, asked for women to be able to choose their working hours: "In this country there is no such possibility and it makes the life of mothers very difficult. I, for instance, have to be out of the home for 12 hours and if I want to deal with any problem related to my children I have to take leave from my job". And Tatiana argued for "new forms of organisation of time, for instance half-time or part-time jobs or other forms of rational working time".

The strong tradition of parental leave under communism, and mothers' ability to return to employment, were reflected in many responses. The level of family income while on childcare leave was one theme. Zofia argued for paid leave, and Dagmara explained her early return to work: "I put Klaudia in a nursery when she was one and a half, but it was very hard for her. I had to go back to work because we had only 600 zlotys [approximately £145 or €99] for the three of us".

More often, respondents commented on the risks to their jobs if they took leave, and the consequent unemployment among mothers, and their swift return to work after childbirth. Janina, currently on parental leave, argues that returning to work after leave is the most important issue at the moment, because returning after leave "is becoming less and less possible at present". Kasia too stressed that "the important thing is that a woman should be protected in practice, not only in theory, and be able to return to her job".

Holiday time was another issue that permeated these responses, reflecting a strong tradition of state and employer involvement in provision for children through the year. Lidia asked for state support with "family holidays and shorter working time", while Irena embedded this in the wider health, educational and cultural needs of children:

> "Children's access to culture ... financial support, in the case of children's serious illness, and to let a child go on vacations, subsidised pre-schools, paid parental leave, shorter working time for mothers of small children, security of work for mothers with small children and the opportunity to take it up at an appropriate time."

This comment about children's access to culture was echoed by many others. Mothers wanted rights that would give them time to combine paid employment with care for their children. But they wanted time for their children enriched by access to culture, education, sport, holidays, not empty time in which their children were purely minded.

In summary, many responses involved demands around working time, especially for women and especially when they had young children. This centred on reduced working hours but included flexibility, better paid and longer parental leave and arrangements for holiday periods. Respondents acknowledged with Róża that they already spent more time than their partners did with their children: "Women devote more time to their children". Sometimes they argued that men did not spend enough time with the children, but when they discussed policy, and how it should support parenthood, they thought mainly about how it could support them as mothers, and enable them to fit motherhood around their jobs. This fitted rather oddly into their accounts of fathers' responsibility for childcare, where they asserted men's obligations and acknowledged their participation.

Women's unpaid work responsibilities were already seen as disadvantages in the labour market, and some of these proposals might tip the balance against women's position in the labour market and men's increasing participation in care.

Care

There was very broad acceptance of men's role and responsibility in childcare and, in general, accounts of partners who accepted this (see Chapter Five): "If parents undertake a decision to conceive a child, then the responsibility for bringing it up rests on both of them" (Róża). But very few respondents indeed followed this through into proposals that would involve the government in encouraging or supporting men's increasing role in the household. Edyta was rare in expressing a commitment to a Swedish system of maternal and paternal leave, because it "motivates fathers to take care of children, and it gives good results in the form of good relations between fathers and children". Responses were more coloured by national history, with respondents drawing on their own experience of state care as children. There were very general demands for the state to play a much wider role in funding and providing care for children of all ages.

Marlena argued for the role of the family as the crucial one: "Only the help of grandparents and good organisation or cooperation between husband and wife can really help". But much more often respondents expanded on the state's role in providing care and education, and sometimes on the need for state regulation of private provision and stronger subsidies for pre-school places. The obligation of the state to underpin parents was frequently and emphatically expressed. Monika argued that "the state should support parents. ... Closing pre-schools, and state schools, and allowing private schools – this is no help on the part of the state, too little assistance is given in the struggle against drug abuse, alcoholism, robberies among children". Róża made a similar claim: "The state has a duty to open nurseries, pre-schools and schools in which children could be safe and gain knowledge". Hanna complained of the lack of available facilities: "The authorities should guarantee parents access to these elementary forms of help. In our neighbourhood there is no pre-school, not to mention a nursery". Stanisława expressed her demand in terms of equal opportunities, which could be approached only through effective state support for children and parents:

> "The care of pre-school children, nurseries, schools, equipment of schools and securing them professional personnel of the same level in cities and villages, which could give all children equal chances in life, are obligations belonging to the state."

Similarly, Marta argued that the poor circumstances of some families required state intervention:

> "If there are any exceptional circumstances then the state's care is necessary and indispensable. Among my relatives there are two girls – their father died of cancer and now his wife has lost her job and has got cancer too – so there are two girls who need an education and a start in life."

Recreational provision for the holidays was a theme taken up by many: "If children are of school age there should be summer camps or something like that" (Aleksandra), and "funding for vacation camps" (Urszula).

Alicja regretted the closure of centres catering for children's recreational, cultural and educational needs. Again, she saw this as an area of state responsibility, where parents could not, on their own, offer a secure and enriching environment for children:

> "Free cultural centres should be restored, because a lot of families are not able to take care of children on their own, just to learn how to draw, play the piano, speak a foreign language. It would distract children away from some social problems, because they often steal out of boredom."

Patrycja agreed that "clubs would also help to remove children from negative environments", while Urszula felt the need for places of safety where she "could leave my child under someone's care so that I could meet my obligations".

There were also demands for state regulation of the quality of private provisions: "I think that someone should supervise these private solutions, for instance, private pre-schools" (Marta), and for higher subsidies for pre-schools or for children attending pre-school: "Financial support for pre-schools, because they are very expensive" (Patrycja).

Most respondents emphasised family responsibility in caring for children, especially parents' responsibility and especially mothers'. But there were many demands for the state to underpin parents, both in terms of the respondents' own needs, and in terms of principled arguments about the need for a socialised response to care. Many respondents noted the increasing inequality in Poland and the difficulty of poorer families in meeting care costs. Many were critical of the state's reduction of support for pre-school children, and withdrawal from any responsibility for school-age children during holidays or after school; from responsibility for enriching the cultural environment for children outside school hours, and for equal opportunities for children from different socioeconomic backgrounds.

Consequences for gender equality today

Some respondents noted the freedoms and opportunities of post-communism. Jolanta argued that "women are now more valued, educated and are successful in their chosen professions"; Karolina felt that "women can now do what they wish ... they feel important and useful"; and Kasia said that a woman "has more opportunities for development because she can educate herself, gain experience and is not limited by stereotypical rules". But in their accounts of being parents, the much wider sense was that women have lost ground. Combining employment and motherhood is seen as essential to survival but is extremely difficult. At the household level, men have undertaken more, but the costs of parenthood fall much more on women than they did under communism. Unfettered competition has brought discrimination against women, who are seen as a risk to businesses: "There is discrimination against women. They work, they run homes and despite all this they are thought of as less efficient and able than men" (Lidia). But it has also brought unpaid work sharply into conflict with paid work, instead of both being seen and supported as they were under communism: "It was easier to regulate the time of work, to find a job that guaranteed more spare time and better finances" (Krystyna). Our respondents raged about these losses, about authorities they saw as abrogating their responsibilities to support working parents, and to provide a safe and enriching environment for children.

Discussions of the social policies that respondents would like to see are fraught with difficulties. They are very aware that the change from communism brings a competitive environment in which any concessions to them as mothers may be punished by employers. So, while the sense of government obligation is usually strong, there is also a strong sense of the problem of bringing solutions that will support them in the new situation. Many respondents criticised the situation of women in Poland, discriminated against through their rights as mothers and potential mothers. But most also argued for regulation of companies, while recognising that "it is difficult to suggest a solution to this problem, but it should be resolved somehow". The broad conclusion, then, was for a more regulated capitalism in which there was more room for families through a level of government support which their own parents had been able to take for granted.

There was widespread acknowledgement of partners who cared for their children in ways that their own fathers rarely did. A strong sense of change in households, then, was conveyed by our respondents. But in all the discussion of social policies, there was an underlying assumption that social policies should support mothers in their ability to combine paid work with care for their children, rather than supporting the change that many identified towards more equal households. Alicja wanted "work at home on a 'mom-typical' job". Liliana argued that "women should work shorter hours". Urszula held that "the authorities should also regulate the working hours of parents ... I think that six hours should be the maximum for mothers of little children".

It could be argued that social policies supporting parents and children, rather than mothers and children, would be more likely to support gender equality in Poland. The environment described by some respondents seems particularly to expose women to discrimination in the labour market, but is relatively favourable to men's participation in care. Policies that supported men's care work as well as women's (as in Sweden) or reduced paid working hours for men and women (as in France) would be less likely to expose women to discrimination, and might seize the moment for public acknowledgment of men as caring fathers.

What about gender discrimination in former USSR?

Conclusion

There was little evidence in our study of a return of the male breadwinner regime in terms of the respondents' experience or expectations. Few respondents saw themselves as depending on partners, or saw governments' obligations in terms of supporting men's employment rather than women's. Essentially, respondents saw themselves as workers, needing social/collective level support for their paid work, for their parenting and for their children (see Chapter Two, Figure 2.1).

Respondents argued, in general, that governments should regulate working time and parental leave and support nurseries, cultural and holiday provision for children. There is great complaint from these respondents about the inadequacies of government, indeed much more complaint against the inadequacies of government than about the inadequacies of husbands. Governments are seen as abrogating an essential duty.

Discussions of state support are suffused with women's experience of growing up under a regime that did take responsibility for the meshing of paid and unpaid work, for paid work and parenting, and that did take responsibility for children's needs across time, and beyond school. The change from communism has been accompanied by a much less noticed change in households. Our respondents condemn the withdrawal of the state from services and responsibilities which they see as essentially collective.

Changes in men's attitudes are acknowledged and applauded: responses suggest moves towards egalitarian principles in men and women and a move towards men as carers in practice. They applaud their partners for meeting their children's needs in a way that their own fathers would never have contemplated. But the changes in expectations of men, and their accounts of men in practice, do not amount to seeing men as equal partners in care, and themselves as equal partners in paid work. Respondents tend to see themselves as mother-workers and their partners as worker-fathers: the policies they seek would mainly make women's lives more flexible so that they can fit paid work around motherhood. In their demands for regulating working time and for maternal leave, mothers show themselves as still accepting the primary role and responsibility in childcare: respondents are more likely to ask for policies that enable women to be mothers and workers than for policies that would encourage men to be fathers and carers. Men's working time and working practices are challenged in these accounts, but only a little. These solutions could bring problems of their own, in their emphasis on women's responsibility for childcare, which appears to contradict respondents' claims about the obligations of men. Policies supporting equal parenting, such as reducing working hours and establishing fathers' rights to share parental leave, would go with the flow of changing masculine identity among the young fathers described here. It would also offer women a better chance of gender equality in the workplace and could bring better resources to families.

SEVEN

Gender equality in the wider Europe

Introduction

The recent accessions to the European Union brings new questions about the aspirations of mothers in the new CEE member states. Will there be support in Europe for their social agenda, for more collective responsibility for children? Will women's employment be supported in quality as well as quantity? Will there be support for gender equality in households and policies to allow work–life balance for both men and women? What are the implications of European Union enlargement for gender equality in the new CEE member states?

As argued in Chapter Two, the merging of CEE countries within the European Union brings together gender regimes with contrasting histories and trajectories. The male breadwinner model of household and social policy has dominated most of Western Europe with, in the 1960s and 1970s, Scandinavian countries turning away from it and leading towards a dual earner model. But most of Western Europe remains at a one-and-a-half earner norm at best, and far from gender equality in income, power or respect. In contrast, CEE countries have had social policy support for a dual earner system for the best part of half a century. Under communism, despite the lack of civil society, a women's movement and a traditional division of labour within households, gender equality could be seen as one of the strengths of social policy in these countries. These systems have been battered by the transition from communism, which has brought unemployment and reductions in state support for childcare and families. We have argued that the claims of increasing gender inequality and re-traditionalisation towards a male breadwinner model have been overstated. Nevertheless, state support for the dual earner model has been challenged and reduced in the context of transition from communism and the development of markets. Can the dual earner traditions of CEE countries survive another transition into a European Union, which is also a common market? Will the result be more gender equality or less, especially in the eight new member states whose history is of communist dual earner regimes, but also in the European Union at large?

The widening of Europe has also been discussed more in terms of economics, and where there is a high public profile for social concerns it has centred on migration rather than other aspects of social policy. Amid the many debates about gender equality in the European Union, very little commentary indeed has centred on the impact of this momentous change on women or gender equality in CEE countries, although the accession process has now generated some reviews (Choluj and Neusuess, 2004; Velluti, 2005). A useful literature about accession sheds some light on gender issues. In particular, *EU expansion to the East: Prospects and problems* (Ingham and Ingham, 2002); special editions of the *Journal of European Public Policy* (2000); *West European politics* (2002) also published as *The enlarged European Union: Diversity and adaptation* (Mair and Zielonka, 2002); and the *Journal of European Social Policy* (2003, 2004) now provide some developed debates and insights into the social aspects of this significant transformation. And the European Union, through the structural indicators in particular, gives comparative statistical information as well as assessments of CEE accession countries and their gender policies as they join Europe (Sloat, 2004).

It matters a great deal to women in CEE countries what will be the impact of the European Union in terms of economy, employment and social support for motherhood and care. But the meaning and significance of social Europe are much debated. The importance of gender equality within European Union social policy is also contested, as is the construction to be put on a work–life balance agenda that appears to put changing gender relations at the heart of the European Union social policy. The direction of change in each of these cases is also contested. The complexity of European Union decision making makes it difficult to come to a conclusion about the overall impact of European Union policy. The balance and relationship between social and economic policy, the development of the Open Method of Coordination, the meaning of the shift from equal opportunities to gender mainstreaming, the development of work–life balance policies: the combined impact of these is difficult to interpret. It is also subject to change, in the "ups and downs of European gender equality policy" (Rubery et al, 2004). This suggests that the balance between social Europe and market Europe is an open question with a changing answer: "Its contours are unfixed and its heart and soul elusive" (Threlfall, 2003, p 136).

We shall argue that the tension at the heart of the European Union – between a European social model based on social solidarity and social cohesion and an economic model based on liberal markets – is also at the heart of the transition process, and the way that it will impact on women in the new CEE member states and on gender relations in households and in public. The accession process so far has been dominated more by the market model than by the social model. In this process as well as in transition from communism, the systems of support for mothers in the labour market have lost some ground. The European Union has had some impact on the development of civil society and systems of governance; on the development of discussion about social exclusion and on benchmarks, through the Open Method of Coordination, all of which may put gender issues into stronger relief in the politics and households of CEE countries. But European Union social policy is a system of regulation not of taxation, and the development of free markets has gone along with the development of inequalities, often in the context – in Central and Eastern Europe – of falling national incomes. The current level and distribution of the structural funds are wholly inadequate to the task of drawing the new members in: for example the levels of transfers in the budget for 2000–06 are equivalent to one tenth of the sum given to the former East Germany after unification (Rhodes, 2003, p 56). Previous enlargements have brought economic and social growth to new members, and accession may bring new members closer to EU15 levels of income. But also, increasing women's labour market participation is at the heart of current European Union economic policies. The need for social support for children and childcare – central to the CEE gender model – could become more evident in the new Europe, to the benefit of East and West. But this social model needs social spending at the European Community level in order to reduce the differences between old members and new, and it needs European Union-level support for national spending to shore up the dual earner system, protecting women's earning capacity and children's care. One vision is of a European social model in which social cohesion and social spending, high quality employment and economic growth reinforce one another, as described in the Social Policy Agenda (European Commission, 2000a). The alternative vision is of a 'race to the bottom', as richer welfare states reduce entitlements to avoid migration based on fears of social raids, however unfounded. Migration may be "a problem for the sending countries and a solution for the receiving countries" but acting as if migration would inevitably take place has already brought measures to cut social policies or close labour markets (Kvist, 2004, pp 303-8).

The European Union: market model or social model?

The first much-debated question is about the importance of social Europe. Streeck argues trenchantly for the "insignificance of Community social policy in the integration process" (Streeck, 1995, p 407), while others argue for the growing importance of European Union social powers (Walby, 1999, p 118; Duncan, 2002). Similarly, some see the Open Method of Coordination as a new development of the social possibilities in Europe, bringing shared social objectives (Atkinson, 2003), while others emphasise the change from hard-wired directives to softer forms of implementation. Does the Open Method of Coordination represent a softening of the social agenda, a drift away from directives with bite? Or does the adoption of social objectives and indicators pursued after the Lisbon summit of 2000 mean a re-birth of the social dimension of Europe?

There is clearly no single social policy or welfare regime in Europe to compare with the single market and no social policy instruments to compare with the Central Bank or single currency. Social policy regimes at national level remain the key. But an empirical picture of Europe's decision-making structures in the social policy arena has to take account of the existence of supra-national powers and their expression through the European Court of Justice, to which nation states are subject. The effectiveness of these bodies in delivering social policy is open to question, but there can be no argument about making it: "The EU possesses competencies, unified judicial control, and significant capacities to develop or modify policies" (Pierson and Leibfried, 1995, p 1). The present structure falls short of a federal model, but it is one in which "national welfare states remain the primary institutions of European social policy, but they do so in the context of an increasingly constraining multi-tiered polity" (Leibfried and Pierson, 2000, p 268). Social policy has not flowed freely in the wake of economic policy: its development has been contested, and remains open to negotiation.

The notion and practice of Europe as a single market clearly precedes Europe as a power in social policy. The European Union's beginnings as a coal and steel community are evidenced in the original European Economic Community Treaty: only 12 of the 248 articles were devoted explicitly to social policy (Hantrais, 2000, p 2). But the implications of these beginnings for the nature, significance and momentum of social Europe are open to discussion. Some argue that the dream to integrate social Europe is history: western welfare states were built on the struggle between labour and capital. Now, in the context of a weakening of labour power in relation to increasingly mobile capital, there is no force for social policy: the battle for social Europe has been fought and lost (Streeck, 1995; Bornschier and Ziltener, 1999). A middle view is of a more open-ended contest between a Europe based on free trade and one based on welfare states. The emphasis on 'negative integration' (removing barriers to free trade) rather than 'positive integration' (developing social policy) is seen as risking the end of the European social model before it began (Wickham, 2002). Alternatively, some view the European Union as having been vigorous and proactive in developing strategies against the global market, reconfiguring and developing itself as a polity in response to globalisation (Walby, 1999, p 134).

So, what is the European social model? One account is that Europe is distinguished from the US or Japan by its welfare states, albeit mainly at national rather than European Union level: "The density of rights and obligations in Europe means that Europeans are of necessity more entangled in the state than Americans" (Wickham, 2002, p 3). This suggests that social policy and social spending are a core part of the European social model. The Social Policy Agenda sees the social model more in terms of the relationships between economic, employment and social objectives as it "sets out to ensure the positive and dynamic interaction of economic, employment and social policy", as in Figure 7.1:

Figure 7.1: Social Policy Agenda

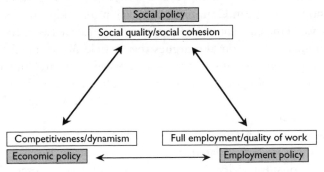

The policy mixes to be established to create a virtuous circle of economic and social progress should reflect the interdependence of these policies and aim to maximise their mutual positive reinforcement.

Source: European Commission (2000a), p 6

The emphasis here is on the relationship between economic employment and social policies and their interdependence, developing "mutually reinforcing economic and social policies" to raise the quantity and quality of employment, to combine "good social conditions with high productivity and high quality goods and services" (European Commission, 2000a, pp 7-8). If the European social model is defined in this Social Policy Agenda, its aim is to develop mutually reinforcing economic, employment and social policies to improve the quality of life as well as the quality of work.

But if the character of Europe is to have welfare states, it is also the case that the change in welfare states is from rights based on citizenship towards rights based on employment. So, while the Social Policy Agenda describes economic, employment and social goals as equally important and mutually reinforcing, the European Commission does not always stick to this version of the relationship between them. While social cohesion is described as an objective in itself, with equal weighting with economic and employment policy as instruments of social policy, these ideas are balanced by a more instrumental view of social policy in increasing employment and economic growth: "A guiding principle will be to strengthen the role of social policy as a productive factor" (European Commission, 2000a, pp 7-8). And a more recent Social Agenda prioritises growth and jobs over social objectives, in the context of globalisation and ageing populations (European Commission, 2005, p 7).

Many commentators see in the Lisbon summit of March 2000, a new phase in the development of Europe's social power. This brought a commitment from heads of state to become "the most competitive and dynamic knowledge-based economy capable of sustainable economic growth with more and better jobs and greater social cohesion" (European Commission, 2000a, p 3). Atkinson sees this as "a revival of the conception of Europe as a social as well as an economic community". Atkinson also argues that Article 3b of the Treaty on European Union means that national governments are "not free to determine the *objectives* of redistributive policy, and that the freedom lies solely in the choice of means towards commonly agreed ends" (Atkinson, 2003, pp 261-3).

Following the Lisbon summit and the Social Policy Agenda in 2000, these ideals were translated into social indicators. Because of the principle of subsidiarity, the primary social indicators agreed by the European Union in 2001 are outcome indicators, allowing for a variety of routes towards the same objectives. Current structural indicators on social inclusion encompass: at risk of poverty, in-work poverty risk, income inequality (comparing top and bottom income quintiles and Gini coefficients), long-term unemployment, jobless households, early school leaving, low educational attainment, life expectancy and inequality of self-defined health (comparing top and bottom income quintiles). Gender breakdowns allow analysis of the effectiveness of member states in reducing women's poverty (see Chapter Two). Structural indicators on employment include employment rates by gender, while measurements of the quality of work and childcare facilities are being developed. These indicators have also been a part of the accession process: "The adoption of the European social indicators conveys a clear message to countries currently applying to join the European Union. The indicators embody the social goals that must be endorsed by the accession countries" (Atkinson, 2003, p 270).

Three years from the Lisbon summit and the publication of the Social Policy Agenda, in *The social situation in the European Union (2003)* (European Commission, 2003a), the European Commission's account of "the resilience of the European social model" emphasises markets as well as social policies: "We have witnessed not the withering away of European approaches built on a combination of market dynamics and public efforts, but a strengthening and further development of the European Social Model" (European Commission, 2003a, p 26). Here, the Commission comments on positive trends in employment, education, health and general well-being, as well as "a process of catching up and convergence".

A new development resulting from the development and publication of the indicators is the possibility of comparing countries' 'performance' as well as measuring progress towards the European Union goals on a systematic and regular basis. Academic social policy has for some time debated different welfare regimes (Esping-Andersen, 1990) and argued the benefits of the social democratic model in economic as well as social terms: "Far from being 'horses for courses', the social democratic welfare regime turns out to be the best choice", whatever the goal (Goodin et al, 1999, p 260). But the new evidence brings a new dimension of support in Europe for 'active welfare states' with high levels of spending and social commitment. In two publications in 2003, the European Commission argues that high-quality social policies will deliver strong economic performance: "Those Member States that perform best on all crucial indicators are those where the principles of active welfare states are applied with the greatest consistency and commitment" (European Commission, 2003a, p 26). In *Choosing to grow: Knowledge, innovation and jobs in a cohesive society*, the report on the Lisbon strategy of economic, social and environmental renewal, the Commission points to Denmark, Sweden and Finland as consistently the 'best performers' on the Lisbon targets, whether in terms of general economic performance, employment, research and innovation, economic reform, social cohesion or the environment

(European Commission, 2003b, p 29). The Joint report by the Commission and the Council on social inclusion, adopted in March 2004, commented that "the most socially progressive countries within the Union are also among the most economically advanced" (Council of the European Union, 2004, p 3).

This integration of social and economic objectives in this version of the European social model shows one current of belief in the European Union that markets alone cannot deliver economic objectives, let alone social ones. It has brought social objectives higher up the priority list in developing higher-quality work, especially increasing equal opportunities and reducing social exclusion. But it does tend to make social objectives second to economic ones, as social policies are usually successful provided they do not conflict with economic aims (Taylor-Gooby, 2003, p 554). And while evidence may accumulate of the effectiveness of particular policies or 'active welfare states', it has been argued that the European Employment Strategy, which pioneered the Open Method of Coordination, shows little evidence of policy learning, of participation by social partners, while building social policy around employment raises all kinds of questions (de la Porte and Pochet, 2004).

In an account of the European social model from an accession country perspective, Ferge and Juhasz highlight the values of social solidarity and cohesion, the agenda of social and civil rights and ideals of participatory decision making with institutionalised processes for involving social partners in decisions (Ferge and Juhasz, 2004). From the point of view of accession countries, the revival of a social policy agenda after the Lisbon summit, although vital, came 10 years too late. It became part of the accession process in 2002, nearly a decade after the first accession agreement (Potucek, 2004) and after a period in which the International Monetary Fund and the World Bank influenced decisions about the transition from communism, restructuring, and the reduction of welfare spending. But a reviving European Union Social Policy Agenda may still offer support to those in CEE countries who want to promote 'active welfare states'.

Gender equality in the European Union

A second question is about gender policies within the European Union. If anywhere you might expect to find significant social policies it is in gender policies: provisions for equal pay were written into the Treaty of Rome and gender policies have been widely agreed to be among the most successful aspects of social policy making. But if the European

Union is formed as a labour market, with social policy – including gender policy – targeted at workers, this may have significant implications for women, who are more likely to have low-paid employment and less likely to have paid employment of any kind. So how important is gender equality policy in the European Union, and what is its nature and direction?

Does 'gender mainstreaming' mean that social policy is developing from a concern with equal pay in paid employment to the social underpinning of gender inequality (Rees, 1999; Walby, 2004)? Gender mainstreaming was brought into European Union debates in the mid-1990s, and was intended to organise or reorganise all policy processes to incorporate a gender equality perspective in all policies, at all levels and at all stages (Beveridge and Shaw, 2002). Some critics see a preoccupation with the processes rather than with the objective of gender equality, while Stratigaki asks whether gender policies have been co-opted for other agendas (2004) and whether gender mainstreaming has been used as an "alibi for neutralising positive action" (Stratigaki, 2005, p 165). And Rubery asks whether gender mainstreaming and the Open Method of Coordination bring more priority to gender equality, or allow gender equality policy to become thinned out and marginalised as equal opportunities are removed from the position as one of four pillars of the European Union employment strategy to one among ten guidelines. "Is the Open Method too open for gender equality policy?" (Rubery, 2005).

Constitutional commitments to gender equality have been extended. The Treaty of Rome incorporated equal pay for men and women and was primarily concerned with labour markets and competition. A more general commitment to gender equality is now embedded in the Treaty of Amsterdam, which lays down that the Community shall have as its task the promotion of equality between men and women. Even critical commentators acknowledge that in this area European Union intervention has been "rich and innovative" (Rossilli, 1997, p 64). These tendencies have been enhanced by the accession of Finland and Sweden in the mid-1990s, bringing new political pressure to gender equality policies in the European Union. They could be further extended by the new CEE member countries with deeper traditions of more equal treatment: the process of implementing European Union gender equality and mainstreaming legislation in new member states is reviewed by Velluti (2005).

If the market element of social Europe is often in tension with the social, another contradiction is between different gender models (see Chapter Two and Figure 2.1). One is a gender model in which men and women work and care, and both are the subject of work–life balance. This lifts the issue from the individual woman to the household level and calls for men to be involved in care as well as for social policies to support men's care. In Europe, the new millennium began with a resolution on the balanced participation of women and men in family and working life, supporting a new 'social contract on gender', agreed by the Council of the European Union and the Ministers for Employment and Social Policy:

> The beginning of the twenty-first century is a symbolic moment to give shape to the new social contract on gender, in which the de facto equality of men and women in the public and private domains will be socially accepted as a condition for democracy, a prerequisite for citizenship and a guarantee of individual autonomy and freedom, and will be reflected in all European Union policies. (Council of the European Union, 2000)

While this appears to offer an ideal of work–life balance for men as well as for women, alternative models – in which work–life balance is for women – persist alongside this more radical vision. At the nation state level, work–life balance may be interpreted in different ways: with a one-and-a half ideal in the Netherlands; in Spain, a model in which women are allowed extended leaves to continue their care responsibilities; and a UK model of individual choice, in which men's choice of long hours may restrict their partners' choices (Rubery, 2005). There is little evidence of policies in Poland or other CEE countries to encourage men's participation in care: rather a reactive response by governments relating to parental care by men, and no serious debates about working-time policies (Open Society Institute, 2005). But at the household level, policies for work–life balance for men and for women would support a household model in which men's responsibility for care is widely assumed, and – rather less widely – practised.

We should also ask about the room for collective policies, and how far the European Union is open to social spending. A model in which care is shared between men and women proposes a more radical transformation than one based on state support or provision of childcare. But the evidence of those regimes that have achieved a degree of gender equality is that care has been provided and funded by governments as well as by households (Gornick and Meyers, 2003; Pascall and Lewis, 2004). Collective solutions are also a crucial part of the dual earner system in CEE countries. Our respondents expressed their partners' responsibility for childcare, but they raged about government irresponsibility and the need for state involvement in the circumstances of growing inequality and increasing pressure on them as workers. The Lisbon summit and the Social Policy Agenda could be seen as triggering a climate more favourable to more collective solutions, as social policy is seen as intrinsically connected to economic and employment policies, and official evidence is gathered, through the Open Method of Coordination, of the superiority of the Scandinavian 'active welfare states'. This would be particularly important for CEE countries whose gender model has been based on more collective solutions.

We ask about the implications of accession for gender models in CEE countries in terms of key aspects of gender regimes: paid work, care work, time and voice. The historic record of the European Union in each dimension will be examined, as well as the implications for gender equality in CEE countries as they join the European Union. Will membership of the European Union destroy, protect or develop the social supports that have made it possible for women in CEE countries to combine paid and unpaid work?

Gender equality in paid work?

The 1957 Treaty of Rome committed member states, under Article 119, to the principle that men and women should receive equal pay for equal work. This built gender equality into the European Union at the foundation. It also built in a connection with the European Union as a market, in its concern with a level playing field and fair competition, although discussion of rights was also part of the context (Shaw, 2002, p 216). It was the second wave of the women's movement in the 1970s that put the treaty commitment to use, stimulating legal testing and directives on equal pay (1975) and equal treatment at work (1976). In 1986, there followed directives on self-employment and occupational pensions. The Social Charter (1989) and the Social Chapter of the Maastricht Treaty (1992) brought further development of these core principles of the Treaty of Rome about equal pay for men and women. The 1997 Treaty of Amsterdam brought a crucial development in equality legislation, empowering the Council of Ministers to take action against discrimination based on sex, racial or ethnic origin, religion or belief, disability, age or sexual orientation. The European Court of Justice has been central in the development of gender equality law. It has often been seen as interpreting the equal pay principle expansively (Neilson, 1998; Walby, 1999), producing legislation of considerable scope that forces policy change on national governments and providing individuals with redress against them when governments fail (Mazey, 1998). While the European Court of Justice has often been seen as 'activist' in its developing understanding of indirect discrimination, for example in recognising the undervaluation of part-time work, it has taken a more restrictive view of unpaid care work, and has shown "little adaptation to the changed environment of gender mainstreaming" (Shaw, 2002, p 223).

The European employment policy brought gender equality into focus in 1997, making it one of the four pillars of its strategy, and adding gender mainstreaming in 1998. Childcare targets, and targets to reduce the gender pay gap substantially as well as the gender gaps in employment and unemployment are also now agreed by the European Council. According to von Wahl, a European equal employment regime has emerged (von Wahl, 2005, p 90). Rubery sees these developments as a significant pushing of equal opportunities up the agenda of the employment strategy. But she also identifies problems: in particular, the alternative – more economistic – conceptions of employment policy within other policy-making elements of the European Union, as well as varied employment regimes at the national level (Rubery, 2005). The "ups and downs of European gender equality policy" made gender equality into one of ten new guidelines in 2003, reducing its earlier prominence as one of the four pillars. There was also a shift towards integrating women into employment at the expense of gender equality in employment (Rubery et al, 2004).

While the legal framework of rights has tended to expand to produce a body of some scope, implementation is another question (Beveridge and Nott, 2002). Problems at national level make it hard for women to take up their rights: "The fragmented policy process, arduous legal procedures and scarce resources of equal-opportunity agencies (leading to insufficient financing and support of individual claimants) have hindered successful legal representation" (Ostner and Lewis, 1995, p 173). Such criticism of legally regulated rights is not confined to the European Union. Most accounts of national UK policy implementation of equal opportunities legislation have told the same story (Morris and Nott, 1991). Neither have national governments always hastened to meet their legal obligations and, even when they have, it has sometimes been in terms of levelling down. Furthermore, some states have had opt-outs from European Union legislation.

Making legal regulation work in practice is a serious problem. The processes of law are cumbersome and expensive and individuals tend to become locked in unequal struggles with employers or government departments. Legal institutions themselves tend to be male dominated, and while no one seeking greater equality between men and women would dispense with equality legislation, neither should they place too much faith in the ability of the law to bring it about. Such difficulties may be more exaggerated in CEE countries, disabled by their brief history of access to law in defence of individual freedoms, extreme constraints of economy, and minimal infrastructure in the form of equal opportunity commissions and legal aid. All the region's former communist countries have signed and ratified the 1979 United Nations Convention on the Elimination of All Forms of Discrimination against Women, but the development of machinery to implement it has been slow and there have been "few mechanisms to strengthen the prosecution of discriminatory actions against women" (UNICEF, 1999, p 17). New means by which central governments can monitor women's issues (for example, equal opportunities secretariats) have to work against a historic deficit of civil society institutions and social action to implement broad claims as rights for individuals (UNICEF, 1999, p 106; Pascall and Manning, 2000). The evidence from CEE countries is that few gender equality cases have reached the courts (Sloat, 2004, p 80), while "gender mainstreaming remains limited to formal statements that are not translated into practice" (Choluj and Neusuess, 2004, p 6).

Despite rights to gender equality being built into the constitution and legal practice of the European Union, women in Europe earn less than men, have less secure work, receive fewer benefits from work and have lower pensions in old age (Arber, 1999; Hantrais, 2000, p 113). Innovative legislation has not so far succeeded in containing gender inequalities, even in the rewards from paid employment. The gender pay gap in 2003 in the EU15, was 16%, and varied little between 1994 and 2001, despite the increasing profile of gender equality at European policy level. The gender pay gaps in CEE countries are varied: some countries, such as Slovenia with 11%, have maintained low pay gaps, but for others, going to market has meant a growing inequality between men and women, with a high of 24% in Estonia (see Chapter Two, Table 2.3). Policy for reducing these gender gaps is as critical in CEE countries as in Western Europe.

It has been argued that in the 1990s, the European Union's preoccupation with deregulating the labour market may have had more real impact on women than the extension of legislation to protect them (Rossilli, 1999). Similar points have been made about the

European Union's relationship with CEE countries, with early messages from the European Union being more concerned with developing markets than with protecting gender equalities (Ferge and Juhasz, 2004; Potucek, 2004). We have to ask whether the European Union as a single market is a powerful underlying force in the polarisation of incomes, security and the difference in advantages from work between men and women, and between women, as well as between other groups of socially included and excluded (Duncan, 1996).

Increasing women's labour market participation is a high priority of the European Commission, if mainly as a solution to demographic and economic problems. European Commission documents are now peppered with the problems of population: low fertility below replacement rates and the increasing numbers of the very old, are seen as the key social developments. "Maintaining the labour supply will increasingly depend on raising the activity and employment rates of women" (European Commission, 2003a, pp 11-13). The structural indicators show women's employment rate for the EU25 as 55.1%. CEE figures are not far from this average, with Estonia at 59% and Poland at 46%, and, in this case, still falling. The highest figure, for Sweden at 71.5%, shows just how serious women's employment situation is in the new CEE member states. As noted in Chapter Two, men's employment is also low in most CEE member states and only in the Czech Republic is there a gender gap in employment wider than the EU15 average. However, in this respect the current European Union preoccupation with increasing women's participation could be important to CEE countries (European Commission, 2004b). The interconnectedness of the economic and other domains is important here, and may increase the prospects for European Union influence on gender equality (Walby, 2004).

The concept of a European social model in which economic and social policy and employment policy support one another, as in the Social Policy Agenda (European Commission, 2000a, p 8), may show a climate useful to CEE countries. The Commission connects social quality, social cohesion, full employment and quality work to competitiveness and dynamism, and may justify social spending, and 'active welfare states' (European Commission, 2003a, p 26). To balance this, however, the emphasis in the most recent employment policy has been on women's participation in employment, rather than on low pay, or working time, which would affect employers (Rubery, 2005). Labour market participation is clearly important for women in CEE countries, but without increasing pay, it will not bring gender equality.

Gender equality in care work?

Paid employment has been central to European legislation and action for gender equality. Most hard law – the treaties and directives – has concerned rights attaching to paid work. Unpaid work is not covered by this approach:

> Students of gender issues have repeatedly stressed the problems of treating labour-market issues in isolation from the broader environment that encompasses gender relationships. The EU builds on a narrow notion of equality that implies treating working women like working men. EU law applies only to the working population or to people 'actively seeking employment'. Only the family concerns of continuously employed wage earners attract political attention. (Ostner and Lewis, 1995, p 159)

The European Court of Justice has been a force for wide interpretation of equal pay, but it has drawn the line to exclude unpaid work, arguing that "it was not the job of the Court to settle questions concerned with the organisation of the family or to alter the division of responsibility between the parents" (Ostner and Lewis, 1995, p 165). The maternity leave directive was enacted finally on health grounds rather than as an issue of gender equality. The Social Charter was about workers, not citizens.

State involvement in childcare has been a key source of variation between western welfare states (Gornick and Meyers, 2003). One part of the widening European Union agenda has been a concern with childcare, with accounting provision, establishing best practice and promoting policy learning (Moss and Brannen, 2003). CEE countries have a stronger tradition of state involvement in childcare but, for children under three years of age, many services have disappeared. Ferge and Juhasz comment on the lack of any support from the European Union accession process in this case. But not all has been lost since the transition: for 3- to 6-year-olds, kindergarten remains popular, especially in Hungary (See Chapter Two). The European employment strategy has led to childcare targets agreed at Barcelona (Rubery, 2005), in which childcare services should reach 90% of pre-school children and 33% of children aged under three. This may help to stem further losses, and rebuild some provision for the very young. The economic case for increasing women's labour market participation may be crucial here.

An alternative strategy is to develop policies to encourage fathers to care. The resolution on work–life balance, above, agreed by the European Council and the Ministers for Employment and Social Policy proposes a radically new gender model, in which the European Union will foster:

> the objective of balanced participation of men and women in family and working life, coupled with the objective of balanced participation of men and women in the decision making process and member states would adopt: reinforcing measures to encourage a balanced sharing between working men and women of the care to be provided for children, elderly, disabled or other dependent persons. (Council of the European Union, 2000)

These ideas of 'balanced sharing' of care work are a long way from the early equal opportunities agenda, in which women were offered equality on men's terms. They are not so far from the ideals expressed by our respondents and other current quantitative data (see Chapter Five). But how much force has a resolution? The trends are of widening agendas: from economy to social policy, from paid work to care work. But they are also of decreasing force, from directives down to recommendations and then finally resolutions. There are important symbolic changes in the switch from an individual opportunity perspective to one that encompasses fathers in childcare, but the impact in practice is uncertain.

The increasing trend towards seeing women's labour market participation as a solution to European problems, and the increasing evidence and understanding of the importance of welfare states in producing the environment in which they can: these may be important contributions towards collective solutions for care. But there is a danger that the employment agenda is prioritised over the equality agenda.

Gender equality in time?

Time policies are gaining ground, with the Combination Scenario in Holland, Daddy Months in Norway and Sweden, Time in the City beginning in Italy, and shorter working weeks agreed in several countries, notably the 35-hour week in France. The European Union, too, has working-time policies, with directives on working time, parental leave, and part-time work all legislated for in the 1990s. A directive establishing 14 weeks' maternity leave with 80% pay conditional on employment was agreed as a health issue in 1992. Whatever the mixed motives of these policies, they all have implications for the gender division of work, paid and unpaid. Current European Union policy limits weekly working hours to 48, while the European Council resolution referred to previously has a more radical purpose:

> to step up their efforts to ensure balanced participation of men and women in family and working life, notably through the organisation of working time and the abolition of conditions which lead to wage differentials between men and women. (Council of the European Union, 2000, para 5a)

No society in practice resembles this balanced participation: unequal paid working hours contribute to gender inequality in public and private. Can time policies enable the shift that would be needed in men's working lives to match women's working lives? And would such policies have anything to offer women in CEE countries, who now have relative equality in paid working time, with little part-time work but long working hours?

Shorter working weeks have fought with flexibility – that is employer flexibility – and in many countries, such as the UK – have lost. But they have been part of trades union demands in Western Europe, and have been won for French workers, with the Aubry laws reducing working hours to 35 per week, in larger firms from January 2000 and in smaller firms from January 2002. Interestingly from the point of view of CEE countries, this legislation was aimed primarily at reducing unemployment and sharing work between households rather than within them. But it has enabled parents to reconcile their working life and family life: the evidence of surveys is that people – especially parents – are highly satisfied, and reluctant to return to longer working weeks. Obviously, men may use the free time for leisure rather than for childcare, but there is some evidence that shorter working hours are associated with men's participation in meeting children's day-to-day needs (Boulin, 2000; Fagnani and Letablier, 2004).

Long working hours are clearly a major problem in CEE countries, currently averaging 44 a week (Paoli and Parent-Thirion, 2003) and making the reconciliation of paid work and family responsibility particularly problematic. A shorter working week for men in CEE countries could bring women out of unemployment, and enable the sharing of childcare within households. If it brings men or women out of unemployment it should bring benefits to poor households as well as to better-off ones. Of course, the low levels of income in CEE countries make these policies problematic, but reducing men's hours would make more contribution to work–life balance than the importation of part-time and flexible hours for women, enabling mothers to better reconcile the competing demands on them.

European Union policies themselves need to be reconciled if they are to offer serious change. The Working Time Directive sets a limit to the working week of 48 hours, but this is well above the hours that people would choose for themselves (Fagan and Warren, 2001), and well above a level which would enable parents to share childcare between them. Can we expect that the European Union will reduce the maximum hours in order to reach the balanced participation of the new millennium resolution? This is a real test point where the interests of men and women at work and the goal of social cohesion could compete with the interests of employers and the goals of competitiveness and dynamism. There is a wider social and economic case that goes beyond individual employers for enabling women's fuller participation in employment through policies reducing working hours for men and women. If European Union policy makers are to enable the 'balanced participation' in care, especially childcare, of the resolution, there will need to be more directives reducing working time from 48 hours.

Gender equality of voice?

Gender regimes are also systems of power, whether at the household level, in civil society or in European governance. To what extent do European policies enable the development of civil society and the participation of women in civil society and public politics?

The European Union has created a political forum in which interpretations of gender equality issues can be challenged and changed and from which policy networks can emerge (Hoskyns, 1996). It has also provided a forum for policy learning, and for pressure to develop policies supporting women in the labour market, work–life balance and so on, especially since Swedish membership has brought pressure to produce a more Scandinavian model in the rest of Europe (Duncan, 2002).

It has also developed policies for increasing women's participation in decision making. In 1996, Council Recommendation (2-12 1996) recommended member states to promote balanced participation of women and men in the decision-making process, improve the collection of data with which to monitor this, and promote participation at all levels in governmental bodies and committees. This has been followed up in *Towards a Community framework strategy on gender equality (2001-5)* (European Commission, 2000b), which is fostering the development of networks and understanding of electoral systems and monitoring the European Union's own decision-making processes. Thus the principles of parity democracy have "seeped into the European Union's portfolio of gender equality policies" (Shaw, 2002, p 224). The Open Method of Coordination brings social indicators on women and men in decision-making positions in politics, in the economy and in social life: these are now in a European database (Women's Computer Centre, Berlin). Europe has therefore stimulated the awareness of this issue, and enabled the collection of systematic comparative data. Unfortunately the data show that there is still far to go before women have a full part in decision making. To take the example of national parliamentary bodies: the percentage of seats in European Union member countries was 23%, with a low of 9% in Greece and a high of 45% in Sweden. There is not very good evidence here of the European Union's effectiveness so far in bringing about more equality in decision-making processes (European Commission, 2003a, p 156; see Chapter Two, Table 2.8 for CEE countries). Nor do the decision-making processes of the European Union stand up to critical scrutiny (Shaw, 2002).

In the new CEE member states, the European Union has had an identifiable impact in social and civil dialogue, democratising the policy-making processes and developing civil society. In Hungary, civil dialogue has been the most affected, bringing innovative legislation in 2003: "A path-breaking piece of legislation attempting to create genuine political legitimation for civil participation" (Ferge and Juhasz, 2004, p 239). This creates a civil fund, to be distributed by elected commissions. Similarly, Poland now has 37,000 voluntary organisations or foundations officially registered (60% estimated active), a new law (2003) on public utility and voluntary service to stimulate these organisations, and legislation to fund them through 1% taxation, with proceeds to organisations nominated by the individual taxpayer. Among these organisations are 300 women's organisations. As part of implementing accession, there has been a national programme of activities in aid of women, fighting unemployment and developing childcare.

While there are dangers that state-centred traditions will marginalise the social partners rather than include them, 'cognitive Europeanisation' and the new comparative statistical data are welcomed for bringing new discussions about gender and social inclusion (Lendvai, 2004).

These changes may enable women's participation in civil society and bring women more fully into public decision making. They are crucial for keeping issues of gender equality in work, care, time, income and voice on the agenda.

Conclusion

We have asked about the tension between social and economic objectives in Europe, historically, and at the point of enlargement in 2004. What are the implications of that tension for social policy and gender models in the new CEE member countries?

The gender model underpinning European social policy has widened from its focus on paid employment to working motherhood, childcare and parental leave (Hantrais, 2000, p 112), gender mainstreaming (Rees, 1999), working time, work–life balance, and the wider structures of power (Rossilli, 1997, p 65). This has politicised questions of responsibility for care, especially childcare, bringing official support for a 'new social contract on gender' in which men and women have work and family responsibilities, and which is to be supported by the European Union, the individual states and the social partners (Council of the European Union, Resolution 2000/C 218/02).

This model also lifts the level of intervention above the individual (which offered women equal opportunities if they could show themselves to be like men), to policies which involve households – and men in households – as well as social partners and civil society. Is this enough to bring support to a dual earner model in CEE countries and enough to bring the European spending that is also needed if CEE women – and men – are to do more than work?

There are numerous reasons for a cautious assessment of the likelihood of the European Union supporting women and gender equality in CEE.

First, the European Union is primarily a regulatory system rather than a system of taxation and spending. Social spending at the European level remains small, and there is no integration of welfare systems to match the integration of currencies and markets. The social aspects of the European social model, as distinct from the market ones, have been slow to emerge. This was true in the early period of the Common Market, and in the period before enlargement. The accession process began with the launching of the Copenhagen criteria of accession in 1993. These emphasised the development of market economies able to compete and be compatible with existing member states. Reforms of economic, political, legal and administrative systems came first in the Copenhagen criteria and with "genuine social goals at the bottom of the list" (Potucek, 2004, p 263). It was not until 2000, with the Lisbon strategy, that social policy resurfaced in the accession agenda, with the re-emergence of ideals of social cohesion and quality of life. This agenda was offered to the accession countries in 2002. It was therefore a crucial decade – from the beginning of the accession process – before social policy became a serious part of the accession agenda. Welfare state restructuring in the transition period was therefore dominated, not by the European social model, but by the World Bank and the International Monetary Fund. Economic policies stressed markets, and social policies stressed constraint and privatisation. CEE countries therefore join the European Union with a significant social deficit in terms of the Lisbon strategy and the European social model (Ferge and Juhasz, 2004; Potucek, 2004).

The economic policy of monetary management, the Stability and Growth Pact, has often been in conflict with the objectives of social cohesion and solidarity. The European Commission itself acknowledges problems of implementation in a report on the Lisbon strategy to the European Council: *Choosing to grow: Knowledge, innovation and jobs in a cohesive society* admits the need for "better integration of Lisbon strategy priorities into the Union's instruments and monitoring mechanisms for macroeconomic policy coordination" (European Commission, 2003b, p 33). This acknowledges the existence of different voices in different parts of the European Union policy world, with economic priorities often more narrowly defined than they are in the Lisbon strategy and the Social Policy Agenda

The tendency, while stretching the canvas of European Union social policy, has been to reduce its legal standing, moving from legally binding treaties and directives towards recommendations and resolutions and the Open Method of Coordination. There is plenty of room for doubt about the willingness of member states and social partners to implement European Union social policy.

Also the rhetoric of social Europe is much stronger than the reality. Again, in *Choosing to grow*, the Commission admonishes: "The credibility of the Lisbon reforms depends most on transforming policy declarations into action, allowing Member States to be judged by what they do and not just by what they say" (European Commission, 2003b, p 31).

What hope is there now for European Union gender policies that will sustain women's position in CEE countries? In the context of all the obstacles, pessimism about the gender equality project in Europe may be the more rational approach (Rubery, 2005). But there are perhaps three reasons for hope among the debris of rather defeated expectations in Central and Eastern Europe.

First is the currently very high profile of women's employment among the economic objectives of the European Union. Across Europe, low birth rates and ageing populations make women a source of untapped labour; high levels of education, especially in CEE countries, make them a valuable one. Increasing women's labour market participation seems the answer to every problem, but only if it is supported in such a way that they can have children too.

Second, the current development of the European social model is bringing measurement and recognition of the success of the Scandinavian, higher spending, version of the welfare state, in meeting economic and social objectives. This has been well known in the social policy literature, of course (Goodin, 1999). But the Commission itself is now producing data under the Open Method of Coordination, and officially and systematically highlighting the effectiveness of higher spending welfare models (European Commission, 2003a, 2003b). As commentators from CEE countries all note, this is tragically late in terms of the losses to public spending and services sustained during the transition from communism, about which the European social model has done very little. But the social model may be strengthening with social science supporting social Europe (Atkinson, 2003). As Szalai argues, in debate with Vobruba, European Union accession – if agreed on appropriate terms – offers the possibility of ending the "desertion of the state" and re-establishing its welfare functions (Szalai, 2003; Vobruba, 2003a, 2003b).

The third reason emerges out of this, in an understanding at the European Commission and Council level, that European economic goals need more than markets. The social aspects of the European social model are increasingly seen as supporting the economic ones. This instrumental view of social policies may have limitations and dangers (Ostner, 2000), but the present convergence is of ideals connecting competitiveness to quality of labour and quality of life. This may make a difference to women in CEE countries, whose high levels of education and employment fit with European solutions to economic problems, and with ambitions for raising the quality of work everywhere, but especially among women. This may bring support for measures to enable women's participation in the workplace, including support for changing working hours, control and flexibility with families rather than employers, and support for collective services –especially childcare services – that are necessary to a European social model that has women as equal partners.

EIGHT

Conclusion

What kind of gender regimes are emerging in the new CEE member states? We have argued that we need to understand the gender impact of welfare states in terms of gender differences in work, care, time, income and voice. But we also need to understand them in terms of different levels of intervention, and the extent to which social policies support gender equality at the social/collective level, in civil society and in households or whether social policies expect individuals to make gender equality for themselves. *Do women participate in social policies?*

The movement from collective solutions to more individual ones is an intrinsic part of the movement from communism. But does it also bring new gender differences in welfare? We have examined this in terms of key components of gender regimes, work, care, income, time and voice through a range of indicators such as gender gaps in pay, employment and unemployment, working time, part-time work, welfare systems' impact on poverty and the gender differences in exposure to poverty. In particular, we have looked at the extent of gender difference/gender equality on these measures, and how the new CEE member states compare with the EU15, and states representing particular positions on the dual earner/breadwinner spectrum, with Sweden at one end and Ireland and Malta at the other. In CEE countries, women's labour market participation has diminished, but so has men's; concomitantly, women's unemployment has increased, but so has men's. But in every country except the Czech Republic the gaps between women's and men's employment and unemployment rates are below the EU15 average and everywhere they are well below representative countries with a male breadwinner tradition. Women's working hours in the new CEE member states are also more similar to men's than in the EU15. In particular, there is a relative absence of part-time work, and it is less characteristically women's work than in the EU15 where women's part-time work contributes five times as much to total employment as men's. All of these statistical comparisons show less gender-differentiated work and working time.

The evidence of welfare transfers suggests that they are as successful in reducing women's risk of poverty as in reducing men's. In Estonia the gender gap in risk of poverty after transfers is 3% and compares with Ireland, but in all other CEE countries the gender gap after transfers is below the EU15 average, and in one case – Poland – is negative. The political arena shows women at a serious disadvantage, with a lack of participation in decision making: political representation at ministerial level and in Parliament is below the European Union average of 23%. But, decision making apart, on most indicators there is not a gender gulf approaching that in the traditionally male-breadwinner countries such as Ireland and Malta, and they are above average on these indicators in comparison with the EU15.

If reducing collective solutions to more individual ones is an intrinsic part of the transition from communism, it does involve key changes from the point of view of women and gender equality. Reducing support for working motherhood in terms of nurseries and kindergartens, leave entitlements, educational and cultural services for children is one key feature. The state no longer guarantees work, so transition also propels mothers into a competitive labour market in which motherhood is a competitive disadvantage. There is a change in the structure and financing of systems towards private sector solutions and towards means testing with more contingent and stigmatising benefits. The new freedoms bring new opportunities for women as well as men but these are unequally distributed. Some women are able to sustain working motherhood through well-paid jobs or family support (especially from grandmothers) but for many the loss of services has reduced their ability to combine paid work and family work. Radically reducing family size is one strategy parents are using in the context of these constraints, but it is also an indication of the pressures under which parents are managing work and family. The dual earner model of the communist years is less supported at the collective level as national governments reduce spending on services which support families. This brings major losses in the security of systems supporting parents.

There is some evidence of measures supporting extended parental leave, which may be seen as keeping mothers at home; however, there is no general development of policies to sustain women as dependants. Abortion legislation in Poland may carry the message that motherhood is a core responsibility for women but declining family size suggests that women are finding ways to avoid motherhood. And elsewhere in CEE countries women's reproductive rights are not challenged. The extension of insecurities makes labour market participation crucial for women. The dual earner model has suffered blows but is still embedded in economic and social structures, social welfare systems and everyday expectations.

We also address the question of how much we can see similarities or differences between the new CEE member states. What have our data shown about differences between the regimes of the new CEE member states in gender terms? Slovenia emerges on a number of indices as more gender equal than other CEE countries, with a low gender pay gap, high representation of women in decision-making positions in the civil service, paternity leave and benefits and equality of working hours. Hungary has strong provision for 3- to 6-year-olds and has enabled women to sustain their labour market participation much more effectively than Polish women, to the extent that some authors see different gender regimes emerging (Fodor et al, 2002, pp 486-7). In some ways Poland can be seen as the strongest case of a return to tradition, with the Roman Catholic Church playing a large role in decision making, legislation against abortion, high unemployment for women, and more limited and contingent support for parental leave, including means-tested family allowances and childcare benefits. But transition has not altered women's need for employment. Low wages mean that families are much more likely to suffer poverty if women are not in paid employment, and the desire for an income figures largely in accounts of women's need for jobs. The declining use of maternity leave, as described previously, shows women rejecting this model of motherhood in the face of labour market discrimination in Poland. Many respondents saw maternity and childcare leave as damaging in the economic and political climate, and spoke of early return to work to protect their jobs. A partnership or dual carer model of the family begins to appear in legislation, bringing more equal rights in the use of leave for fathers as well as mothers. Men are much less likely to take such leave than women, but these are important changes of principle towards equal rights to care and towards a partnership, dual carer model of the family. Poland's gender gaps in unemployment, employment and working time are not at all similar to those in the traditional male breadwinner regimes and on these indicators Poland is a middle-ranking CEE country.

If we turn to what these CEE countries have in common, first is the 40-year rule of communism that brought support for a dual earner system much earlier than elsewhere. The experience of transition, while it brings the possibility of different trajectories, has shared components: more political freedom and access to international ideas, but also economic shocks to the systems that supported working motherhood. European Union accession now brings a common set of pressures to develop civil society, support women's labour market participation and sign up to gender equality as an objective of national governments.

The dual earner tradition leaves women with a common expectation about their desire for employment as well as motherhood, as well as a need for employment to keep themselves and their children out of poverty. These are powerful common factors: they leave a gender system in work, income, time and care that is a more deeply rooted dual earner system than in most EU15 countries. On none of the indices we have used do the new CEE member states match Sweden, but neither have they changed in character to become male breadwinner societies such as Ireland or Malta. We see them as dual earner regimes but, after the transformation with its losses in social support for motherhood and for gender equality, they are more challenged dual earner regimes than the Scandinavian ones.

Inside Poland: is a welfare state possible after communism?

We argue that, even in Poland, the changes of the transition period have been more about the loss of collective provision supporting motherhood and dual earner households, rather than a change towards male breadwinner assumptions, with roles and resources differentiated by gender. The gender regimes of the new era frame the experience of our respondents as mothers in the transition period. Of course our respondents expressed every kind of view, including the liberal rejection of the 'nanny state'. But angry and principled responses about the responsibilities of governments, their duties to citizens and to families put the loss of collective services at the top of most mothers' agendas. Their rage was directed to governments more than to partners for the lack of resources, security, time for children and childcare, and their feeling of being neglected as mothers, and their anxieties about their children's care and futures.

The lack of feminist politics has been widely noted and we questioned this and what it might mean. Did the lack of organisations with an explicitly feminist agenda mean that women did not identify with issues of paid and unpaid work, the need for state support and the need for the state to support men's involvement in care? There was little sign of these citizens celebrating their freedom from the state. Their situation as parents of young children was often of being under great pressure of time, money and security for themselves and their children. The responses of mothers of young children in Poland were indeed not often explicitly feminist, but they shared an international feminist agenda in terms of the need for men to be responsible for children, and the need for governments' involvement in the welfare of children. Most responses suggest that parenting was not seen as an individual lifestyle choice, but as a social decision and responsibility, and one in which governments and men should share (Gornick and Meyers, 2003). Certainly, the overthrow of communism represented a rejection of one kind of government. But our respondents' rejection of authoritarianism did not equate to a rejection of government. Respondents were highly critical of the state's withdrawal from welfare and the support of families. The widening social divisions in Poland were seen as generating problems of disadvantage that could not be addressed by individual action. As our respondent Anna argued: "There are a lot of problems that only the authorities with their means can solve". Governments were seen as having a moral responsibility which they had abrogated.

High levels of women's unemployment, a discriminatory labour market, the Roman Catholic Church and legislation against abortion: these have led some commentators to diagnose a culture and polity in which motherhood is prioritised and men are very resistant to household work. But our respondents offer a more complex picture: in particular they take a strong stand about the responsibility of men in caring for children, and their accounts are of a significant change in the gender relations of households, a picture which is supported by emerging quantitative data from the European Foundation for the Improvement of Living and Working Conditions and shared across CEE countries (Paoli and Parent-Thirion, 2003). The accounts of parenting and of parental responsibility are not of gender equality; but they are of more gender equality than appears in Western Europe, and a rapid change from the traditional gender roles typically described in the former communist region and in Poland in particular.

If their accounts were not of gender equality in assumptions or practices about gender roles, especially parental roles, neither were they of a return to tradition. Our respondents' accounts of their households were of strong assumptions about men's responsibility for children and of more commitment to carrying this through into practice than in most accounts from the West. Respondents spoke of men's responsibility as part of the decision to have children: "If parents undertake a decision to conceive a child, then the responsibility for bringing it up rests on both of them" (Róża); of men's own sense of obligation and increasing competence, compared with their own fathers: "A man did not touch children. ... My husband devotes a lot of time to our child. If he could he would feed her" (Aneta). These accounts suggested a shared sense of responsibility, while the division of labour in practice was still unequal. There was little sense from households that they were seeking traditional gender roles or relationships of dependency within partnerships.

The accounts of the parents we interviewed suggest that there is some contradiction in Poland between the gender assumptions of government and the gender assumptions in households with young children. Governments have reduced support for working motherhood; restricting abortions shows them in this respect prioritising traditional motherhood over working motherhood. Most of our respondents wanted employment for themselves as well as for their partners, most assumed men's responsibility for care, and most assumed that government policy should support this partnership model of the family, not only dual earner but also dual carer.

The pleas for more state intervention particularly emphasise a need for control over working time and support for childcare. One respondent, Eleanora, exemplified the argument for an idea of citizenship involving state responsibilities towards parents in the form of school, pre-school and cultural centres: "The state is obliged to take responsibility for the development of the younger generation, to render knowledge accessible, to make children and young people equal. Worse-off parents cannot secure the development of a child by themselves". When respondents discussed social policies they tended to assume that state support should involve support for motherhood rather than for fatherhood or radically changed gender roles. But their accounts did not suggest the move back to the male breadwinner family that is sometimes assumed. These households were not havens of gender equality but they have radically changed in the course of transition from communism. Poland has experienced more challenges to the dual earner tradition than elsewhere in the former communist region. While our respondents offered a variety of accounts of households, they make room for the interpretation that men have compensated at home for the withdrawal of the state from family support. This picture fits with the quantitative account of working conditions in the then accession countries given by the European Foundation for the Improvement of Living and Working Conditions (Paoli and Parent-Thirion, 2003).

State policies in Poland are therefore in contradiction to the ideas and ideals of mothers in households, and perhaps of their partners, insofar as we can read them. Women's accounts are very critical of the state's position on families, and of the emptiness of government family policies. As argued by our respondent Urszula: "A woman who gives birth to a child should be favoured, and this does not happen. On the contrary, she is persecuted". Their accounts of themselves and their households are of commitment to paid work and to sharing care for children. This includes partners who accept responsibility for children, even if not equal responsibility for childcare. The ideal of a return to the male breadwinner model of the family is also at odds with movements in the rest of Europe towards dual earner households, an increasing women's participation in the labour market. Care work is increasingly recognised in the European Union as a barrier to women's paid work, and the male breadwinner model as an obstacle to gender equality. It may be particularly difficult in the post-communist countries to argue for a welfare state, but most respondents were very clear about the need for the kind of support to parenting that they had themselves experienced as children: namely kindergartens, holidays, cultural activities after school, and especially security of care through time. They saw childcare as a family responsibility, especially mothers' responsibility, but were also powerful advocates of a shared model of parenting, with fathers' responsibility and the states' responsibility supporting their own acceptance of their obligations as mothers.

What prospects are there for change, either through civil society, national politics or the European Union?

Freedom from authoritarian government has brought democratic involvement and new developments in civil society across the region. But there is strong evidence that men have benefited more than women, especially in terms of participation in formal politics. There is some development in women's civil action: a number of active groups have formed but they are not yet a major force. Some of our respondents had been active in groups of various kinds; most were angry but not politically active. The dominance of men in politics and the relative quiet of civil society have allowed very dramatic changes to happen to women, in particular, their reduced welfare coverage and the declining value of support to working parenthood. Such changes are not uniform across post-communist countries, and have been most radical in Poland where male authority has been reinforced by Roman Catholic authority, weakening women's position and the dual earner model of the family. Losses have occurred in state support for parents as workers: a tradition of women's place in public life has been undermined.

But among households themselves the need for both men and women to earn remains. We found respondents doing their own benchmarking (Wickham, 2002), comparing their situations with Swedish women. Membership of the European Union brings access to networks which may enable sharing of ideas among parents as well as among academics (Pető, 2004). These may support developing ideals of partnership in care, which are stronger than has been generally recognised.

Will joining Europe bring benefits to CEE countries in terms of gender equality?

The Lisbon strategy, the Social Policy Agenda, the Open Method of Coordination and national action plans have focused attention on increasing employment, especially quality employment and especially women's employment. The European Commission sees these as promoting economic growth and competitiveness and addressing the problems of ageing populations. Women's employment is now a core concern of the European Union. The concerns of the European Union have concomitantly widened, extending from issues of gender at work, towards covering broader issues of the differences behind the experience of men and women at work. Working parenthood has become subject to recommendations such as the one on childcare. Directives on working time and on parental leave bring rights enabling women's participation in the labour market. The European Union resolution on work–life balance agrees the need for a balance for both parents. Scandinavian 'active welfare states' with high levels of social spending and support for parents are now demonstrably better at achieving European Union goals, with the structural indicators providing evidence of their superiority at increasing quality employment, social cohesion and economic growth.

The literature shows very mixed feelings about the success of European Union policies in practice, but there are some grounds for optimism about the impact of accession on gender politics in European Union countries. European Union accession has brought some support for developing civil society in Hungary and Poland, supporting innovative legislation to fund new organisations and consultative processes with social partners. There is evidence (see Chapter Seven) that the European legislation has brought gender issues into the public arena, protecting against further damage to the systems supporting women's employment. And current debates in the European Union, where work–life balance is a live and important issue, may be illuminated and changed by the presence of CEE members, in that the balance of Europe itself will change with a presence of CEE members, shifting the balance from male breadwinner towards dual earner gender regimes.

Contemporary debates about gender equality and welfare regimes

There is an emerging consensus that gender equality depends on care as well as paid employment, and on men changing as well as women. Ideas for changing men's working lives as well as women's, which would once have been the preserve of feminist social policy, have become part of the mainstream: "True gender equality will not come about unless, somehow, men can be made to embrace a more feminine life-course" (Esping-Andersen et al, 2002, p 95). Policies to produce this more feminine life-course have been proposed for CEE countries in academic commentary:

> To effectively counteract discrimination against women, changes in that unfriendly environment are imperative. Social policy solutions should recognise the need for dual family earnings and support choices regarding the division of labor between paid and unpaid activities on the part of both parents. The past regulations on leaves due to family reasons, which gave some privileges to women, were in fact gender-oriented. Childrearing and household activities in general ought to be considered as an investment in social capital – defined as resources inherent in family and in community social organisation for developing human capital of family and community members. (Kotowska, 1995, p 87)

> Stressing the importance of male parental roles would strengthen family ties and enhance children's socialisation process while, at the same time, allowing married women with children to pursue their careers. (Łobodzińska, 2000, p 67)

These ideas begin to appear in the literature of the international agencies as well. A paper about the CEE countries, written for the United Nations Economic Commission (UNECE) for Europe argues that "the reformed system of social protection should create conditions to provide women and men with equal choices between paid work and family. This involves redistribution of responsibilities not only among social partners but also within a family" (Ruminska-Zimny, 2002, p 9).

The European Council has committed member states, through its new millennium resolution, to policies bringing gender equality into private life as well as public (Council of the European Union, 2000). Thus all European governments are committed in principle to work–life balance policies that would support men as carers in the family as well as women as employees in the labour market. The European Union's work–life balance policy will not by itself bring transformation of traditional roles – because national governments will often ignore it – but it will lend support to changes that are happening for other reasons.

There is international agreement about gender equality as an objective of national governments and international agencies; everywhere there are policies aiming to bring women into paid work and politics on a similar basis to men. And everywhere, to some extent, these have failed. CEE countries have had, in this context, some of the most successful, with a strong history of women's participation in paid employment and of structures to support it through care services and parental leave. But these are threatened in the new competitive environment by a falling public expenditure and also by market forces. There is little protection in Poland against discrimination, and there are many possibilities for women to lose out in jobs, security and income: policies which offer women protection to bear and care for children may, in capitalist competitive economies, make them vulnerable to discrimination. Post-communist countries are particularly weak in systems of protection of individual rights, and women are particularly exposed to the cold draft of market forces.

The proposal to feminise men's lives is a proposal to bring gender equality at a deeper level, in parenting as well as in employment, in households as well as in the labour market. It is also a proposal to bring care work to the forefront of public policy, and to make having children and looking after them, possible again. Most of our respondents were looking for ways to bend their own lives to meet their children's needs rather than to bend their husbands' lives: few of our respondents made social policy proposals that conformed with this idea. But they were very aware of the problems resulting from such policies: that women were seen as bad employees, found it difficult to go back to work after parental leave, and were discriminated against. The evidence they offered about the treatment of mothers, when governments and employers expect only mothers to do childcare, adds weight to the emerging view in international agencies as well as in academic contributions: regimes need to support men's care work if they are really to pursue gender equality.

The literature has painted fathers in Poland as very traditional in orientation to the family, and very reluctant to see fatherhood as care. Under communism, gender regimes were indeed characterised by a dual earner system in employment and traditional model of care work in families. The closure of civil society allowed very limited access to outside sources of change, in particular to the women's movement. The very different account of fathers offered by the respondents (and supported in new quantitative data) suggests that a dual carer model may be developing among young parents, perhaps in response to the radically changing and demanding experience of the transition period. Although clearly households did not enforce gender equality entirely there was a widespread sense that the current generation of young fathers had no 'complexes' about caring for their children. But they did lack support from their governments. There was little evidence of government action against employers who discriminated against women, or regulating working time so that childcare could be more equally shared, or promoting equality of parental leave. Men in power in Poland appear to be offering policies that accord with the expectations of their own generation rather than those of their sons and daughters. Men's responsibility for care and willingness to care were among the clearest messages to come from our Polish mothers.

Transition from communism is synonymous with changes in the state and welfare services. Welfare services and employment structures that supported women's employment under communism brought gender regimes in which working motherhood was assumed and in which gender equality in public life was greater than in most countries of Western Europe in the second half of the 20th century. Transition has brought reductions in public expenditure and reductions in mothers' ability to sustain continuous working lives. In this respect, regimes in Central and Eastern Europe have lost some of their edge over the West. But we have also asked what is the legacy of 'statist feminism' in terms of women's relationship with the state now? It is clear that women are under-represented in formal politics. There may also have been some reluctance to identify with 'feminist' ideas. But transformation has brought developments in civil society that make it more possible for people to find their own solutions. The new transition into the European Union brings support for developments in civil society and now puts gender equality on the political agenda. The Social Policy Agenda, with women's employment at the forefront of European Commission policies for economic growth and social cohesion, makes it more likely that women in the former communist countries can find the political impetus and support to sustain collective systems of care. The importance of those systems, and the obligations of the wider society to children and to their parents, were the strongest message from our respondents: they could see no other way to meet children's needs or their own needs for employment and incomes. Rejection of the communist past did not amount to rejection of state or collective solutions: on the contrary, the respondents expressed a strong sense of the moral responsibilities of governments to themselves and their children.

References

Abrahamson, P. (1999) 'The welfare modelling business', *Social Policy and Administration*, vol 33, no 4, pp 394-415.

Alber, J. and Fahey, T. (2004) *Perceptions of living conditions in an enlarged Europe*, Dublin: European Foundation for the Improvement of Living and Working Conditions.

Alber, J. and Köhler, U. (2004) *Health and care in an enlarged Europe*, Luxembourg: Office for Official Publications of the European Communities.

Arber, S. (1999) 'Gender inequalities in European societies today', in T. Boje, B. van Steebergen and S. Walby (eds) *European societies: Fusion or fission?*, London and New York: Routledge.

Atkinson, A.B. (2003) 'Social Europe and social science', *Social Policy and Society*, vol 2, no 4, pp 261-72.

Balcerzak-Paradowska, B. (1995) 'Polityka społeczna na rzecz rodziny w Polsce' (Social policy towards the family), in S. Golinowska and B. Balcerzak-Paradowska (eds) *Rodziny w Polsce: Ewolucja, zróżnicowanie, okres transformacji (Families in Poland: Evolution, differentiation, transformation period)*, Warszawa: IPiSS, pp 51-72.

Balcerzak-Paradowska, B. (1997) 'Publiczne instytucje usług społecznych a rodzina' ('Public institutions providing social services and the family'), in *Partnerstwo w rodzinie i na rzecz rodziny (Partnership in the family and for the family)*, Warszawa: IPiSS, pp 55-69.

Balcerzak-Paradowska, B. (2003) 'Możliwość godzenia obowiązków zawodowych z rodzinnymi' ('Possibilities of combining family and work duties'), in B. Balcerzak-Paradowska (ed) *Praca kobiet w sektorze prywatnym: Szanse i bariery (Work of women in the private sector: Opportunities and barriers)*, Warszawa: IPiSS, pp 305-22.

Balcerzak-Paradowska, B. (2004a) 'Social policy, legal and institutional provisions: an incentive or barrier to hiring women?', in *Gender and economic opportunities in Poland: Has transition left women behind?*, Warsaw: The World Bank, Report no 29205, pp 18-44

Balcerzak-Paradowska, B. (2004b) *Rodzina i polityka rodzinna na przełomie wieków (Family and family policy at the turn of century)*, Warszawa: IPiSS.

Balcerzak-Paradowska, B., Hebda-Czaplicka, I. and Kołaczek, B. (2003a) 'Zmiany własnościowe w polskiej gospodarce: rozwój sektora prywatnego i jego wpływ na rynek pracy' (Ownership changes in the Polish economy: development of the private sector and its influence on the labour market), in B. Balcerzak-Paradowska (ed) *Praca kobiet w sektorze prywatnym: Szanse i bariery (Work of women in the private sector: Opportunities and barriers)*, Warszawa: IPiSS, pp 23-92.

Balcerzak-Paradowska, B., Głogosz, D., Hebda-Czaplicka, I. and Kołaczek, B. (2003b) 'Przekształcenia własnościowe a aktywność zawodowa kobiet: zmiany i uwarunkowania' (Ownership changes and economic activity of women: changes and conditions), in B. Balcerzak-Paradowska (ed) *Praca kobiet w sektorze prywatnym: Szanse i bariery (Work of women in the private sector: Opportunities and barriers)*, Warszawa: IPiSS, pp 93-155.

Bambra, C. (2004) 'The worlds of welfare: illusory and gender blind?', *Social Policy and Society*, vol 3, no 3, pp 201-12.

Beck, U. and Beck-Gernsheim, E. (2002) *Individualization: Institutionalized individualism and its social and political consequences*, London and New York: Sage Publications.

Beskid, L. (1996) 'Bezrobocie kobiet' (Unemployment of women), in J. Sikorska (ed) *Kobiety i ich mężowie (Women and their husbands)*, Warszawa: IFiS PAN, pp 101-16.

Beveridge, F. and Nott, S. (2002) 'Mainstreaming: a case for optimism and cynicism', *Feminist Legal Studies*, vol 10, no 3, pp 299-311.

Beveridge, F. and Shaw, J. (2002) 'Introduction: mainstreaming gender in European public policy', *Feminist Legal Studies*, vol 10, no 3, pp 209-12.

Björnberg, U. and Sass, J. (1997) *Families with small children in Eastern and Western Europe*, Aldershot: Ashgate.

Bornschier, V. and Ziltener, P. (1999) 'The revitalization of Western Europe and the politics of the "social" dimension', in T. Boje, B. van Steebergen and S. Walby (eds) *European societies: Fission or fusion?*, London and New York: Routledge.

Boulin, J.-Y. (2000) *Actual and preferred working hours in the EU: National background for France*, Dublin: European Foundation for the Improvement of Living and Working Conditions.

Bryman, A. (1988) *Quantity and quality in social research*, London and New York: Routledge.

Buckley, M. (1997) *Post-Soviet women: From the Baltic to Central Asia*, Cambridge: Cambridge University Press.

Camilleri-Cassar, F. (2005) *Gender equality in Maltese social policy?: Graduate women and the male breadwinner model*, Malta: Agenda.

Castles, F.G. (2003) 'The world turned upside down: below replacement fertility, changing preferences and family-friendly public policy in 21 OECD countries', *Journal of European Social Policy*, vol 13, pp 209-27.

CBOS (Centrum Badania Opinii Społecznej [Public Opinion Research Centre]) (1993) *Postawy wobec pracy i aspiracje zawodowe kobiet (Attitudes towards work and professional aspirations of women)*, Research report, Warszawa: Public Opinion Research Centre.

CBOS (1996) *Polityka państwa wobec rodziny: Ocena, społeczne postulaty (Policy of the state towards the family: Assessment and social postulate)*, Research report, Warszawa: Public Opinion Research Centre.

CBOS (1997a) *Kobiety o podziale obowiązków domowych w rodzinie (Division of housework in the family: The views of women)*, Research report, Warszawa: Public Opinion Research Centre.

CBOS (1997b) *Aspiracje zawodowe kobiet a życie rodzinne (Professional aspiration of women and family life)*, Research report, Warszawa: Public Opinion Research Centre.

CBOS (1998) *Wychowanie dzieci w rodzinie i opieka nad nimi (Upbringing and care of children in families)*, Research report, Warszawa: Public Opinion Research Centre.

CBOS (2000) *Sytuacja polskich rodzin: Ocena i postulaty (Situation of Polish families: Assessment and postulates)*, Research report, Warszawa: Public Opinion Research Centre.

Central Statistical Office (2001) *Podstawowe informacje o rozwoju demograficznym Polski w latach 1990-2000 (Basic information on demographic development of Poland)*, Warszawa: GUS (Central Statistical Office).

Central Statistical Office (2003a) *Dzieci w Polsce (Children in Poland)*, Warszawa: GUS (Central Statistical Office) and Biuro Rzecznika Praw Dziecka (Bureau of the Spokesman of Children Rights).

Central Statistical Office (2003b) *Gospodarstwa domowe i rodziny (Households and families)*, Warszawa: GUS (Central Statistical Office).

Central Statistical Office (2003c) *Rocznik Demograficzny (Demographic yearbook of Poland)*, Warszawa: GUS (Central Statistical Office).

Central Statistical Office (2004a) *Rocznik Demograficzny (Demographic yearbook of Poland)*, Warszawa: GUS (Central Statistical Office).

Central Statistical Office (2004b) *Kobiety i mężczyźni na rynku pracy (Women and men in the labour market)*, Warszawa: GUS (Central Statistical Office).

Choluj, B. and Neusuess, C. (2004) 'EU enlargement in 2004: East-West priorities and perspectives from women inside and outside the EU', UNIFEM discussion paper.

Corrin, C. (1992) *Superwomen and the double burden: Women's experience of change in Central and Eastern Europe and the former Soviet Union*, London: Scarlet Press.

Council of the European Union (2000) Resolution of the Council and of the Ministers for Employment and Social Policy on the balanced participation of women and men in family and working life, *Official Journal* 2000C 218/02.

Council of the European Union (2004) Joint report by the Commission and the Council on social inclusion, Brussels: Council of the European Union.

Cousins, C. and Tang, N. 'Working time, gender and family in west and central east Europe', unpublished Working Paper, Hertfordshire: University of Hertfordshire.

Creighton, C. (1999) 'The rise and decline of the "male breadwinner family" in Britain', *Cambridge Journal of Economics*, vol 23, pp 519-41.

Crompton, R. (ed) (1999) *Restructuring gender relationships and employment: The decline of the male breadwinner*, Oxford: Oxford University Press.

Daly, M. (ed) (2001) *Care work: The quest for security*, Geneva: International Labour Office.

Daly, M. and Rake, K. (2003) *Gender and the welfare state*, Cambridge: Polity Press.

de la Porte, C. and Pochet, P. (2004) 'The European employment strategy: existing research and remaining questions', *Journal of European Social Policy*, vol 14, no 1, pp 71-8.

Doniec, R. (2001) *Rodzina wielkiego miasta (The family of a large city)*, Kraków: Wydawnictwo Uniwersytetu Jagiellońskiego.

Duch-Krzystoszek, D. (1996) 'O podziale władzy i obowiązków w rodzinie' (Division of power and duties in the family), in J. Sikorska (ed) *Kobiety i ich mężowie* (*Women and their husbands*), Warszawa: IFiS PAN, pp 137-57.

Duncan, S. (1996) 'Obstacles to a successful equal opportunities policy in the European Union', *European Journal of Women's Studies*, vol 3, no 4, pp 399-422.

Duncan, S. (2002) 'Policy discourses on "reconciling work and life" in the EU', *Social Policy and Society*, vol 1, no 4, pp 305-14.

Einhorn, B. (1993) *Cinderella goes to market: Citizenship, gender and women's movements in East Central Europe*, London: Verso.

EISS (European Institute of Social Security) (2002) *MISSCEEC II (Mutual information system on social protection in the Central and Eastern European countries)*, Leuven: EISS.

Erler, G.A. and Sass, J. (1997) 'Family policy measures – the parents' view', in U. Björnberg and J. Sass (eds) *Families with small children in Eastern and Western Europe*, Aldershot: Ashgate.

Esping-Andersen, G. (1990) *The three worlds of welfare capitalism*, Cambridge: Polity Press.

Esping-Andersen, G. and Micklewright, J. (1991) 'Welfare state models in OECD countries: an analysis for the debate in Central and Eastern Europe', in G.A. Cornia and S. Sipos (eds) *Children and the transition to the market economy*, Aldershot: Avebury Publishing, pp 35-68.

Esping-Andersen, G., Gallie, D., Hemerijck, A. and Myles, J. (2001) *A new welfare architecture for Europe?*, Report submitted to the Belgian presidency of the European Union, Brussels: Commission of the European Communities.

Esping-Andersen, G., Gallie, D., Hemerijck, A. and Myles, J. (2002) *Why we need a new welfare state*, Oxford: Oxford University Press.

European Commission (2000a) *Social Policy Agenda: Communication from the Commission to the Council, the European Parliament, the Economic and Social Committee and the Committee of the Regions*, Luxembourg: Office for Official Publications of the European Communities.

European Commission (2000b) *Towards a Community framework strategy on gender equality (2001-05)*, Brussels: Commission of the European Communities.

European Commission (2003a) *The social situation in the European Union (2003)*, Luxembourg: Office for Official Publications of the European Communities.

European Commission (2003b) *Choosing to grow: Knowledge, innovation and jobs in a cohesive society*, Report to the spring European Council, 21 March (2003) on the Lisbon strategy of economic, social and environmental renewal, Luxembourg: Office for Official Publications of the European Communities.

European Commission (2004a) *The social situation in the European Union (2004)*, Luxembourg: Office for Official Publications of the European Communities.

European Commission (2004b) *Delivering Lisbon: Reforms for the enlarged Union (COM 2004)*, Report from the Commission to the spring European Council, Brussels: Commission of the European Communities.

European Commission (2005) *The Social A genda 2005-10*, Luxembourg: Office for Official Publications of the European Communities.

Fagan, C. and Warren, T. (2001) *Gender, employment and working-time preferences in Europe*, Report for the European Foundation for the Improvement of Living and Working Conditions, Luxembourg: Office of Official Publications of the European Communities.

Fagnani, J. and Letablier, M.T. (2004) 'Work and family-life balance: the impact of the 35-hour laws in France', *Work, Employment and Society*, vol 18, no 3, pp 551-72.

Fahey, T. and Spéder, S. (2004) *Fertility and family issues in an enlarged Europe*, Luxembourg: Office for Official Publications of the European Communities.

Fajth, G. (1996) 'Family support policies in Central and Eastern Europe', National Academy of Sciences and National Research Council Task Force on Economies in Transition Workshop, Washington, DC.

Ferber, M. and Kuiper, E. (eds) (2004) 'Feminist economic inquiry in Central and Eastern Europe', *Feminist Economics*, vol 10, no 3, pp 81-118.

Ferber, M. and Raabe, P. (2003) 'The Czech Republic', in L. Walter (ed) *Women's issues worldwide*, Westport, CT: Greenwood Press.

Ferge, Z. (1997a) 'The changed welfare paradigm – the individualization of the social', *Social Policy and Administration*, vol 31, no 1, pp 20-44.

Ferge, Z. (1997b) 'A Central European perspective on the social quality of Europe', in T.W. Beck, L. Maesen and A. Walker (eds) *The social quality of Europe*, The Hague/London/Boston: Kluwer Law International, pp 165-81.

Ferge, Z. (1997c) 'The perils of the welfare state's withdrawal', *Social Research*, vol 64, no 4, pp 1381-94.

Ferge, Z. (1998) 'Women and social transformation in Central-Eastern Europe: the "old left" and the "new right"', in the Social Policy Association's *Social Policy Review*, no 10, pp 217-36.

Ferge, Z. (2001a) 'Welfare and "ill-fare" system in Central-Eastern Europe', in R. Sykes, P. Prior and B. Palier (eds) *Globalization and European welfare states*, Basingstoke: Palgrave Macmillan.

Ferge, Z. (2001b) 'Disquieting quiet in Hungarian social policy', *International Social Security Review*, vol 54, no 2-3, pp 107-26.

Ferge, Z. (2002) 'European integration and the reform of social security in the accession countries', *European Journal of Social Quality*, vol 3, no 1, pp 9-25.

Ferge, Z. and Juhasz, G. (2004) 'Accession and social policy: the case of Hungary', *Journal of European Social Policy*, vol 14, no 3, pp 233-51.

Ferge, Z. and Tausz, K. (2002) 'Social security in Hungary: a balance sheet after twelve years', *Social Policy and Administration*, vol 36, no 2, pp 176-99.

Firlit-Fesnak, G. (1997a) 'Kobiety i mężczyźni w rolach rodzinnych i zawodowych: marzenia o partnerstwie a żywotność tradycji' (Women's and men's family and professional roles: dreams about partnership and the strength of tradition), in *Partnerstwo w rodzinie i na rzecz rodzin (Partnership in the family and for the family)*, Warszawa: IPiSS, pp 21-31.

Firlit-Fesnak, G. (1997b) 'Polish families in the transformation period', in U. Björnberg and J. Sass (eds) *Families with small children in Eastern and Western Europe*, Aldershot: Ashgate, pp 143-58.

Fodor, E. (1997) 'Gender in transition: unemployment in Hungary, Poland, and Slovakia', *East European Politics and Societies*, vol 11, no 3, pp 470-500.

Fodor, E. (2002) 'Gender and the experience of poverty in Eastern Europe and Russia after 1989', *Communist and Post-Communist Studies*, vol 35, no 4, pp 369-82.

Fodor, E., Glass, C., Kawachi, J. and Popescu, L. (2002) 'Family policies and gender in Hungary, Poland, and Romania', *Communist and Post-Communist Studies*, vol 35, no 4, pp 475-90.

Förster, M.F. and Tóth, I.J. (2001) 'Child poverty and family transfers in the Czech Republic, Hungary and Poland', *Journal of European Social Policy*, vol 11, no 4, pp 324-41.

Fraser, N. (1997) *Justice interruptus: critical reflections on the 'post-socialist' condition*, London and New York: Routledge.

Fudała, T. (1996) 'Skala polskiego ubóstwa' (The scale of Polish poverty), *Problemy Rodziny*, no 4, pp 9-11.

Funk, N. and Mueller, M. (eds) (1993) *Gender politics and post-communism: Reflections from Eastern Europe and the former Soviet Union*, London and New York: Routledge.

Fuszara, M. (1993) 'Abortion and the formation of the public sphere in Poland', in N. Funk and M. Mueller (eds) *Gender politics and post-communism: Reflections from Eastern Europe and the former Soviet Union*, London and New York: Routledge, pp 241-52.

Fuszara, M. (1994) 'Market economy and consumer rights: the impact on women's everyday lives and employment', *Economic and Industrial Democracy*, vol 15, no 1, pp 75-87.

Fuszara, M. (1997) 'Women's movements in Poland', in C. Kaplan, S. Keates, and J.W. Wallach (eds) *Transitions, environments, translations: Feminisms in international politics*, London and New York: Routledge, pp 128-42.

Fuszara, M. (2000a) *Gender equality measures in Poland – is there a chance to introduce them?*, Ljubljana: The Peace Institute.

Fuszara, M. (2000b) 'New gender relations in Poland in the 1990s', in S. Gal and G. Kligman (eds) *Reproducing gender: Politics, publics, and everyday life after socialism,* Princeton, NJ: Princeton University Press.

Fuszara, M. (2000c) *The new gender contract in Poland,* Vienna: IWM (Institute for Human Sciences).

Fuszara, M. (2000d) 'Feminism, the new millennium and ourselves: a Polish view', *Signs*, vol 25, no 4, pp 1069-75.

Gal, S. and Kligman, G. (2000) *Reproducing gender: Politics, publics, and everyday life after socialism*, Princeton, NJ: Princeton University Press.

Gal, S. and Kligman, G. (2004) 'Reproduction as politics in East-Central Europe', *Nouvelles Questions Feministes*, vol 23, no 2, pp 10 et seq.

Gershuny, J. (2000) *Changing times: Work and leisure in post-industrial society*, Oxford: Oxford University Press.

Gershuny, J. and Sullivan, O. (2003) 'Time use, gender, and public policy regimes', *Social Politics*, vol 10, no 2, pp 205-28.

Gładzicka-Janowska, A. (2003) 'Czas pracy w Polsce na tle Unii Europejskiej' (Time of work in Poland and the European Union), *Wiadomości Statystyczne*, no 1, pp 28-39.

Glass, C. and Kawachi, J. (2001) 'Winners or losers of the reforms: gender and unemployment in Hungary and Poland', *Review of Sociology of the Hungarian Sociological Association*, vol 7, no 2, pp 109-40.

Głogosz, D. (1997) 'Organizacje pozarządowe partnerem dla rodziny' ('Non-governmental organisations – partners for the family'), in *Partnerstwo w rodzinie i na rzecz rodziny (Partnership in the family and for the family)*, Warszawa: IPiSS, pp 70-7.

Golinowska, S. (1995a) 'Historyczny zarys formowania się rodziny w Polsce' (Family formation in Poland: brief historical approach), in S. Golinowska and B. Balcerzak-Paradowska (eds) *Rodziny w Polsce: Ewolucja, zróżnicowanie, okres transformacji (Families in Poland: Evolution, differentiation, transformation period)*, Warszawa: IPiSS, pp 17-24.

Golinowska, S. (1995b) 'Przemiany w warunkach życia polskich rodzin w okresie transformacji' (Poland's family living-condition changes in the transfomation period), in S. Golinowska and B. Balcerzak-Paradowska (eds) *Rodziny w Polsce: Ewolucja, zróżnicowanie, okres transformacji (Families in Poland: Evolution, differentiation, transformation period)*, Warszawa: IPiSS, pp 243-56.

Goodin, R.E., Heady, B., Muffels, R. and Dirven, H.-J. (1999) *The real worlds of welfare capitalism*, Cambridge: Cambridge University Press.

Gornick, J.C. and Meyers, M.K. (2003) *Families that work: Policies for reconciling parenthood and employment*, New York: Russell Sage Foundation.

Gospodarka (2004) 'Dlaczego kobiety zarabiają mniej? Analiza sytuacji w Polsce i w Unii Europejskie' (Why do women earn less? Analysis of the situation in Poland and European Union), *Gospodarka*, no 3(472), pp 65-9.

Goven, J. (2000) 'New Parliament, old discourse? The parental leave debate in Hungary', in S. Gal and G. Kligman (eds) *Reproducing gender: Politics, publics, and everyday life after socialism*, Princeton, NJ: Princeton University Press, pp 286-306.

Graniewska, D. and Balcerzak-Paradowska, B. (2003) 'Praca zawodowa – rodzina w opiniach respondentek' (Economic activity – family according to respondents), in B. Balcerzak-Paradowska (ed) *Praca kobiet w sektorze prywatnym: Szanse i bariery (Work of women in the private sector: Opportunities and barriers)*, Warszawa: IPiSS, pp 286-304.

Haas, A., Kawachi, J. and Laas, A. (2003) 'Estonia', in L. Walter (ed) *Women's issues worldwide: Europe*, Westport, CT: Greenwood Press.

Haney, L. (2002) *Inventing the needy: Gender and the politics of welfare in Hungary*, Berkeley, CA: University of California Press.

Hantrais, L. (2000) *Social policy in the European Union*, Basingstoke: Macmillan.

Hantrais, L. (2002a) 'Central and East European states respond to socio-demographic challenges', *Social Policy and Society*, vol 1, no 2, pp 141-50.

Hantrais, L. (2002b) *Gendered policies in Europe: Reconciling employment and family life*, Basingstoke: Palgrave Macmillan.

Heinen, J. (1995) 'Unemployment and women's attitudes in Poland', *Social Politics*, vol 2, Spring, pp 91-110.

Heinen, J. (1997) 'Public and private: gender – social and political citizenship in Eastern Europe', *Theory and Society*, vol 26, pp 577-97.

Heinen, J. and Portet, S. (2002) 'Political and social citizenship: an examination of the case of Poland', in M. Molyneux and S. Razavi (eds) *Gender justice, development and rights*, Oxford: Oxford University Press.

Hoskyns, C. (1996) *Gender, women, law and politics in the European Union*, London: Verso.

Ignatowicz, J. (2000) *Prawo rodzinne (Family law)*, Warszawa: Wydawnictwa Prawnicze PWN.

Ingham, H. and Ingham, M. (2002) *EU expansion to the East: Prospects and problems*, Cheltenham: Edward Elgar.

International Labour Organization (ILO) (2005) 'Conditions of Work and Employment Programme' (www.ilo.org/).

Jalusic, V. (2002) 'Between the social and the political – feminism, citizenship, and the possibilities of an arendtian perspective in Eastern Europe', *European Journal of Women's Studies*, vol 9, no 2, pp 103-22.

Jalusic, V. and Antic, M. (2000a) *Gender equality and equal opportunities policies in Central and Eastern Europe*, Vienna: IWM (Institute for Human Sciences).

Jalusic, V. and Antic, M. (2000b) *Prospects for gender equality policies in Central and Eastern Europe*, Vienna: IWM (Institute for Human Sciences).

Janowska, Z. (2000) 'Uczestnictwo kobiet w życiu zawodowym i politycznym: Polska rzeczywistość a wymagania Unii Europejskiej' (Women's partcipation in professional and political life: Polish reality and demands of European Union), *Polityka Społeczna*, no 1, pp 15-18.

Kiernan, K. (2000) 'European perspectives on union formation', in L.J. Waite and C. Bachrach (eds) *The ties that bind: Perspectives on marriage and cohabitation*, New York: Walter de Gruyter, pp 40-58.

Knijn, T. (2001) 'Care work: innovations in the Netherlands', in M. Daly (ed) *Care work: The quest for security*, Geneva: International Labour Office, pp 159-74.

Knijn, T. and Selten, P. (2002) 'Transformations of fatherhood', in B. Hobson (ed) *Making men into fathers: Men, masculinities and the social politics of fatherhood*, Cambridge: Cambridge University Press, pp 168-90.

Kocourkova, J. (2002) 'Leave arrangements and childcare services in Central Europe: policies and practices before and after the transition', *Community, Work and Family*, vol 5, no 3, pp 301-18.

Kołaczek, B. (2001a) 'Kobiety na rynku pracy w krajach Europy Środkowo-Wschodniej' (Women on the labour market in Central and East European countries), *Polityka Społeczna*, no 2, pp 10-14.

Kołaczek, B. (2001b) 'Szanse podjęcia pracy na lokalnych rynkach pracy' (Chances of undertaking employment in the local labour market), in B. Balcerzak-Paradowska (ed) *Kobiety i mężczyźni na rynku pracy: Rzeczywistość lat 1990-99 (Women and men on the labour market: Reality of the years 1990-99)*, Warszawa: IPiSS, pp 110-29.

Kołaczek, B. (2001c) 'Zatrudnienie kobiet i mężczyzn w Polsce w latach 1990-99: tendencje zmian' (Employment of women and men in Poland during the period 1990-99: tendencies of changes), in B. Balcerzak-Paradowska (ed) *Kobiety i mężczyźni na rynku pracy: Rzeczywistość lat 1990-99 (Women and men on the labour market: Reality of the years 1990-99)*, Warszawa: IPiSS, pp 43-72.

Korpi, W. (2000) 'Faces of inequality: gender, class, and patterns of inequalities in different types of welfare states', *Social Politics*, vol 7, pp 127-91.

Kotowska, I.E. (1995) 'Discrimination against women in the labour market in Poland during the transition to a market economy', *Social Politics*, vol 2, pp 76-90.

Kurzynowski, A. (1995a) 'Aktywność zawodowa kobiet a rodzina' (Women's professional activity versus family), in S. Golinowska and B. Balcerzak-Paradowska (eds) *Rodziny w Polsce: Ewolucja, zróżnicowanie, okres transformacji (Families in Poland: Evolution, differentiation, transformation period)*, Warszawa: IPiSS, pp 40-50.

Kurzynowski, A. (1995b) 'Sytuacja materialna a bezpieczeństwo ekonomiczne rodzin' ('Material situation and economic security of families'), in A. Kurzynowski (ed) *Rodzina w okresie transformacji systemowej (The family in the transformation period)*, Warszawa: Wyzsza Szkoła Pedagogiczna Towarzystwa Wiedzy Powszechnej, pp 57-76.

Kvist, J. (2004) 'Does EU enlargement start a race to the bottom? Strategic interaction among EU member states in social policy', *Journal of European Social Policy*, vol 14, no 3, pp 301-18.

Kwak, A. (1998) 'Family policy and family life in Poland', in A. Kwak and R. Dingwall (eds) *Social change, social policy and social work in the new Europe*, Aldershot: Ashgate, pp 59-72.

Land, H. (2004) *Women, child poverty and childcare: Making the link*, London: Daycare Trust.

Leibfried, S. and Pierson, P. (2000) 'Social policy', in H. Wallace and W. Wallace (eds) *Policy-making in the European Union*, Oxford: Oxford University Press.

Lendvai, N. (2004) 'The weakest link? EU accession and enlargement: dialoguing EU and post-communist social policy', *Journal of European Social Policy*, vol 14, no 3, pp 319-33.

Leszkowicz-Baczyńska, Ż. (2002) 'Między domem a pracą — wewnętrzne i zewnętrzne uwarunkowania zadowolenia z życia kobiet' (Between home and work – inner and outer conditions of women's satisfaction from their lives), in A. Wachowiak (ed) *Przemiany orientacji życiowych kobiet zamężnych (Transformation of life orientation of married women)*, Poznań: Wydawnictwo Fundacji Humaniora, pp 75-122.

Lewis, J. (1992) 'Gender and the development of welfare regimes', *Journal of European Social Policy*, vol 2, no 3, pp 159-73.

Lewis, J. (1997) 'Gender and welfare regimes: further thoughts', *Social Politics*, vol 4, no 2, pp 160-77.

Lewis, J. (1998) *Social care, gender and welfare state restructuring*, Aldershot: Ashgate.

Lewis, J. (2001a) 'The decline of the male breadwinner model: the implications for work and care', *Social Politics*, vol 8, no 2, pp 152-70.

Lewis, J. (2001b) *The end of marriage: Individualism and intimate relations?*, Cheltenham: Edward Elgar.

Lewis, J. (2002) 'Gender and welfare state change', *European Societies*, vol 4, no 4, pp 331-57.

Lewis, J. (2003) 'Developing early years childcare (1997-2002): the choices for mothers', *Social Policy and Administration*, vol 37, no 3, pp 219-38.

Łobodzińska, B. (1995) *Family, women and employment in Central-Eastern Europe*, Westport, CT: Greenwood Press.

Łobodzińska, B. (1996) 'Women's employment or return to "family values" in Central and Eastern Europe', *Journal of Comparative Family Studies*, vol 27, no 3, pp 519-44.

Łobodzińska, B. (2000) 'Polish women's gender-segregated education and employment', *Women's Studies International Forum*, vol 23, no 1, pp 49-71.

McLaughlin, E. and Glendinning, C. (1994) 'Paying for care in Europe: is there a feminist approach?', in L. Hantrais and S. Mangen (eds) *Family policy and the welfare of women*, Cross-National Research Papers, Third Series, Leicestershire: The Cross-National Research Group, pp 52-69.

Mair, P. and Zielonka, J. (2002) *The enlarged European Union: Diversity and adaptation*, London: Frank Cass.

Makkai, T. (1994) 'Social policy and gender in Eastern Europe', in D. Sainsbury (ed) *Gendering welfare states*, London and New York: Sage Publications, pp 188-205.

Mazey, S. (1998) 'The European Union and women's rights: from the Europeanization of national agendas to the nationalization of a European agenda?', *Journal of European Public Policy*, vol 5, no 1, pp 131-52.

Milic-Cerniak, R. (1995) *Social costs of transition national report: Poland*, Vienna: IWM (Institute for Human Sciences).

MISSOC (Mutual Information System on Social Protection in the European Union Member States and the European Area) (2004) *Social protection in the 10 new member states*, Europa website http://europa.eu.int

Moghadam, V.M. (1993) *Democratic reform and the position of women in transitional economies*, Oxford: Clarendon Press.

Molyneux, M. (1990) 'The "woman question" in the age of perestroika', *New Left Review*, vol 183, pp 23-59.

Morris, A. and Nott, S. (1991) *Working women and the law: Equality and discrimination in theory and practice*, London and New York: Routledge.

Moss, P. and Brannen, J. (2003) *Rethinking children's care*, Maidenhead: Open University Press.

Mueller, M. and Funk, N. (eds) (1993) *Gender politics and post-communism: Reflections from Eastern Europe and the former Soviet Union*, London and New York: Routledge.

Nagy, B. (2003) 'Hungary', in L. Walter (ed) *Women's issues worldwide: Europe*, Westport, CT: Greenwood Press, pp 281-95.

Neilson, J. (1998) 'Equal opportunities for women in the European Union: success or failure?', *Journal of European Social Policy*, vol 8, no 1, pp 64-79.

O'Connor, J., Orloff, A.S. and Shaver, S. (1999) *States, markets and families: Gender, liberalism and social policies in Australia, Canada, Great Britain and the US*, Cambridge: Cambridge University Press.

OECD (Organization for Economic Co-operation and Development) (1999) *A caring world: The new Social Policy Agenda*, Paris: OECD Publications.

OECD (2002) *Babies and bosses: Reconciling work and family life (2 vols)*, Paris: OECD Publications.

Open Society Institute (2005) *Equal opportunities for women and men: Monitoring law and practice in new member states and accession countries of the European Union*, Network women's programme, New York: OSI.

Ostner, I. (2000) 'From equal pay to equal employability: four decades of European gender policies', in M. Rossilli (ed) *Gender policies in the European Union*, New York: Peter Lang, pp 25-42.

Ostner, I. and Lewis, J. (1995) 'Gender and the evolution of European social policies', in S. Liebfried and P. Pierson (eds) *European social policy*, Washington, DC: The Brookings Institution, pp 432-66.

Paci, P. (2002) *Gender in transition*, Washington, DC: The World Bank.

Pailhe, A. (2000) 'Gender discrimination in Central Europe during the systemic transition', *Economics of Transition*, vol 8, no 2, pp

Paoli, P., Parent-Thirion, A. and Persson, O. (2002) *Working conditions in candidate countries and the European Union*, Dublin: European Foundation for the Improvement of Living and Working Conditions.

Paoli, P. and Parent-Thirion, A. (2003) *Working conditions in the acceding and candidate countries*, Dublin: European Foundation for the Improvement of Living and Working Conditions.

Pascall, G. and Lewis, J. (2004) 'Emerging gender regimes and policies for gender equality in a wider Europe', *Journal of Social Policy*, vol 33, no 3, pp 373-94.

Pascall, G. and Manning, N. (2000) 'Gender and social policy: comparing welfare states in Central and Eastern Europe and the former Soviet Union', *Journal of European Social Policy*, vol 10, no 3, pp 269-96.

Pascall, G. and Manning, N. (2002) 'Social Europe East and West', in H. Ingham and M. Ingham (eds) *EU expansion to the East: Prospects and problems*, Cheltenham: Edward Elgar.

Pető, A. (2004) 'Feminisms and social sciences in European countries with a statist feminist heritage: networks and strategies', *Feminist Economics*, vol 10, no 3, pp 101-18.

Pető, A., Szabó, S. and Kuhl, A. (eds) (2004) *The situation of women in transition*, Budapest: Hungarian Section of the Party of European Socialists.

Pierson, P. and Leibfried, S. (1995) 'The dynamics of social policy integration', in S. Liebfried and P. Pierson (eds) *European social policy*, Washington, DC: The Brookings Institution, pp 432-66.

Pine, F. (1995) 'Kinship, work and state in post-socialist Poland', *Cambridge Journal of Anthropology*, vol 18, no 2, pp 47-58.

Piotrowski, J. (1980) 'Wpływ pracy zawodowej kobiet na życie rodzinne z uwzględnieniem zróżnicowania społeczno-ekonomicznego' ('Influence of women's professional work on family life: the role of socio-economic differentiation'), in *Rodzina i polityka społeczna na rzecz rodziny w PRL (Family and social policy towards family in the Polish People's Republic)*, Warsaw: Krajowa Konferencja Naukowa, Rada do Spraw Rodziny, Warszawa, pp 79-91.

Plakwicz, J. (1992) 'Between church and state: Polish women's experience', in C. Corrin (ed) *Superwomen and the double burden: Women's experience of change in Central and Eastern Europe and the former Soviet Union*, London: Scarlet Press, pp 75-96.

Plantenga, J. (2002) 'Combining work and care in the polder model: an assessment of the Dutch part-time strategy', *Critical Social Policy*, vol 22, no 1, pp 53-71.

Plantenga, J., Schippers, J. and Siergers, J. (1999) 'Towards an equal division of paid and unpaid work: the case of the Netherlands', *Journal of European Social Policy*, vol 9, no 2, pp 99-110.

Pollert, A. and Fodor, E. (2005) *Working conditions and gender in an enlarged Europe*, Dublin: European Foundation for the Improvement of Living and Working Conditions.

Potucek, M. (2004) 'Accession and social policy: the case of the Czech Republic', *Journal of European Social Policy*, vol 14, no 3, pp 253-66.

Rake, K. (2000) *Women's incomes over the lifetime*, Women and Equality Unit, London: The Stationery Office.

Redmond, G., Schnepf, V. and Suhrcke, M. (2002) *Attitudes to inequality after ten years of transition*, Florence: UNICEF Innocenti Research Centre.

Rees, T. (1999) *Mainstreaming equality in the European Union: Education, training and labour market policies*, London and New York: Routledge.

Regulska, J. (1998) 'Transition to local democracy: do Polish women have a chance?', in M. Rueschmeyer (ed) *Women in the politics of post-communist Eastern Europe*, New York: M.E. Sharpe, pp 33-63.

Regulska, J. (2001) 'Gendered integration of Europe: new forms of exclusion', *Berliner Journal Für Soziologie*, vol 11, no 1, p 51.

Report on the situation of Polish families (1995) *(Raport o sytuacji polskich rodzin)* Pełnomocnik Rządu do Spraw. Rodziny i Kobiet. Warszawa.

Report on the situation of Polish families (1998) *(Raport o sytuacji polskich rodzin)* Pełnomocnik Rządu do Spraw Rodziny. Warszawa.

Rhodes, M. (2003) 'The enlargement crisis of the European Union', *Journal of European Social Policy*, vol 13, no 3, pp 54-7.

Ritchie, J. and Lewis, J. (2003) *Qualitative research practice: A guide for social science students and researchers*, London and New York: Sage Publications.

Rossilli, M. (1997) 'The European Community's policy on the equality of women: from the Treaty of Rome to the present', *The European Journal of Women's Studies*, vol 4, no 1, pp 63-82.

Rossilli, M. (1999) 'The European Union's policy on the equality of women', *Feminist Studies*, vol 25, no 1, pp 171-82.

Rossilli, M. (2000) *Gender policies in the European Union*, New York: Peter Lang Publishing.

Rubery, J. (2005) 'Gender mainstreaming and the open method of coordination: is the open method too open for gender equality policy?', in J. Zeitlin, and P. Pochet (eds) *The open method of coordination in action: The European social inclusion and employment strategies in action*, Madison, WI: European Union Center.

Rubery, J., Smith, M. and Fagan, C. (1999) *Women's employment in Europe: Trends and prospects*, London and New York: Routledge.

Rubery, J., Smith, M., Fagan, C. and Grimshaw, D. (1998) *Women and European employment*, London and New York: Routledge.

Rubery, J., Figueiredo, H., Smith, M., Grimshaw, D. and Fagan, C. (2004) 'The ups and downs of European gender equality policy', *Industrial Relations Journal*, vol 35, no 6, pp 603-28.

Ruminska-Zimny, E. (2002) *Gender aspects of changes in the labor markets in transition economies*, New York and Geneva: United Nations Economic Commission for Europe.

Sainsbury, D. (1996) *Gender, equality and welfare states*, Cambridge: Cambridge University Press.

Sass, J. and Jaeckel, M. (1997) 'The compatibility of work and family', in U. Björnberg and J. Sass (eds) *Families with small children in Eastern and Western Europe*, Aldershot: Ashgate, pp 61-92.

Semenowicz, A. and Antoszkiewicz, D. (1996) 'Elementy ochrony rodziny w polskim ustawodawstwie' (Elements of family protection in Polish jurisdiction), in *Wybrane zagadnienia z zakresu polityki rodzinnej – część I (Selected issues of family policy – part I)*, Warszawa: Zeszyty Biura i Analiz Kancelarii Senatu, pp 11-25.

Shaw, J. (2002) 'The European Union and gender mainstreaming: constitutionally embedded or comprehensively marginalized?', *Feminist Legal Studies*, vol 10, no 3, pp 213-26.

Siemieńska, R. (1996) *Kobiety: Nowe wyzwania: starcie przeszłości z teraźniejszością (Women: New challenge: encounter of past with present)*, Warsaw: Instytut Socjologii Uniwersytetu Warszawskiego.

Siemieńska, R. (1998) 'Consequences of economic and political changes for women in Poland', in J. Jacquette and S. Wolchick (eds) *Women and democracy: Latin America and Central and Eastern Europe*, Baltimore: The Johns Hopkins University Press, pp 125-52.

Siemieńska, R. (1999) 'Elites and women in democratising post-communist societies', *International Review of Sociology*, vol 9, no 2, pp 197-219.

Siemieńska, R. (2000) *Political representation of women and mechanisms of its creation in Poland*, Ljubljana: The Peace Institute.

Siemieńska, R. (2002) 'Intergenerational differences in political values and attitudes in stable and new democracies', *International Journal of Comparative Sociology*, vol 43, nos 3-5, pp 368-90.

Sloat, A. (2004) *Legislating for equality: The implementation of the EU equality acquis in Central and Eastern Europe*, Jean Monnet Working Paper 08 and 04, New York: New York University School of Law.

Stavarska, R. (1999) 'EU enlargement from the Polish perspective', *Journal of European Public Policy*, vol 6, no 5, pp 822-38.

Stratigaki, M. (2004) 'The cooptation of gender concepts in EU policies: the case of reconciliation of work and family', *Social Politics*, vol 11, no 1, pp 30-56.

Stratigaki, M. (2005) 'Gender mainstreaming versus positive action – an ongoing conflict in EU gender equality policy', *European Journal of Women's Studies*, vol 12, no 2, pp 165-86.

Streek, W. (1995) 'From market making to state building? Reflections on the political economy of European social policy', in S. Liebfried and P. Pierson (eds) *European social policy*, Washington DC: The Brookings Institution.

Szalai, J. (2002) 'From opposition in private to engagement in public: Motives for citizen participation in the post-1989 new democracies of Central Europe', *Social Research*, vol 69, no, 1, pp 71-82.

Szalai, J. (2003) 'Whose claim and whose risk?', *Journal of European Social Policy*, vol 13, no 1, pp 58-60.

Szatur-Jaworska, B. (2001) 'Zadania polityki rodzinnej w Polsce na tle sytuacji demograficznej' (Goals of family policy in Poland in the light of the demographic situation), in B. Rysz-Kowalczyk (ed) *Problemy społeczne wybranych grup demograficznych (Social problems of selected demographic groups)*, Warszawa: Instytut Polityki Społecznej Uniwersytet Warszawski, pp 51-74.

Szeman, Z. (2003) 'The welfare mix in Hungary as a new phenomenon', *Social Policy and Society*, vol 2, no 2, pp 101-8.

Taylor-Gooby, P. (2003) 'Introduction: open markets versus welfare citizenship: conflicting approaches to policy convergence in Europe', *Social Policy and Administration*, vol 37, no 6, pp 539-54.

Taylor-Gooby, P. and Hastie, C. (2003) 'Paying for "world class" services: a British dilemma', *Journal of Social Policy*, vol 32, no 2, pp 271-88.

Taylor-Gooby, P., Hastie, C. and Bromley, C. (2003) 'Querulous citizens: welfare knowledge and the limits to welfare reform', *Social Policy and Administration*, vol 37, no 1, pp 1-20.

Threlfall, M. (2003) 'European social integration: harmonization, convergence and single social areas', *Journal of European Social Policy*, vol 13, no 2, pp 121-39.

UNICEF (United Nations Children's Fund) (1998) *Education for all? The TransMONEE project regional monitoring report, No 5*, Florence: UNICEF International Child Development Centre.

UNICEF (1999) *Women in transition: Regional monitoring report No 6*, Florence: UNICEF International Child Development Centre.

UNICEF (2001) *A decade of transition: Regional monitoring report No 8*, Florence: UNICEF Innocenti Research Centre.

UNICEF (2002) *Social monitor 2002*, Florence: UNICEF Innocenti Research Centre.

UNICEF (2003) *Social monitor 2003*, Florence: UNICEF Innocenti Research Centre.

van der Lippe, T. and Fodor, E. (1998) 'Changes in gender inequality in six Eastern European countries', *Acta Sociologica*, vol 41, no 2, pp 131-49.

Velluti, S. (2005) 'Implementing gender equality and mainstreaming in an enlarged European Union – some thoughts on prospects and challenges for Central Eastern Europe', *Journal of Social Welfare and Family Law*, vol 27, no 2, pp 221-33.

Vobruba, G. (2003a) 'The enlargement crisis of the European Union: limits of the dialectics of integration and expansion', *Journal of European Social Policy*, vol 13, no 1, pp 35-62.

Vobruba, G. (2003b) 'Debate on the enlargement of the European Union', *Journal of European Social Policy*, vol 13, no 1, pp 35-62.

von Wahl, A. (2005) 'Liberal, Conservative, Social Democratic or European? The EU as an equal employment regime', *Social Politics*, vol 12, no 1, pp 67-95.

Walby, S. (1999) 'The new regulatory state: the social powers of the European Union', *British Journal of Sociology*, vol 50, no 1, pp 118-37.

Walby, S. (2004) 'The European Union and gender equality: emergent varieties of gender regime', *Social Politics*, vol 11, no 1, pp 4-29.

Watson, P. (1993) 'The rise of masculinism in Eastern Europe', *New Left Review*, vol 198, pp 71-82.

Watson, P. (1997) 'Civil society and the politics of difference in Eastern Europe', in J.W. Scott, C. Kaplan and D. Keates (eds) *Transitions, environments, translations: Feminisms in international politics*, London and New York: Routledge.

Watson, P. (2000a) 'Politics, policy and identity: EU eastern enlargement and East-West differences', *Journal of European Public Policy, special issue*, vol 7, no 3, pp 369-84.

Watson, P. (2000b) 'Rethinking transition: globalism, gender and class', *International Feminist Journal of Politics*, vol 2, no 2, pp 185-213.

Wickham, J. (2002) 'The end of the European social model before it began?', Dublin: Irish Congress of Trade Unions. http://www.ictu.ie and html and publications and ictu and Essay2.pdf

Wolchick, S. (2003) 'Slovakia', in L. Walter (ed) *Women's issues worldwide: Europe*, Westport, CT: Greenwood Press, pp 587-600.

World Bank (2001) *Engendering development: Through gender equality in rights, resources, and voice*, New York and Oxford: Oxford University Press.

World Bank (2002) *Transition: The first ten years: analysis and lessons for Eastern Europe and the former Soviet Union*, Washington, DC: European Bank for Reconstruction and Development and the World Bank.

Zielińska, E.(1990) *Przerywanie ciąży: Warunki legalności w Polsce i na świecie (Abortion: Legal conditions in Poland and in the world)*, Warszawa: Wydawnictwo Prawnicze.

Zielińska, E. (2000) 'Between ideology, politics, and common sense: the discourse of reproductive rights in Poland', in S. Gal and G. Kligman (eds) *Reproducing gender: Politics, publics, and everyday life after socialism*, Princeton, NJ: Princeton University Press.

Zielińska, E. (2002) 'Sytuacja kobiet w Polsce w świetle zmian legislacyjnych okresu transformacji' (Situation of women in Poland in the light of jurisdiction changes in the transformation period), in M. Fuszara (ed) *Kobiety w Polsce na przełomie wieków: Nowy kontrakt płci? (Women in Poland at the turn of the century: New gender contract?)* Warszawa: Instytut Spraw Publicznych, pp 84-102.

Websites

European Commission Europa Database on Women and Men in Decision-making, http://europa.eu.int/comm/employment_social/women_men_stats/index_en.htm

Europa NewCronos website: Eurostat structural indicators, http://epp.eurostat.cec.eu.int

UNICEF Innocenti Research Centre TransMONEE database, www.unicef-icdc.org/resources

Appendix: The sample

Location

31 respondents from Skierniewice and 31 from Warsaw

Selection criteria

- married or cohabiting women
- at least one child under seven (but they could have more)
- employed but, at the time of interview, they could be on maternity or childcare leave
- living in Skierniewice or Warsaw.

The research was carried out first in Skierniewice, and then in Warsaw. The sample in Warsaw was matched to the Skierniewice group in terms of age, level of education, number of children, employment, maternity or childcare leave and pattern of shift-work.

Characteristics of both groups together (62 women)

62 were married, none living with a partner outside marriage
5 were on maternity or childcare leave, 57 were working at the time of the interview.

Working patterns

One shift (including one night shift)	31
Two shifts	15
Three shifts	3
Worked part time	1
Without regular working hours	7

Years in the marriage

5 and less	17
6–10	23
11–15	15
16–18	7

Age (years)

20-24	3
25-29	19
30-34	21
35-39	14
40-44	5

Number of children (aged up to 17) in families

One	21
Two	24
Three	15
Four	2

Level of education

Elementary	2
Vocational	5
Secondary	30
Above secondary but below university (college)	3
University	22

Index

Page numbers in *italic* refer to tables or figures.